Digital Culture & Society

Vol. 2, Issue 1/2016

Pablo Abend, Mathias Fuchs (eds.)
Quantified Selves and Statistical Bodies

The journal is edited by
Pablo Abend, Mathias Fuchs, Ramón Reichert,
Annika Richterich, Karin Wenz

Editorial Board
Maria Bakardjieva, Brian Beaton, David Berry, Jean Burgess, Mark Coté, Colin Cremin, Sean Cubitt, Mark Deuze, José van Dijck, Delia Dumitrica, Astrid Ensslin, Sonia Fizek, Federica Frabetti, Richard A. Grusin, Orit Halpern, Irina Kaldrack, Wendy Hui Kyong Chun, Denisa Kera, Lev Manovich, Janet H. Murray, Jussi Parikka, Lisa Parks, Christiane Paul, Dominic Pettman, Rita Raley, Richard Rogers, Julian Rohrhuber, Marie-Laure Ryan, Mirko Tobias Schäfer, Jens Schröter, Trebor Scholz, Tamar Sharon, Roberto Simanowski, Nathaniel Tkacz, Nanna Verhoeff, Geoffrey Winthrop-Young, Sally Wyatt

[transcript]

The Journal *Digital Culture & Society* appears twice a year, in March (spring) and September (fall).
It is available for annual subscription directly from the publisher. The subscription begins with the current issue and includes all issues of one year. Delivery of the subscribed issues occurs immediately after their appearance. Invoicing occurs with delivery of the first issue of a year. The subscription is automatically continued by one year, unless canceled with the publisher by February 1st.

Annual subscription	*Germany*	*internationally*
print, incl. postage:	55,00 €	65,00 €
e-journal:	55,00 €	55,00 €
bundle (print and digital), incl. postage:	66,00 €	76,00 €

Single issue		
print:	29,99 €	
e-journal:	29,99 €	
bundle (print and digital), incl. postage:	36,00 €	

For more information, please see: http://transcript-verlag.de/dcs

Bibliographic information published by the Deutsche Nationalbibliothek
The Deutsche Nationalbibliothek lists this publication in the Deutsche Nationalbibliografie; detailed bibliographic data are available on the Internet at http://dnb.d-nb.de

© 2016 transcript Verlag, Bielefeld

All rights reserved. No part of this book may be reprinted or reproduced or utilized in any form or by any electronic, mechanical, or other means, now known or hereafter invented, including photocopying and recording, or in any information storage or retrieval system, without permission in writing from the publisher.

Cover layout: Kordula Röckenhaus, Bielefeld
Typeset: Michael Rauscher, Bielefeld

ISSN 2364-2114
eISSN 2364-2122
Print-ISBN 978-3-8376-3210-1
PDF-ISBN 978-3-8394-3210-5

Printed and bound in Great Britain by Marston Book Services Ltd, Oxfordshire

Content

Introduction
The Quantified Self and Statistical Bodies
Pablo Abend and Mathias Fuchs 5

I Situating the Quantified Self Phenomenon

From Quantified to Qualified Self
A Fictional Dialogue at the Mall
Andréa Belliger and David J. Krieger 25

Total Affect Control
Or: Who's Afraid of a Pleasing Little Sister?
Marie-Luise Angerer and Bernd Bösel 41

Theorising the Quantified Self and Posthumanist Agency
Self-Knowledge and Posthumanist Agency in Contemporary US-American Literature
Stefan Danter, Ulfried Reichardt and Regina Schober 53

II Investigations in Quantifying Practices

Bodies, Mood and Excess
Relationship Tracking and the Technicity of Intimacy
Alex Lambert 71

Unhappy? There's an App for That
Tracking Well-Being through the Quantified Self
Jill Belli 89

III Conceptual and Legal Reflections

Casual Power
Understanding User Interfaces through Quantification
Alex Gekker 107

My Quantified Self, my FitBit and I
The Polymorphic Concept of Health Data
and the Sharer's Dilemma
Argyro P. Karanasiou and Sharanjit Kang   123

IV Entering the Field

How Old am I?
Digital Culture and Quantified Ageing
Barbara L. Marshall and Stephen Katz   145

Games to Live With
Speculations Regarding NikeFuel
Paolo Ruffino   153

Quantified Bodies
A Design Practice
James Dyer   161

Quantified Faces
On Surveillance Technologies, Identification
and Statistics in Three Contemporary Art Projects
Mette-Marie Zacher Sørensen   169

Coupling Quantified Bodies
Affective Possibilities of Self-Quantification beyond the Self
*Robert Cercós, William Goddard, Adam Nash
and Jeremy Yuille*   177

V In Conversation with

**I Think it Worked Because Mercury
was in the House of Jupiter!**
*Tega Brain and Surya Mattu in Conversation with Pablo Abend
and Mathias Fuchs*   185

Biographical Notes   195

Introduction
The Quantified Self and Statistical Bodies

Pablo Abend and Mathias Fuchs

> 'And now,' the doctor said, tapping Mae's wrist monitor, 'now it's active. It'll collect data on your heart rate, blood pressure, cholesterol, heat flux, caloric intake, sleep duration, sleep quality, digestive efficiency, on and on. [...] When we see non-normative rates of stress in a Circler or a department, we can make adjustments to workload, for example. It measures the pH level of your sweat, so you can tell when you need to hydrate with alkaline water. It detects your posture, so you know when you need to reposition yourself. Blood and tissue oxygen, your red blood cell count, and things like step count.'
> DAVE EGGERS "THE CIRCLE", 2013, 154-155

Just like her colleagues at *The Circle* – the fictional IT company in David Eggers' eponymous novel – new entrant Mae is asked to swallow a tiny sensor, which is able to monitor important vital functions in real-time, visualising the results on a wristlet's display and reporting the data to the company's medical centre. While in Egger's fictional work the idea of a fully quantified and numerical body presages a dystopian society of control, contemporary quantified self enthusiasts are tempted by the possibilities of the surveyed body. Thus, joggers can keep track of their accomplishments, snorers can monitor their sleep, and chronically ill patients can readjust their medication. "Self-knowledge through numbers" became the mantra of the emerging communities of self-trackers (cf. Lupton 2014), and quantified self, lifelogging, and personal informatics are the terms used to describe the use of digital technology to track physical activity, quantify bodily processes, and monitor one's own conduct of life.

Not completely dissimilar to *The Circle*, a non-fictional association that calls themselves "Quantified Self" and "a network" was set up in the San Francisco Bay area in 2007 by Gary Wolf and Kevin Kelly. With a background in editing for *Wired* magazine and the *Whole Earth Review*, both founders were hippyish enough to promote technology as a means for "personal evolution", "self-improvement" and "self-awareness" (Wolf 2010), and straightforward enough to understand that "self-knowledge through numbers" can be big business. No wonder that the global brand of QS has a centralised organisational structure and that, briefly, after the phase of "looking 10,000 years into the future" (Kelly 2015), the team was expanded to seek assistance from *McKinsey* consultant Joshua Kauffman and former *eBay* executive producer Kate Farnady. With application areas such as sports, finance, health, productivity and the military/surveillance complex, and with the declared goal to become "globally active", it seems likely that profitmaking will not have to wait for 10,000 years.

It might, however, be useful to change the direction and scale of the observation: forget about the distant future for a moment and have a close look at the near past instead. Individual attempts to measure, digitise and document personal information can be found in various forms of household books, handwritten budget diaries, body size measurements on door frames, gardening notes and hiking diaries.

One of the more systematic and large-scale projects on quantified selves was the British "Mass Observation" movement that started in the 1930s, or what has been described as "direct observations" by Schütz (1964) and others. These shared efforts to quantify aspects of everyday life can be seen as pre-digital precursors that have anticipated what now has become a digitally enhanced practice of self-observation. Mass observation was conceived as a programme for the scientific study of social behaviour in Great Britain via observers and diarists who wrote down what they experienced and measured. In a letter to the *New Statesman* on January 30, 1937, Tom Harrison, Humphrey Jennings and Charles Madge announced a new form of "anthropology of ourselves" (Harrison/Jennings/Madge 1937). The idea was to motivate citizens to create notes based on their own observations of eating habits, alcohol consumption, housing, fashion, sports, wartime activities, media consumption and any other conceivable aspect of daily life. In the late 1930s, it was reported to be not an unusual sight in Bolton or Blackpool to see diarists monitor their drinking habits in the local pubs. Mass observation records report that the average pub-goer in Bolton drank 3.45 pints of beer in the evening (Smart 2013). Other observations report activities of the "Working Man's Hair Specialist" at Bolton Open Market, love at the beach in Blackpool and other fascinating details of everyday life.

The founders of mass observation must have appeared to be equally hip and out-of-the box in those days as Kelly and Wolf seem to be now. Harrison was an ornithologist and self-taught anthropologist who published on "cannibals" for the *Left Book Club* edition. Jennings was a documentary filmmaker, painter and surrealist, and a friend of André Breton. The communist poet Madge wrote for the *Daily Mirror* and for the *Left Review*, during those days a journal that would easily compete in popularity and cult-status with what the *Whole Earth Review* represented in the 1980s. But, different to Wolf and Kelly's "self-knowledge", the results of mass observation were thought to create a social asset that would help to analyse and change society, rather than the individual. Starting with the self-observation of the Bolton-based working class diarists, the work-town and common (wo)man's problems were reflected as problems of humans in a specific political situation. This is quite different to what the contemporary Quantified Self (QS) movement intends to achieve. James Hinton (2010: 6) points out that mass observation was a "discipline and a context which transcended the purely private, meeting a need to frame individual quests in relation to larger public purposes."

It has to be mentioned here that the ambitious goals the mass observation movement had in 1937 have not always been achieved. Very much in a similar way that contemporary quantified self-observation might become the target of interest for observers beyond ourselves, the mass observation movement of the 1940s became instrumentalised by the interests of the Ministry of Information, the secret services and the commercial sector. It was not only "The Pub and the People" that became a topic for directive replies by the volunteer diarists, but also "War begins at Home" (Harrisson/Madge 1940). After the war, mass observation, or what was left of it, worked mainly for market analysis and consumer studies; a transformation that might well happen to today's idealistic goal of "personal evolution", as proclaimed by QS.

Today we find an abundance of hard- and software for the quantification of data that stems from individual metabolisms, emotions and affective states: *Mindbloom* for the measurement of feelings, *Stresscheck* for anxiety awareness *Moodscope* for mood tracking, *Livescan* for glucose levels, *MealSnap* for food intake, *DigIFit* for the heart rate, *My Monthly Cycles* for the menstrual period, and many more. The goal of apps like these is to facilitate body management and control through monitoring and feedback, with the ambition to transform the body and its activities into numeric representations of what can be measured, monitored, evaluated and transmitted. Digitisation and connectivity are therefore at the core of quantified selves and the QS ideology. We have become accustomed to the assumption that digitisation and connectivity have been made available by digital technology, but both, the process of turning measurement data into discrete numbers and the pervasiveness of communication technology can be achieved without digital computers.

The concept artist On Kawara works on issues of the quantification of personal data and does so by using manual quantification and the postal system for his art pieces. His multiannual experiment of measuring, monitoring and communicating the time when he gets up was conducted from 1968 to 1979. *I GOT UP* is a continuous piece in which the artist sends picture postcards to two different addressees, each stamped with the exact time he arose that day and the addresses of both sender and recipient.

On July 9, 1970 he sent a picture postcard from the Triborough Bridge, New York to his friend Richard Kostelanetz, who lives in New York as well, with the rubber stamp "I GOT UP AT 1.18 P.M." imprinted on the card. On March 29, 1974, another standard tourist picture postcard from an Orlando Travelodge was sent to On Kawara's gallerist Roger Mazarguil in Paris' 17th district: "I GOT UP AT 7.38 A.M."

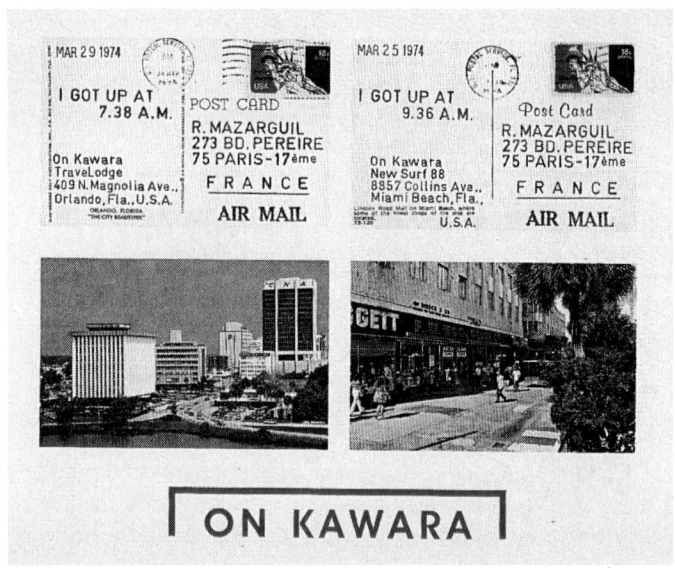

Image 1: Two copies of postcards (front and back) from the On Kawara postcard series *I GOT UP*. 29 March 1974 (left) and 25 March 1974 (right).

The seemingly banal messages contain more meaning for On Kawara than just the simple fact of when he got out of bed. Kawara's postcards do not record the time of his waking up, as an Apple watch or any other contemporary quantified self device would do, but his "getting up", with its ambiguous conflation of bodily and existential implications (getting up as opposed to not getting up). For a long time he made a map of his daily walks and cab rides. He created and stored lists of the people he met. He sent postcards, letters and telegrams to friends and colleagues around the world, telling them that he was still alive: "I am still alive – On Kawara". For the artist, self-observation is therefore not a tool for the optimisation of his health or lifestyle. Obviously waking up at 7 is as good as waking up at 8 in the morning. On Kawara's concern was about quantification of an aspect of his self as a statement confirming his existence. The numerical value of his statement "I GOT UP AT ..." is actually completely irrelevant. The numbers contain no meaning. "Self-knowledge through numbers" would be the opposite of what On Kawara has in mind. The numbers are just distracting from what is at stake. The artist exemplifies what David Hume investigates in his *Treatise of Human Nature* (1738). Hume states: "though we commonly be able to distinguish pretty exactly betwixt numerical and specific identity, yet it sometimes happens, that we confound them, and in our thinking and reasoning employ the one for the other" (Hume 1738). Hume's numerical identity can only hold between a thing and itself. It requires absolute qualitative and quantitative sameness and can only be applied to values that can be counted. The "quantified self" mingles two concepts that are otherwise disconnected: numerical identity and the unquantifiable self. It might be that the inconsistent notion of a "quantified self" is so seductive to many because it promises that the self and quantification could go together well. On Kawara's work demonstrates in an ironic way that numerical identities do not constitute specific personal identities. The QS movement tries to suggest the opposite.

Quantified Self Care

When we follow the enthusiasts and listen to the communities' and industries' claims on personal evolution, self-improvement and self-awareness, the quantified self purports to be a modern means to fulfil the Greek tenets of "knowing yourself" *(gnōthi seautón)* and "taking care of yourself" *(epimelēsthai sautou)*, through which one gains access to the truth concerning oneself in order to reflect on the limits of knowledge of the world (Foucault 1993: 204). These principles allow for a kind of introspection (Foucault 2005: 11), which is necessary, broadly speaking, to be at peace with the world and oneself (Hellenistic and Roman philosophy), or to find salvation in the eyes of God (Christianity) with purification of the consciousness and the soul as a common denominator (Foucault 1988: 33, 40). According to Foucault, these transformations of the self are achieved by applying various techniques (ibid; 1993):

"[T]echniques which permit individuals to effect, by their own means, a certain number of operations on their own bodies, on their own souls, on their own thoughts, on their own conduct, and this in a manner so as to transform themselves, modify themselves, and to attain a certain state of perfection, of happiness, of purity, of supernatural power, and so on." (Foucault 1993: 203)

As Mark Butler observes in his book subtitled *Popular Technologies of the Self at the Beginning of the 21st Century* (2014), Foucault's techniques of the self have a history that involves a changing mode of how we take care of and engineer ourselves. Antiquity was characterised by the need to care for ourselves, which involved "actions exercised on the self by the self" (Foucault 2005: 11), including techniques of meditation, memorisation of the past, examination of conscience, and checking mental representations. In medieval Christianity, the dominant technique of the self took the form of the verbal confession, which became a ubiquitous and permanent activity. According to Butler, modernity focuses on an economically driven work on the self as a way of productive self-engineering, and for the contemporary and postmodern phase, he identifies actions that involve an aesthetic play with the notion of the self and identity. There is some evidence that the quantified self contains aspects of each of these phases: caretaking, working, and playing with our mental and physical selves. QS technologies encompass techniques of the self that reflect practices from antiquity, modernity and postmodernity. The very same technologies can be applied to take care, work or play – depending on the context and attitude of the users. An Apple watch that is in the hands (or on the wrist) of a meditative mind can well lead to relaxation and contemplation. The same device can, on the contrary, induce stress-generating exercises and agonistic competition with others. A third group of users might not take the device seriously and play with it, mock it, misuse it or deconstruct it creatively. Butler's observation of a convergence of recreational drugs, fashion and techniques of the self finds a match in the repurposing of QS technology for cannabis consumers in Oregon, USA. The substance consumers use modern technologies to optimise the effect of cannabis. This is the optimisation of a particular health and wellness practice – if one wants to see it that way – but it is also a subversive way of dealing with mainstream technology from Silicon Valley. Amelia Abreu reports: "Quantified stoners wear FitBit and Jawbone wristbands to track their daily activity, log their runs and bike rides … and now optimize their buzzes with high grade weed and a range of data-enriched gadgets to go with it." (Abreu 2015) In a cultural climate that favours quantity before quality any activity has to be quantified. No wonder that cannabis consumption has to follow such guiding principles: "A schoolteacher showed me a homemade vaporizer he'd made out of a gas mask in his garage workshop. He rattled off data points: energy efficiency, growth conditions, and of course, the THC levels in the White Widow and Obama Kush clones." (ibid)

Such burlesque and possibly naïve deconstructions of QS technology perform a mode of excessive play that crosses borderlines of intended territorialisation of an apparatus like QS and opens up spaces for experimentation. Through the tinkering with technology and data the community develops an ethics which can scrutinize socio-technological moral frames. It does so by using the very same technologies and principles in place to territorialise the space of QS which are otherwise authoritative in nature when implemented by technology companies and policy makers. Nafus and Sherman (2014) have identified practices emerging within the QS community, they categorise under the term "soft-resistance" (ibid). Soft resistance means that even within authoritative data structures, practices emerge that challenge the basic building blocks of the structure not by introducing alternatives but by playfully engaging with the technology in ways unintended by the industry and policy makers.

"Soft resistance happens when participants assume multiple roles as project designers, data collectors, and critical sense-makers, rapidly assessing and often changing what data they collect and why in response to idiosyncratically shifting sets of priorities and objectives. Such plasticity fragments data sets and disrupts current algorithmic logics, and thus creates both material and social resistance to traditional modes of data aggregation." (ibid: 1785)

The example mentioned above together with the notion of soft-resistance illustrates that the data of QS is a good example for what Latour calls a "factish". A "factish" mediates between scientific knowledge as absolute truth and the putative naïve believe in a thing which is "nothing in itself" (Latour 1999: 270) but merely a projection surface. The compound neologism of the terms fact and fetish indicates that both are at the same time fabricated, constructed, invented, devised, real and also powerful (ibid: 273). Therefore, truth is neither accessible by looking at so-called facts alone, nor can the fetish be dismissed of being a purely illusionary projection. The meaning and ramification of the "factish" can only be accessed by looking at the actions involved in its production, circulation and usage, and the way "arguments and actions are everywhere facilitated, permitted, and afforded by factishes" (ibid: 274). Seen as "factishes", data about the body obtained by QS can be put into action in ever unknown ways. It can even be used as connection into the afterlife, as in the example from the QS conference in Amsterdam:

"Dana has been using lifelogging to process her grief and maintain a connection to her memories of her mother. She keeps track of "mom sightings" [...] along with her location, comments (micro journal), and her mood or affect at that moment. She noted that her mood is usually multifaceted, with sometimes incongruent feelings co-existing. [...] This process has made her realize that she wishes she had done something like this while her mother was still alive. She'd love to have a record of what she was thinking and feeling each time her mother gave her a porcelain figurine (which she never appreciated at the time, but now they are like a collection of moments when her mom was still alive)."

While there are numerous examples of this kind of playful appropriation by the user, for the most part, QS is marketed as a productive method of self-engineering, in Butler's sense a very modern form of technocratic self-optimisation. The tracking and quantifying of bodily functions precedes the assumption of a body that can be changed and shaped in reconciliation with the results obtained from measurement. In advertisements for wearables, not only self-knowledge but also self-improvement is promised, ranging from "Tools to help you get your best rest" (Fitbit) over "A better brain in 3 minutes a day" (Muse Headband) to "Your path to a better you" (Jawbone). These ads can make these claims because the self of the quantified self is malleable and deficient, improvable only by technologically driven introspection. Necessary to this end, media technologies provide mirrors that point inwards and help to look into the body, as Gary Wolf states in a TED-talk on QS (2010): "The self is just our operation centre, our consciousness, our moral compass. So if we want to act more efficiently in the world, we have to get to know ourselves better." (ibid) Even though Wolf grants the self the ultimate agency over the direction of thought, the self as operation centre is reduced to its function to operate and react according to incoming data. From this position it has to initiate sustainable operations on the body, like behaviour modifications through the adjustment of one's own conduct according to the advice given by the technology. Perhaps the most unconcealed illustration of this underlying behaviourist concept of self-control and ultimately behavioural change through sensor feedback is the wristband called Pavlok by a company called the Behavioural Technology Group. The device sends out weak power surges ("zaps") to the wearer whenever a bad habit is detected by its sensors.

In this sense, the quantified self lines up with a novel understanding of the self, which evolves from the use of digital technology by ourselves on ourselves. This emphasis on the tracking of movement and activities with the help of technology hints to certain transformations of the original concept of techniques of the self.

First of all, self-tracking and methods of the quantified self signify a shift away from the examination of the consciousness and soul towards the examination of the body. In Greek and Christian terms, the self mainly consisted of the soul and the consciousness; in the present, however, the quantified self is concerned with the body and the mind as its control room. Quantifying the self encourages a somatisation of the self, which is well in line with modern "techniques of the body" described by Marcel Mauss in the 1930s. Techniques of the body is the term for activities that adjust the body to its purpose, and this purpose is predefined by the social (cf. Schüttpelz 2010: 7). In contrast to Foucault's techniques of the self, Mauss' techniques of the body are a subset of cultural techniques that put emphasis on the gestures, postures and daily activities that are both effective and traditional (Mauss 1973: 75).

"The techniques of the body can be classified according to their efficiency, i.e. according to the results of training. Training, like the assembly of a machine, is the search for, the acquisition of an efficiency. Here it is a human efficiency. These techniques are thus human norms of human training. These procedures that we apply to animals men voluntarily apply to themselves and to their children. The latter are probably the first beings to have been trained in this way, before all the animals, which first had to be tamed. As a result I could to a certain extent compare these techniques, them and their transmission, to training systems, and rank them in the order of their effectiveness." (Mauss 1973: 77-78)

The mode and method of the training as well as the form of the activity are historically contingent and determined by the social context. The techniques of sleep, rest or movement (e.g. the human gait) vary in different societies according to the different conditions and understandings of efficiency. The term "technique" is used by Mauss in the sense of the Greek *techné*, which refers to all kinds of useful activities of daily living that are taught and learned with the help of instructions, exercises or imitation of role models (cf. Schüttpelz 2010). This definition shares certain attributes with Foucault's techniques of the self and both authors describe the involvement of (media) technologies that accompany subject centred techniques (e.g. mnemonic devices).

Seen in this light, self-tracking, personal informatics and other practices of the quantified self portend a shift from subject centred techniques (e.g. meditation, keeping a diary) to the use of digital technology (e.g. live-logging, self-tracking and tracing). Due to this shift, the practice of introspection by means of temporal exercises gives way to constant automated monitoring and feedback. While subject centred techniques were bound to an iterating search for partial truths, the practice of quantifying the self and the data it generates are framed as direct access to a truth about the self. This entails the promise that acting according to the data, interpreting data, and comparing the data leads us towards accessing our true self.

This kind of permanent feedback is a step away from introspection and spontaneous human action towards a life that is permanently evaluated by others. Foucault reminds us that "governing people is not a way to force people to do what the governor wants; it is always a versatile equilibrium, with complementarity and conflicts between techniques which assure coercion and processes through which the self is constructed or modified by himself" (Foucault 1993: 204). Besides the tangible threat of direct surveillance through sensor technologies, life-logs can become a means of "sousveillance", not in the sense of corrective counter-surveillance to "surveil the surveillers" (Mann/Nolan/Wellman 2003: 348), but as a complement to techniques of panoptic data collection (cf. Dodge/Kitchin 2005). Thus, quantified bodies can become a resource for liberal governmental technologies, which seem predestined for a breed of biopolitics using digital behaviour control technologies within a normalising society (cf. Foucault 1978). Nikolas Rose calls this "the politics of Life itself".

"As human beings come to experience themselves in new ways as biological creatures, as biological selves, their vital existence becomes a focus of government, the target of novel forms of authority and expertise, a highly cathected field for knowledge, an expanding territory for bioeconomic exploitation, an organizing principle of ethics, and the stake in a molecular vital politics." (Rose 2007: 4)

But Foucault also reminds us that in the classical texts the practices of self-care are connoted positively throughout and do not have any negative meaning at all: "Thus we have the paradox of a precept of care of the self which signifies for us either egoism or withdrawal, but which for centuries was rather a positive principle that was the matrix for extremely strict moralities" (Foucault 2005: 13). Power is at the same time repressive and productive and the truth obtained about the self can be used in many ways.

Circulating Quantified Selves

Since data is at the same time a precondition of our access to the truth, the process of mapping the body is simultaneously a process of inscription, of giving form to a "myriad fluxes and flows" (Pickles 2004: 145) by creating numerical abstractions. Even if we reject the idea of a self that is expressed as a set of quantified data about the body and mind (as its operation system), this does not mean that the data obtained is not reacting with identity construction through an alteration of the techniques of the body and the self on a micro level. Data precedes the body and develops a productive agency, where the representation renders the abstract forms real once it starts its circulation in various data economies (cf. Nafus 2013). Sharing quantified self data becomes a common practice, with users of wearables leading the way by posting small maps with jogging tracks and lap times on social networking sites in order to compete with others. Health insurance companies are also offering discounts and premiums to those who track themselves and hand over their data. If we accept that, in the process of circulation, representations can develop a productive agency, we have to ask the question: What kind of subjects does a society produce when its members translate their bodies into discrete numerical objects? The salient point here seems to be the transformation of the quantified self as a "Technology of the

Self" or a "Technology of the Body" to a "Technology of the Social" (Lemke 2011): from the mapping of the self as an individual act to the sharing of self-data with others (a functionality afforded by the majority of tracking and tracing technologies). For example, lifelog technologies enable the subject to record and store everyday activities in textual, audio-visual and numerical form with the potential to "replace or complement existing memory preservation practices" (Allen 2008: 52). While these practices remediate traditional mnemonics, they can be turned into a means of surveillance leading to "incivility, emotional blackmail, exploitation, prosecution and social control" (ibid).

Perhaps one of the biggest issues here is the merging of individual measurements into big data and the gamification of the practices attached to self-tracking technologies. While the terms self-tracking as well as personal informatics suggest an individual tracker and that the practice is voluntary, a variety of collectives is emerging. The data obtained and the technologies used in the quantified self do not remain bound to the individual. Knowledge gets shared locally within QS community meetings (in so-called Show & Tells) and data circulates publicly in social and other networks becoming available to the provider of the technology and third-party agents. In addition, self-tracking could be officially advised, promoted, or even required in the future. Socio-economic ramifications arise when data is centrally stored and mined in the server farms. On aggregating platforms, statistical data can change its value and become a commodity when technologies of the self are decontextualised, deterritorialised and disseminated and, thus, the circulation of bodily knowledge is capitalised (cf. Barta/Neff 2016). And, since the technology companies operate worldwide, there is a global attempt to standardise techniques of the body and the self. Here lies the danger of marginalisation through the inscription of moral rules in the technology and infrastructure deployed. As already well observed by the science and technology studies, standards bear the risk of black boxing their underlying parameters, scales and rubrics, while at the same time naturalising the data in question through scientific certification and measurements: "technology freezes inscriptions, knowledge, information, alliances and actions inside black boxes, where they become invisible, transportable, and powerful in hitherto unknown ways as part of socio-technical networks" (Star 1990: 32). Thus, standards, pre-sets and arbitrary scorings in QS technologies can become a means of arrangement and demarcation when physical or psychological weaknesses circulate through the technical and socio-economic infrastructures of the data economy. An ethical issue arises here: the risk that user groups are marginalized by comparing them to a standardised biological self. A person affected with rheumatoid arthritis undergoing an acute exacerbation or a person facing a phase of depression, for example, might not be able to fulfil a specification of several thousand steps per day. But if the levels of insurance contributions are adjusted to these measures, solidary principles within public welfare systems get further eroded – a process though which new concerns arise: On what basis do techniques of the body get standardised and what happens if questionable standards become a norm in parts of the health economy (which overlaps with the public health system and the educational sector)? Who defines the axioms and objectives of this pedagogy? Who decides what kind of behaviour is prudent and what is not? What is a healthy lifestyle? In short: What are the stories behind the standards? (Lampland/Leigh Star 2009)

The first publicly led discussion about the politics and social ramifications of the quantified self concerned the attempt of a couple of insurance companies offering coupons and deductibles to customers committed to a healthy life according to the companies' norms. The companies electronically verified customers' fitness, nutrition and lifestyle on the basis of regularly submitted data about their bodily condition via special apps. Half a year ago it seemed as if insurance companies, government health services and policy makers all agreed on the usefulness of QS monitoring of parameters like glucose level, blood pressure and heart rhythm. A recent study shows that there is little evidence that the high expectations for self-observation and patient-centred care can be met and that self-observation will not necessarily lead to benefits for patients' physicians, or the insurance sector. As STSI Director Eric Topol reports, "A six-month randomized control trial found no short-term benefit in health costs or outcomes for patients monitoring their health with connected devices" (Comstock 2016). It is, however, too early to make final statements about the benefits of QS technologies under different circumstances and problem scenarios.

There is also another facet to the discourse surrounding self-tracking and personal informatics that puts an emphasis on the appropriation of expert knowledge and technology by laypeople, which can lead the way towards an emancipatory usage of data. Here the practice of self-tracking poses a challenge rather a then a threat. It is primarily a medical discourse, revolving around consumer health informatics, mobile health (Lupton 2012; 2013), or the figure of the e-patient, which concerns sociologists who investigate the shifting divide between expert knowledge and non-certified expertise (Brüninghaus/Heyen 2014), the changes in health communication (Fiore-Gartland/Neff 2015; Lomborg/Frandsen 2015) and the transformations in doctor patient relationships, possibly leading to collective and resisting practices within "citizen health" (Fox 2015). While there have been several studies and researches within the laboratory, the clinic, and the medical office, with some of them thematising the technicity of the technologies in place, few are concerned with the significance of the technicity of sensors within consumer electronics for our image of the self.

Researching Quantified Selves

Research into phenomena of the quantified self and statistical bodies has just begun and many publications are forthcoming (e.g. Lupton 2016; Neff/Nafus 2016; Duttweiler/Gugutzer/Passoth/Strübing 2016). But the question remains whether the phenomena of the quantified and statistical self will develop a cultural relevance in so far that it becomes a milestone in the history of the modern subject. For now, a lot of open questions remain: What is the reason for the boom in technologies for self-measurement and their dissemination in Social Media, computer games and other entertainment technologies? What are the explicit and implicit repercussions of the constitution of the subject? What is the cultural significance of statistical bodies? What are the concrete strategies for action and for the conduct of life that are opened up by the quantified self? What is the ratio of subjectification and technology as mediators of normalisation? Some of these questions are the subject matter of the articles in this issue of the *Digital Culture & Society* journal. Our concern is not to give definite answers but to explore a wide range of questions from different angles in order to enter the discourse and start the discussion about the practices of data gathering and quantification.

The first section of this issue *Situating the Quantified Self Phenomenon* takes one step back from the contemporary movement of self-tracking and situates the Quantified Self phenomenon within wider theoretical and historical discourses. Andréa Belliger and David Krieger start off with a discussion of the influence of quantification technologies on the formation of the modern subject. In their experimental piece, a fictional and winking dialogue between Socrates, Kevin Kelly, Gary Wolf and Bruno Latour among others arises. The authors let the protagonists discuss the emergence of an informational self that is constantly caught up in the process of networking and the moral and ethical questions that arise from this development. The growth of affect- and psychotechnologies is the topic of Marie-Luise Angerer and Bernd Bösel's contribution "Total Affect Control. Or: Who's Afraid of a Pleasing Little Sister?" They trace the roots of affect computing back to the 1950s, i.e. to a time when the cybernetisation of psychology joins research into affect sensitive computing and computer-assisted affect detection. After this genealogical derivation of contemporary phenomena of affective computing, a framework for a critical assessment is outlined. The paper "Theorizing the Quantified Self and Posthumanist Agency. Self-Knowledge and Posthumanist Agency in Contemporary US-American Literature" examines the intellectual histories of the quantified self within works of US-American literature. Stefan Danter, Ulfried Reichardt and Regina Schober focus on fictional works and how they reflect and comment on the changes of the human condition through quantification technologies. After a historical examination the current state is reflected using the example of the novel *Super Sad True Love Story* (2010) by Gary Shteyngart. The fictional text becomes a critical system of second-order observation which not only echoes contemporary practices of quantitative self-observation but provides ways to think about the repercussions of technology and even introduces epistemological counter-models to existing logics of technology-supported subjectification.

The second part *Investigations in Quantifying Practices* features two articles that are concerned with specific application scenarios of the quantified self. As distinct to the first part, where quantification is addressed as part of a wider discussion of the modes of modern and postmodern subjectivication. This section allows a closer look on end-user practices of self-measurement and observation. Alex Lambert moves away from body-centred quantifying practices and investigates tracking technologies that promise to assist in managing relationships. In "Bodies, Mood and Excess: Relationship-Tracking and the Technicity of Intimacy" he looks into the technicity of these applications and how new cultural techniques alter the attitude towards intimacy. By means of the application PplKpr (people keeper), Lambert shows how relationship-tracking produces an excess of meaning through which intimacy remains a continuous mystery. The link between mood and emotion tracking and positive psychology is the topic of Jill Belli's paper "Unhappy? There is an App for That. Tracking Well-Being through the Quantified Self." The article starts with an introduction to the ideology of positive psychology that branded itself "the science of happiness". After this introduction Belli gives a comprehensive overview over so-termed "happiness apps" and works out the influence of ideas originating from positive psychology using various examples.

Section three *Conceptual and Legal Reflections* gathers articles that deal with the practical ramifications of quantifying practices. Alex Gekker looks at quantification by interface design. In an autoethnographic exercise he shows how users of digital mapping applications get pulled into a "machine zone" build on quantified information and gamification strategies while using the application. Gekker uses the term "soft power" to characterize this kind of micro initiative to act in a certain way triggered by the technicity of the interface. While it is widely agreed that QS data somehow belongs to the sphere of personal privacy, neither the status of the data as private data nor the approach to assure this status are clear. Therefore, Argyro Karanasiou and Sharanjit Kang ask in their contribution "My Quantified Self, my FitBit and I: The Polymorphic Concept of Health Data and the Sharer's Dilemma" for a new legal framework to account for the privacy issues involved in personal sensor data. They trace the ambiguous concept of privacy through the history of legal discourse and, considering case studies of the private and public health sector, propose a shift from privacy as a demandable right to an autonomy-based concept.

Entering the Field is an experimental section of the *Digital Culture & Society* journal. It features shorter articles and allows for the presentation of early stage research, case studies, and explorative artistic works. With this section, we aim at providing a platform for researchers to enter discourse and start a discussion concerning their materials and methodological approaches. Barbara L. Marshall and Stephen Katz take a look at "quantified ageing" and how this field of inquiry is faced with fundamental changes when ageing bodies are measured, standardized and treated according to the logic of numerically based functionality. They lay out four fields of the research agenda on ageing and quantified selves: the use of wearables and mobile technology, digital apps, the gamification of ageing and the political economy of data sharing. The article "Games to Live With" by Paolo Ruffino deals with the gamification of life through combining quantification and game logics. Taking a closer look at NikeFuel, Farmville, Cookie Clicker and others, Ruffino shows how we do not use these technologies as tools for a specific purpose but rather as things we carry around and live with. Thus, these game and game-like technologies should be characterised as "parasites" and the question arises, how we can cohabit with these entities. In "Quantified Bodies – A Design Practice" James Dyer focuses on the quantified body as a body that is both read and written: a process which he claims to be ultimately a design task.

Dyer uses the notion of design in order to introduce an alternative reading of quantified self contrary to a critique which is all too often entangled in notions of ideology, social control or fetishisation. Looking on quantified self from the angle of design allows to bring back the agency of the tracker and to gain a more nuanced view on practices related to self-tracking without falling into the "well-trodden path of critique". Mette-Marie Zacher Sørensen presents and analyses contemporary art projects that all involve numerical methods to represent the human face and the identification of these faces, for example by applying DNA technology or software for biometric video analysis. In her article "Quantified Faces – On Surveillance Technologies, Identification and Statistics in Three Contemporary Art Projects" three works are situated in and compared to historical approaches that statistically compress physiognomy using Francis Galton's composite portraits from the 1800s and the author examines the technological agency at play. The contribution "Coupling Quantified Bodies Affective Possibilities of Self-Quantification beyond the Self" reports on a system the authors Robert Cercós, William Goddard, Adam Nash and Jeremy Yuille have designed that introduces a structural coupling of human and non-human bodies. In their work "Dataponics: Human-Vegetal Play", human physical activity measured by a Fitbit is mapped to the amount of light and water fed to a potted plant. The moisture in the growing hydroponic medium that surrounds the plant's roots is measured, and the system plays different internet radio stations accordingly. The authors initiate a discussion on the theoretical lessons that can be learned by looking at this setup.

For the interview section *In Conversation with*, the editors talked with the two artist-engineers Tega Brain and Surya Mattu about the quantified self, astrology, and Google galleries. On their website unfitbits.com the artists introduce ways to "[f]ree your fitness data from yourself", "[e]arn insurance discounts!", and promise "fitness solutions for every lifestyle." The website features audits of various homemade appliances that work with step counters, like a Marcel Duchamp style bicycle wheel, a metronome, and an orderable desktop pendulum.

We hope you enjoy this second issue of the *Digital Culture & Society* journal. The editors would like to thank all contributors, our editorial board members and reviewers for their cooperation, commitment and support. The next issue will be a special issue on *Politics of Big Data*, edited by Mark Coté, Paolo Gerbaudo and Jennifer Pybus. It will be published in September 2016.

References

Abreu, Amelia (2015): "The Quantified Stoner", November 26, 2015, (http://motherboard.vice.com/read/the-quantified-stoner).

Albrechtslund, Anders/Lauritsen, Peter (2013): "Spaces of Everyday Surveillance: Unfolding an Analytical Concept of Participation." In: Geoforum 49, pp. 310-16.

Allen, Anita L. (2008): "Dredging up the Past: Lifelogging, Memory, and Surveillance." In: The University of Chicago Law Review 75/1, pp. 47-74.

Barta, Kristen/Neff, Gina (2016): "Technologies for Sharing: Lessons from Quantified Self About the Political Economy of Platforms." In: Information, Communication & Society 19/4, pp. 518-531.

Beltramelli, Tony (2015): Deep-Spying: Spying using Smartwatch and Deep Learning, Master Theses, Copenhagen: IT University of Copenhagen.

Brüninghaus, Anne/Heyen, Nils (2014): "Wissenstransfer von der Gesellschaft in die Wissenschaft? Formen und Potenziale nicht-zertifizierter Expertise für Lebenswissenschaften und Medizin." In: Technikfolgenabschätzung 23/2, pp. 63-66.

Butler, Mark (2014): Das Spiel mit sich. (Kink, Drugs & Hip-Hop). Populäre Techniken des Selbst zu Beginn des 21. Jahrhunderts, Berlin: Kulturverlag Kadmos.

Comstock, Jonah (2016): "Scripps Wired for Health study results show no clinical or economic benefit from digital health monitoring", (http://mobihealthnews.com/content/scripps-wired-health-study-results-show-no-clinical-or-economic-benefit-digital-health).

Crawford, Kate/Lingel, Jessa/Karppi, Tero (2015): "Our Metrics, Ourselves: A Hundred Years of Self-Tracking from the Weight Scale to the Wrist Wearable Device." In: European Journal of Cultural Studies 18/4-5, pp. 479-96.

Dodge, Martin/Kitchin, Rob (2007): "'Outlines of a world coming into existence': pervasive computing and the ethics of forgetting." In: Environment and Planning B: Planning & Design 34/3: pp. 431-445.

Duttweiler, Stefanie/Gugutzer, Robert/Passoth, Jan-Hendrik/Strübing, Jörg (eds.) (2016): Leben nach Zahlen. Self-Tracking als Optimierungsprojekt?, Bielefeld: transcript, forthcoming September 2016.

Eggers, Dave (2013): The Circle, New York: Alfred A. Knopf.

Fiore-Gartland, Brittany/Neff, Gina (2015): "Communication, Mediation, and the Expectations of Data: Data Valences Across Health and Wellness Communities." In: International Journal of Communication 9, pp. 1466-84.

Fox, Nick J. (2015): "Personal Health Technologies, Micropolitics and Resistance: A New Materialist Analysis." In: Health, online first, July 27, pp. 1-18.

Foucault, Michel (1978): "Governmentality." In: Graham Burchell/Colin Gordon/Peter Miller (eds.), The Foucault Effect. Studies in Governmentality, Chicago: The University of Chicago Press, pp. 87-104.

Foucault, Michel (1988): "Technologies of the Self." In: Martin H. Luther/Huck, Gutman/Patrick H. Hutton (eds.), Technologies of the Self. A Seminar with Michel Foucault, London: Tavistock Publications, pp. 16-49.

Foucault, Michel (1993): "About the Beginning of the Hermeneutics of the Self: Two Lectures at Dartmouth." In: Political Theory 21/2, pp. 198-227.

Foucault, Michel (2005): The Hermeneutics of the Subject. Lectures at the Collège de France, 1981-82, New York: Palgrave Macmillan.

Harrisson, Tom/Jennings, Humphrey/Madge, Charles (1937): "Anthropology at Home," In: New Statesman and Nation, January 30, 1937.

Harrisson, Tom/Madge, Charles (1940): War Begins at Home. London: Chatto and Windus.

Hinton, James (2010): Nine Wartime Lives: Mass-Observation and the Making of the Modern Self. Oxford: Oxford University Press.

Hume, David (1738): "Of Personal Identity." In: Of the Understanding. Book I, Part IV, Section 6 of the Treatise of Human Nature.

Kelly, Kevin (2015): "Meet the QS Labs Team", In: QS – Self Knowledge Through Numbers, December 2015 (http://quantifiedself.com/aboutqs-labs/).

Lampland, Martha/Star, Susan Leigh (eds.) (2009): Standards and their Stories. How Quantifying, Classifying, and Formalizing Practices Shape Everyday Life, Ithaca, NY: Cornell University Press.

Latour, Bruno (1999): Pandora's Hope. Essays on the Reality of Science Studies, Cambridge/London: Harvard University Press.

Lemke, Thomas (2011): "Beyond Foucault: From Biopolitics to the Government of Life." In: Bröckling, Ulrich/Krasmann, Susanne/Lemke, Thomas (eds.), Governmentality. Current Issues and Future Challenges. New York: Routledge.

Lomborg, Stine/Frandsen, Kirsten (2015): "Self-Tracking as Communication." In: Information, Communication & Society, online, August 3, 2015, pp. 1-13.

Lupton, Deborah (2012): "M-Health and Health Promotion: The Digital Cyborg and Surveillance Society." In: Social Theory & Health 10/3, pp. 229-44.

Lupton, Deborah (2013): "Quantifying the Body: Monitoring and Measuring Health in the Age of mHealth Technologies." In: Critical Public Health 23/4, pp. 393-403.

Lupton, Deborah (2014): "Self-Tracking Cultures: Towards a Sociology of Personal Informatics." In: Proceedings of the 26th Australian Computer-Human Interaction Conference (OzCHI '14), New York: ACM Press, pp. 77-86.

Lupton, Deborah (2016): The Quantified Self: A Sociology of Self-Tracking Cultures, Cambridge: Polity Press, forthcoming April 2016.

Mann, Steve/Nolan, Jason/Wellman, Barry (2003): "Sousveillance: Inventing and Using Wearable Computing Devices for Data Collection in Surveillance Environments." In: Surveillance & Society 1/3, pp. 331-355.

Mauss, Marcel (1973): "Techniques of the Body." In: Economy and Society 2/1, pp. 70-88.

Nafus, Dawn (2013): "The Data Economy of Biosensors." In: Michael J. McGrath/Cliodhna Ní Scanaill (eds.), Sensor Technologies. Healthcare, Wellness and Environmental Applications, New York: Springer, pp. 137-156.

Nafus, Dawn/Sherman, Jamie (2014): "This One Does Not Go Up to 11: The Quantified Self Movement as an Alternative Big Data Practice." In: International Journal of Communication 8, pp. 1784-1794.

Neff, Gina/Nafus, Dawn (2016): Self-Tracking. Cambridge, MA: The MIT Press, forthcoming May 2016.

Pickles, John (2004): A History of Spaces. Cartographic Reason, Mapping, and the Geo-Coded World, London/New York: Routledge.

Rose, Nikolas (2007): The Politics of Life Itself, Princeton/Oxford: Princeton University Press.

Schüttpelz, Erhard (2010): "Body Techniques and the Nature of the Body. Re-Reading Marcel Mauss", In: Deiters. Franz-Josef/Fliethmann, Axel/Lang,

Birgit/Lewis/Alison/Weller, Christiane (Hg.): Limbus. Australian Yearbook of German Literary and Cultural Studies 2010. Nach der Natur – After Nature. Freiburg: Rombach, pp. 177-194.

Schütz, Alfred (1964): "The well-informed citizen", In: Collected papers. Vol. II. Studies in social theory. The Hague: Martinus Nijhoff, pp. 120-134.

Smart, Alastair (2013): "Mass Observation at the Photographers Gallery", In: The Telegraph August 10, 2013 (http://www.telegraph.co.uk/culture/art/art-reviews/10234037/Mass-Observation-at-the-Photographers-Gallery.html).

Star, Susan Leigh (1990): "Power, Technology and the Phenomenology of Conventions: On Being Allergic to Onions." The Sociological Review 38/S1, pp. 25-56.

Wolf, Gary (2010): The Quantified Self, TED@Cannes, June 2010 (https://www.ted.com/talks/gary_wolf_the_quantified_self?language=de).

Situating the Quantified Self Phenomenon

From Quantified to Qualified Self
A Fictional Dialogue at the Mall

Andréa Belliger and David J. Krieger

Abstract

Quantifying the self is not enough; numbers and statistics must be interpreted, that is, integrated into networks of identity, society, and meaning. The quantified self must become a "qualified" self if body tracking is to have any impact on our lives and society. Data generated by body tracking in all forms are not merely a passive material for interpretation, they do not merely lie around in databases until something from outside makes meaning out of them. Data become information and flow in global networks. Without access to data, individuals must rely on experts and expert systems. Putting body-related data into the hands of those who are directly concerned makes them responsible for doing something with the data, for interpreting and making use of the data. Interpreting the data of body tracking occurs as networking. It breaks out of the constraints of modern subjectivity as well as paternalistic health care structures and occurs by participation, communication, and transparency, that is, by following "network norms." Personal informatics and body tracking is a performative enactment of the informational self. The informational self is neither the product of technologies of power (Foucault), but of an "ethical" technology of the self. The self becomes a hub and an agent in the digital network society. Body tracking transforms the opaque and passive body of the pre-digital age into the informational self. Networking is the way in which order – personal, social, and ontological – is constructed in the digital age.

When Socrates took up the maxim of the Delphic oracle, "know thyself" in order to lead his disciples on the road to wisdom, he could not have known how "personal informatics" would understand this aphorism today. According to the movement's official Website, personal informatics "is a class of tools that help people collect personally relevant information for the purpose of self-reflection and self-monitoring. These tools help people gain self-knowledge about one's behaviour, habits, and thoughts."[1] As this broad definition suggests, personal informatics is concerned with any and all digital information that pertains to one's activities, work, hobbies, finances, family situation, and of course,

---

1   Cf. http://www.personalinformatics.org/.

health, both physical and mental. A more narrow definition focuses primarily on physical and mental health. For this reason, personal informatics are often referred to as "body tracking," "self-tracking," "life logging," and "quantified self." If Socrates lived today, would he encourage the young men of Athens to wear smart watches that continuously monitor their blood pressure, blood glucose levels, nutrition, temperature, movements, heart rate, sleep rhythms, stress, emotional state, posture, surrounding air quality, and much more? This question is not merely rhetorical. If one accepts the claim of the Quantified Self Movement of "self-knowledge through self-tracking with technology,"[2] the road to wisdom leads through a newly accessible land of numbers, charts, graphs, projections, sensors, apps and algorithms. If Socrates met the two "founders" of the Quantified Self Movement, Gary Wolf and Kevin Kelly at the mall, we might suppose he would raise some critical questions about this new form of self-knowledge and attempt to convince his interlocutors that numbers are not enough and that a "quantified" self must go on to become a "qualified" self.

Questioning the validity, objectivity, and usefulness of quantification in any area of human life, and above all in the area of medicine and health, is not easy. We Moderns have come to associate knowledge and truth with scientific methods and hard, empirical facts. Modern medicine is based on accurate measurements of many different bodily processes and functions. Health is defined as "the level of functional and/or metabolic efficiency of an organism."[3] This is usually understood to mean a state of well-being free from illness and disease.[4] Levels of metabolic efficiency are numerical values obtained by technologies of quantification, technologies that in the past were located in specialised laboratories, hospitals, and doctor's offices. Advances in sensorics and wearable computing have brought the laboratory to the patient. Measuring metabolic efficiency no longer requires large expensive machines and perhaps weeks to complete. Everybody today can have inexpensive access to accurate medical- and health-related data continuously and everywhere. We know what the results of the laboratory tests are, before we enter the doctor's office. However, we still go to the doctor. We do this because the meaning of the data depends on understanding medical research and medical science, that is, being a medical expert.

Whatever Gary Wolf and Kevin Kelly might say to Socrates, if a doctor walked by and joined in the discussion, he would certainly say that self-knowledge is a matter of science and not philosophy and that the only oracle worth listening to are laboratory results. These are objective facts. Being able to say this with justification, pride, and perhaps a little complacency, is itself the result of a long history of transformations in what "knowledge" means, and in what it means to know one's self. Just so that Socrates gets it right, and seizing the opportunity to tell Wolf and Kelly what he thinks about so-called e-patients and self-trackers, our doctor might go on to say that not just anybody is qualified for knowledge of the self. He himself went through four hard years of medical school and six

---

2   Cf. Wikipedia https://en.wikipedia.org/wiki/Quantified_Self.
3   Wikipedia https://en.wikipedia.org/wiki/Health_(disambiguation).
4   Cf. Miriam Webster Dictionary http://www.merriam-webster.com/dictionary/health.

years internship. Knowledge of the self requires a self that is properly *qualified* and not just properly quantified. Only those who have undergone rigorous training in the scientific method are qualified for self-knowledge. Finally, he might indignantly add, "You, Socrates, you of all people should know this, for it is you who attempted to lead the young men of your time away from mere opinion to rationality and truth!"

Foucault has pointed out that the idea of a scientific qualification for self-knowledge is the result of a long and changing history. In the ancient world, knowledge of self was always accompanied, if not preceded, by an "ethical" relation to the self. Together with knowing the self, the ancient tradition recognized also the "care" for oneself, *epimelesthai sautou*, 'to take care of yourself,' or 'the concern with self.'

"In Greek and Roman texts, the injunction of having to know yourself was always associated with the other principle of having to take care of yourself, and it was that need to care for oneself that brought the Delphic maxim into operation." (Foucault 1997: 226)

The nearness, if not inseparability, of these two ways of relating to the self highlights at least two important ideas that have gone under in the course of Western history. First, there is the insight that knowing oneself and taking care of oneself are inseparable. This means that there is no value free, objective, impartial, and uninvolved knowledge of the self. Knowledge is always guided, structured, conditioned, and entangled in practices that are "ethical" in some way. Second and closely related to the first insight, there is the ancient view of knowing and caring as essentially *practical activities of relating to the self*. Both self-knowledge and care of the self are that which the ancient Greeks would call *techné*. Foucault speaks of "technologies of the self" in order to emphasize that it is a matter of practices

"which permit individuals to effect by their own means, or with the help of others, a certain number of operations on their own bodies and souls, thought, conduct, and way of being, so as to transform themselves in order to attain a certain state of happiness, purity, wisdom, perfection, or immortality." (ibid: 225)

This explains why the Delphic maxim did not refer to a purely objective knowledge in the modern scientific sense, but linked knowledge of the self to a process of self-qualification and preparedness for the truth. For Plato, caring for the self meant preparing oneself to serve the community in the *polis*. The ideals of the "good" *(kalos)* and the "beautiful" *(kagathos)* were deeply inscribed in what knowing and caring for the self were all about. Only a self that is ethically and practically *qualified* can achieve self-knowledge.

In the course of Western history both the idea that knowing is an "ethical" endeavour and the idea that all such endeavours are practices of self-construction, that is "technologies", have undergone transformations. Heidegger (1977) pointed out that the original Greek idea of technology *(techné)* cannot be equated with what we Moderns understand by technology.[5] The original meaning of *techné* was a way of knowing by which something is brought into being not only with regard to how it functions, but also with regard to values such as beauty and goodness. Modern technology on the contrary is defined by functionality alone. A technological artefact today does not have to be beautiful or ethically good. It has to function efficiently, reliably, and quickly. Originally, *techné* was a making or constructing *(poiesis)* that was not distinguishable from what artists, poets, philosophers, and politicians do. On the basis of the ancient texts, Foucault, at least in his later work, attempts to revive the ideal of a "technology" of the self that is more than pure functionality, but includes "ethical" and "aesthetic" aspects. A technology of the self only concerned with functionality, efficiency, precision, and quantification are what Foucault (1997) calls "technologies of power, which determine the conduct of individuals and submit them to certain ends or domination, an objectivizing of the subject" (Foucault 1997: 225). A technology of the self that returns to the primacy of "caring for the self" and to an original form of *techné* would be more of an "ethics" than a technology. With regard to practices of self-quantification and body tracking, an ethics of the self would not primarily be directed toward the goals of freedom from illness or enhancement of performance and productivity. Instead, coming to know the self would be directed to the self as a work of art and an ethical achievement.

For both Heidegger and Foucault it is clear that modern technologies, including medical technologies, are inherently technologies of power. Foucault emphasizes that technologies of power and technologies of self are always entangled with each other, and also with technologies of production and technologies of language. Nonetheless, it can be shown that specific forms of these entanglements are historical, changeable, and contingent. This is also true for the specific constellation of knowledge, technology, and power characteristic of the modern world. Perhaps the Platonic dialogue in the mall with self-trackers, doctors, and a philosopher might offer an occasion to witness a turning point in our historical constellation of self-knowledge.

Let us suppose that Gary Wolf and Kevin Kelly, our two self-trackers, claim that body tracking provides us with objective, reliable, and accurate knowledge of our bodies, our feelings, and our activities. We may suppose that the doctor who is also participating in the discussion acknowledges this, but claims that people who are not scientifically trained are not qualified to understand or act upon quantified knowledge of the self. The quantified self without the properly

---

5   We base our understanding of Modernity on Latour's description in *We Have Never Been Modern* (1993). Heidegger (1977) emphasized the functional character of the modern view of technology. For Luhmann technology can be considered an evolutionary advance because its functionality reduces the complexity of social order, or as Luhmann (2012: 313) puts it, it supports consensus: "If technical arrangements are preferred in societal evolution, this appears mainly to be because, although they involve artificial objects, they save consensus. What works, works. What proves its worth has proved its worth. Agreement does not have to be reached."

qualified self is a mere hobby, a form of digital recreation with no serious consequences or significance. What would Socrates say about this? If we assume that Socrates did not pass through two thousand years of history to arrive at the mall, the present day Agora, without noticing what was going on, he would probably point out that the rise of Christianity radically changed the original Greek idea of self-knowledge. Christianity led to focusing on self-knowledge as a means of reconciliation with God. This meant closely examining all the temptations to sin associated with the body and earthly life.[6] The true self is therefore the self that heeds the Word of God and renounces sinfulness as well as attachment to the body. The idea of "taking care of oneself" as an ethically guided *techné* is lost under the dominance of spiritual techniques that were aimed to separate the true self from the sinful body. The ethical dimension became thereby merely "moral," that is, a question of *compliance* to God's laws. Foucault distinguishes between the ethical and the moral. Morality is directed toward compliance to given rules, whereas the ethical is a project of self-realisation guided by aesthetic norms and the creativity of *techné*. During the Middle Ages, ethics became morality and the aesthetic dimension was lost entirely, and the gap between technologies of production, technologies of power, and technologies of self widened.

When Christianity became secularised at the beginning of the Modern period, the self had to come to know itself without God's help. "Know thyself" became for Descartes a method to attain certainty by clearly and distinctly separating the self that is transparent to itself in thought from the opaque and extended body. The self appeared to itself as a *res cogitans*, a purely thinking thing in opposition to the physical body and the world in which it was extended. The body, for its part, became an object, a machine, an organism that could be known by means of the physical and biological sciences. After the demise of the transcendental ego of the Cartesian tradition, the conscious subject also became an object of science, the sciences of psychology and sociology. Introspection or simply attempting to turn one's gaze within did not lead to any objective, reliable knowledge at all. At the end of the Modern period, there remains only one kind of knowledge: objective, empirical, quantifiable scientific knowledge. However, as our doctor rightly claims, not just anybody is a scientist. Not just anyone understands what the objective, quantified data of science mean. Even after the subject of modern philosophy disappeared into the data of the psychology, sociology, and medicine, there remained the "qualified" subject of scientific knowing itself. Being a scientist means having attained a position in which knowing is observation untainted by desires, ideologies, historical and cultural limitations.[7] The scientific observer is universal, impartial, disembodied, and only because of this, able to discover the facts. These two, the quantified self that is an object of science and the scientifically qualified self who is capable of making sense of the data now stand opposed in a fictive dialogue with Socrates

---

6 Here we follow Foucault's (1997) history of the ideas of self-knowledge.
7 This is the traditional self-understanding of science in Modernity as is apparent in the debate between "understanding" and "explanation" (cf. Apel 1988).

at the mall. We ask again, what Socrates would say in order to lead his interlocutors on the path to wisdom.

If Heidegger and Foucault are right about the original meaning of self-knowledge as intimately associated with "caring for the self" and thus as an ethical practice, and if self-knowledge is much rather a *techné* in the sense of aiming at aesthetic as well as functional values, we must assume that Socrates would be appalled at the schizophrenic division of human beings into subjects and objects. The cold, quantified data on the one side, and the objective, value-free, disembodied scientific observer on the other. He would also be appalled at the thought that he has nothing to say without a PhD and a long internship. He finds himself in a *polis* made up of objectivized bodies on the one side and a small class of experts on the other, and as bridge between them, a complex state apparatus called Health Care and Public Health, suspiciously exemplifying all the characteristics of tyranny.[8] It is the experts, after all, who set the standard values and norms by means of which data is evaluated. Who says our blood pressure is "too high" or that we have to take ten thousand steps per day? Based on what authority, or sanctions, are we told to change our lives?

At this point, two bystanders who have been listening attentively to the discussion finally decide to join in. Humberto Maturana and Francisco Varela, who are biologists, hasten to assure everyone that there are neither subjects nor objects, but only complex adaptive systems. These systems are self-organising, autopoietic, self-referential, and informationally closed. Maturana and Varela (1987) argue that cognition is a biological function. Self-knowledge is nothing other than the way that a central nervous system processes information in order to maintain its autopoiesis, that is, "self-production." Organisms do not take in information from outside, but construct information according to their own organisation out of undifferentiated perturbations coming from the environment. Body tracking exemplifies this perfectly because it demonstrates how the self relates to itself on the basis of measurements so as to maintain certain values with regard to vital processes. The self is a cybernetic, that is, self-steering system. They explain this in the following way:

"What occurs in a living system is analogous to what occurs in an instrumental flight where the pilot does not have access to the outside world and must function only as a controller of the values shown in his flight instruments. His task is to secure a path of variations in the readings of his instruments, either according to a prescribed plan, or to one that becomes specified by these readings. When the pilot steps out of the plane he is bewildered by the congratulations of his friends on account of the perfect flight and landing that he performed in absolute darkness. He is perplexed because to his knowledge all that he did at any moment was to maintain the readings of his instruments within certain specified limits, a task which is in no way represented by the description that his friends (observers) make of his conduct." (Maturana/Varela 1987: 51)

---

8   Cf. Lupton (1995) for an historical and sociological description of Public Health on the basis of Foucault's analysis of power.

Wolf and Kelly may be assumed to approve of this, because this is exactly what their tracking devices do. They provide real-time measurements of all the important vital functions so that the self can quickly and efficiently respond, just as the pilot responds to the continuous measurements of altitude, speed, wind velocity, and so on shown by the instruments. Self-trackers are confident that when they "live by numbers," that is, follow their instruments, they will fly safely through life and arrive at well-being.[9] Maturana and Varela agree with Socrates that knowing is doing and that self-knowing amounts to constructing the self, much in the original sense of *techné*. Knowledge and truth are forms of adaptation, that is, insofar as they serve to maintain the operations of the system within a specific environment. If they do not do this, the system disintegrates. Maturana and Varela must admit, however, that this reduces the ethical aspect of "caring for the self" to a question of life or death. Truth is viability. Anything short of death is good and beautiful. If there is a problem with the instruments, or the pilot makes an error in judgement, the plane crashes. Maybe others can learn from this, but it is too late for him.

Socrates is at once relieved and troubled by these ideas. We no longer have quantified selves on the one side and qualified, expert selves on the other with nothing to regulate their relations but technologies of power. Instead, we have self-constructing systems using quantitative data in order to monitor and maintain their operations. Nonetheless, Socrates has some questions for Maturana and Varela. If we take the theory of autopoiesis and the biology of cognition as an example of a "technology of the self" in Foucault's sense of ethics, and also in Heidegger's understanding of *techné*, this raises two questions:

1. Where do the parameters of the instruments come from? How does the pilot know that actions he or she undertakes to correct the readings on the instruments have a beneficial effect? Maintaining autopoiesis alone, mere viability amounts to just getting by and not necessarily attaining a state of ethical and aesthetic perfection. Just because natural selection has spared us for the moment, does not mean we are "better" people for that.
2. What effect do the actions of the pilot have on the parameters themselves and not merely on the compliance to the values they dictate? Can the actions of the pilot change the parameters? Or do they merely amount to a kind of "morality," that is, a question of compliance to established standards? What chance of creativity and innovation does the pilot have, when he or she can only react to parameters inscribed in the instruments?

Having heard enough of these strange theories, our doctor re-enters the discussion. He makes it clear that as far as the parameters are concerned, they come from scientific knowledge of the body concerning sickness. Health is nothing other than the absence of sickness and disease. Medical science has decided

---

9   For Lupton (2013: 9) the self-tracker is "a truly cybernetic organism in its attempts to create a closed regulatory system, in which data are produced which then affect behaviours that then create further data and so on."

how high our blood pressure can be, if we are to avoid serious consequences. In addition to this, medical experts, such as the ACSM (American College of Sport Medicine) have established clear "exercise prescriptions" or fitness activities based on research into the relation between physical exercises and certain diseases such as cardiovascular diseases, and body composition diseases (for example, obesity).[10] Objective knowledge of the body sets a norm for health, such as BMI (Body Mass Index), to which one should comply by means of exercises, diet, etc. Body tracking and self-quantification is a means to quickly, easily, and continuously measure the difference between the norm and one's present state. The goal is to attain to the norm or the target value of the cybernetic system. The doctor admits that this is not unlike Maturana's and Varela's description the activities of the pilot who follows instruments in order to maintain the proper altitude and speed of the airplane. However, it is clear that medical experts need to interpret the readings on the instruments and advise the pilot on what to do. Furthermore, he hastens to remind the group, sport medicine, as the name suggests, offers a second meaning of "fitness," namely, that which is necessary for improved performance and skill. Competitive sports are concerned not with absence of disease, but with extraordinary bodily skills, endurance, and abilities that are revealed in competition. Enhancing the body with extraordinary skills and abilities is the goal of fitness and exercises in this second sense. Here one can speak of optimizing, extending, and enhancing the body and the self. Fitness in this sense of the word need not be directly correlated to disease. On the contrary, health takes on the meaning of a certain kind of excellence. Socrates should know this. Was it not the culture of ancient Greece that gave us the Olympics?

Wolf and Kelly probably feel themselves misunderstood at this point and attempt to explain what quantified self really means. Personal informatics should not be subsumed under the traditional meanings of fitness. It is a combination of both and also much more. Personal informatics is not merely "personal" in the sense of being related only to one individual person. It is a kind of self-knowledge that goes beyond the self and involves the environment and the community. As Gary Wolf points out "there is a strong tendency among self-trackers to share data and collaborate on new ways of using it."[11] All the tools and technologies of digitalisation transform the body and the self into information that flows into databases, online platforms, patient communities, social networking sites, etc. Personal informatics encompasses much more than merely body related information. The many different kinds of information that are created, collected, collated, correlated, communicated, and commented become big data, that is, data gathered not merely from body tracking, but from all areas of life, and not exclusively health related. At its best, personal informatics uses big data analytics and social media to discover correlations

---

10   See the discussion of sport medicine from the perspective of Foucault in Markula/Pringle (2006).

11   http://archive.wired.com/medtech/health/magazine/17-07/lbnp_knowthyself?currentPage=all.

and meaning in information that heretofore were hidden from view. Before the advent of the many tracking tools and technologies we have today, the self was informationally opaque and underdetermined. The technologies of personal informatics succeed in turning the self into information so that it becomes transparent and understandable. There is nothing that cannot be digitalised and transformed into information. The self is no longer either an object of scientific knowledge or a trained scientific observer, but is transported onto the plane of information in which every bit counts and everyone is an expert that has something to contribute. It is the "informational self" or the "networked self" that self-tracking reveals.[12] The informational self is not the neo-liberal individual caught within the tensions and contradictions of freedom and self-determination on the one side and macro-social structures such as big government and big industry on the other.[13] As Foucault might put it, the informational self is a product of a specific historical form of "technology of the self," that is, a specific way of relating to the self which constitutes the self in a certain way. The informational self cannot be modelled as an autopoietic system that knows itself self-referentially by means of distinguishing itself from an environment. The many different kinds of information that appear on the screens of self-trackers do not fit into any one system, but link to many other kinds of information throughout the World Wide Web. The Web is non-hierarchical, inclusive, connected, complex, and public.[14] Knowledge, including self-knowledge, is no longer subject to an economy of scarcity as it was in the age of print media. It is more like a cloud than a pyramid. This means that knowledge can best be modelled as a network in which all participate.

Wolf and Kelly go on to point out that what distinguishes the informational self from the neo-liberal, individualistic self that is based on cybernetic models are the affordances of the technologies of self-tracking. Personal informatics supports and encourages connectivity, communication, and flow of information of all kinds. The affordances of self-tracking technologies are socially oriented. Not privacy, but "publicy" (Boyd 2010) is the default. We may still be reading instruments, but the instruments lead us beyond the isolated individual. Once the self has become information, it begins to flow in unforeseeable ways through the myriad connections of global networks. These networks have no clear boundaries. In this "space of flows" (Castells 1996) everything is connected to everything else. The informational self cannot be "informationally closed" as an autopoietic system must be. Instead, it is informationally open to everything else flowing through global networks. Reading the instruments of personal informatics does not show how an organism must maintain certain levels in order to adapt to perturbations in the environment. On the contrary, personal

---

12 Cf. Belliger/Krieger (2015).
13 Cf. Lupton's (2014b) typology of self-trackers, which stretches from "private" and voluntary on one end to collective and "imposed" and "exploited" on the other, is derived from this traditional sociological model.
14 Cf. Weinberger (2012) for a discussion of the nature of knowledge in the age of the Internet.

informatics disclose an "ecology" of information that extends beyond any individual body.[15] The infrastructure of connectivity and flow that makes up the Web hinders any kind of clear boundaries between system and environment. These boundaries, however, as Maturana and Varela admit, are constitutive for autopoietic systems. In their theory, if an organism cannot distinguish itself from its environment, it cannot direct its operations to itself and cannot act to maintain its autopoiesis. It disintegrates into the environment and disappears. Personal informatics, on the other hand, transforms systemic disintegration into forms of network integration. This opens up the possibility of redefining the meaning of "health" and reformulating Foucault's ideal of an ethics as *techné* of the self on the basis of the norms that guide the activity of "networking."[16]

At this moment, the group becomes aware of a tall man standing in the corner who seems to be observing them and writing down everything they say in a small notebook. Out of curiosity, they approach the man and ask him what he is doing. He introduces himself as Bruno Latour and explains that he is a French ethnologist working on the project of an "anthropology of the Moderns."[17] He is very interested in what Wolf and Kelly are saying about networks, since he himself developed a way of seeing the world called "actor-network theory." Since he claims to be an expert on networks, Socrates asks him to explain in plane words the meaning of what Wolf and Kelly are talking about. Latour apologises for not knowing much about personal informatics, but he has studied networks for decades and has discovered that what we call science, technology, and society are forms of associations between human and non-human actors. Nothing can exist alone, all by itself. Everything that comes to be and takes its place in our world does so by means of linking up to other things, forming alliances, delegating actions, entering into hybrid and heterogeneous assemblages that can be described as "actor-networks." Actor-networks are everywhere. Indeed, actors are themselves networks made up of many different associations. Even so-called "cognition" is a network effect, as the recent discussions of "distributed cognition" and "extended mind" show.[18] The self is not a closed system, as Maturana and Varela suppose. It cannot know itself by sharply distinguishing between its own operations and the surrounding environment. Instead, the self is a network and self-knowledge is a process of building, maintaining, dismantling, and transforming networks that extend in all directions and include many different kinds of actors. Ecology is a case in point. Has not the ecological crisis and the advent of the "Anthropocene" shown that there are no boundaries between organisms and environment. The whole planet, Gaia, is one immense ecological network in which every actor is connected in many different ways

---

15   After insisting on the importance of private and individual self-tracking, Lupton (2015: 4) admits that the technologies themselves have social, participatory, and "prosumptive" affordances.
16   In the following, we rely on our discussion of networking in Krieger/Belliger (2014).
17   Cf. Latour (2013).
18   Cf. Rowlands (2010) for a discussion of non-Cartesian cognitive science.

to every other.[19] When Wolf and Kelly talk about the big data of personal informatics, they are talking about networks that include information not just about the blood pressure, heart rate, etc. of individuals, but about the quality of water and air, the effects of urbanisation, climate change, and many other factors that demonstrate exactly the interconnectedness of all things. If there is any pilot flying blindly by instruments than it is not an individual organism, but the human species that is steering Gaia either toward a safe landing or disaster.

Latour insists that if personal informatics are about networking, then they are not merely "personal" or "private." What he has heard about body tracking is mostly complaints and fears about loss of privacy. However, if he is right about actor-networks, then there never was such a thing as privacy anyway.[20] In addition, quite apart from these worries, networking has a positive side. It enables an ethical dimension of responsibility toward the "health" and well-being of the planet. If we have learned anything from ecology, it is the impossibility of drawing sharp boundaries between organisms and environments and the inescapably ethical dimension of self-knowledge. Self-knowledge and care of self cannot be understood as the self-reference of an informationally closed system flying blindly in an environment over which it has no control, an environment which either "selects" it to survive or not. Instead, what networks show us is that "caring for self" and caring for Gaia are the same. He admits that it is not easy to talk about these things and that the chances of being misunderstood are high. Even two thousand years ago, Socrates was considered by many to be a dangerous troublemaker leading the youth of Athens astray. Foucault, at the end of his life, could only formulate a weak hope that the technology of the self could become truly "ethical." The usual understanding of the goals of the quantified self movement does not extend the meaning of health and fitness beyond the individual. How shall we talk about what networking could mean in today's world? Latour tells the group that he has long stopped using the usual vocabulary and concepts of Modernity and has tried to find new words to express our present day situation. He himself has recently attempted to find a name for the activity of networking, an activity that seems so basic and essential for what social order and self-knowledge in the "Anthropocene" are all about. He hesitates a moment, because he is obviously uncertain about telling this distinguished group about the name he would like to propose for what Socrates (along with Foucault) has referred to as "care for the self," and what could be considered a "technology of the self" in an ethical and aesthetic sense. After Socrates urges him to go on, Latour begins to speak about "design."

Design discourse is admittedly mostly technical in the sense of focusing on product development, marketing, and business planning. Nonetheless there is a deeper and, for the social scientist, more interesting background for questions relating to design. At stake is fundamentally a *techné* of the self in the sense of Foucault's ethics. In a well-known book entitled *Sciences of the Artificial*, Herbert

---

19 Cf. https://en.wikipedia.org/wiki/Gaia_hypothesis.
20 Cf. Latour (1993) for an explanation of why we have never been "Modern" and Krieger/Belliger (2014: 151-160) for a discussion of privacy in a global network society.

Simon developed a concept of design that can be traced from Greek *techné* and applied to Foucault's technology of self as ethics. For Simon (1996)

"Engineers are not the only professional designers. Everyone designs who devises courses of action aimed at changing existing situations into preferred ones. The intellectual activity that produces material artifacts is no different fundamentally from the one that prescribes remedies for a sick patient or the one that devises a new sales plan for a company or a social welfare policy for a state. Design, so construed, is the core of all professional training [...] Schools of engineering, as well as schools of architecture, business, education, law, and medicine, are all centrally concerned with the process of design." (ibid: 111)

Latour would agree to this and add that the concept of design today "has been extended from the details of daily objects to cities, landscapes, nations, cultures, bodies, genes, and [...] to nature itself" (Latour 2008: 2). Furthermore, this extension of the idea of design to all aspects of reality means that the concept of "design" has become "a clear substitute for revolution and modernization" (ibid: 5); those two ideals that have led Modernity into an inescapable responsibility for planetary ecology. Finally, for Latour "the decisive advantage of the concept of design is that it necessarily involves an ethical dimension which is tied into the obvious question of *good versus bad design*" (ibid: 5). The ethical dimension that Latour finds at the heart of design joins Foucault's idea of an ethical technology of self for "humans have to be artificially made and remade" (ibid: 10). Understanding self-knowledge as an ethical and technical (in the sense of *techné*) task of design should not lead us into post-humanist speculations and the discussion of cyborgs. Instead, that which makes design both ethically good and aesthetically beautiful is its ability to take many different aspects of what something is and can become into account, to respect all the different claims that can be made on someone or something, to insure that nothing important is overlooked, and to allow for surprises and the unexpected. To design something well, including oneself, in the functional, ethical, and aesthetic dimensions, is to take account of as much information as one can in the process of constructing. Latour proposes that networking, that is, the *techné* of constructing actor-networks, should be understood as *design*. This means that design is a "means for drawing *things* together – gods, non-humans, and mortals included" (ibid: 13).

It is interesting to note that much of the research being done in the area of wearables and personal informatics systems can be classified as design.[21] The well-known five phases model of Li et al. (2010) is used primarily for design research. The central question asked by this research is what motivates, enables, and binds users to a particular constellation of hardware and software? How can automated systems help users set goals and monitor success? This research clearly demonstrates that the information being gathered, aggregated, and interpreted by body tracking technologies also change the parameters of what

---

21 Cf. for example Barua et al. (2012); Epstein et al. (2015a; 2015b).

health and well-being are considered to be. Developers and designers are much more responsive to users' needs and interests than the medical establishment and public health administration. Self-tracking is indifferent to boundaries between primary, secondary, and tertiary health care. This becomes apparent the moment we consider that information aggregated, shared, and evaluated in large quantities can yield new and unforeseen knowledge about health. Health is not a given, but a goal that is to be discovered by practice of gathering data, aggregating, and sharing the data so that further research can discover new and unforeseen correlations. The influential President's Report on Big Data (2014) claims that "Big data can identify diet, exercise, preventive care, and other lifestyle factors that help keep people from having to seek care from a doctor" (ibid: 22). Big Data analytics can "help identify clinical treatments, prescription drugs, and public health interventions that may not appear to be effective in smaller samples, across broad populations, or using traditional methods" (ibid: 23). Big Data enable "predictive medicine" which "peers deeply into a person's health status and genetic information, allowing doctor's to predict whether individuals will develop a disease and how they might respond to specific therapies" (ibid: 23). These possibilities raise important questions with regard to privacy. For example, predictive medicine "extends beyond a single individual's risks to include others with similar genes […]". The Report acknowledges that current legal and cultural notions of privacy "may not be well suited to address these developments" (ibid: 23), and concludes that "Using big data to improve health requires advanced analytical models to ingest multiple kinds of lifestyle, genomic, medical, and financial data" (ibid: 23) all of which are needed to develop personalised health services. Despite the concerns for privacy, many patient community platforms are becoming major contributors to medical research and it is on the basis of this research that the parameters for data selection and evaluation are being adjusted and built into wearables and body tracking tools. It is from this research that the values of what counts as healthy with regard to vital data are set, that is, are fed back into the instruments as goals and markers of health. Not simply gathering more and more data from more and more sensors is the defining characteristic of personal informatics as a technology of self, but the sharing of this data in communities of research, consultation, support, and care. Only when personal informatics and body tracking are not confined to mere compliance to fixed parameters, but guided by network values of connectivity, flow, communication, transparency, participation, and authenticity and only when users are actively and constructively engaged in creating parameters and defining health does the "quantified" self become a "qualified" self. The qualified self is no longer subject to the *morality of compliance*, but is guided by the *ethics of design*.

The goal of design is not to pilot the "machine" successfully on the basis of certain very limited instruments and within given parameters – which is the typical meaning of morality as compliance with given standards – but also to question and change the parameters of functionality and the standards themselves. This practice corresponds with Foucault's notion of ethics. Ethics are not morality. They are much more a *techné* in the sense of design as proposed by Latour. The ethical life is lived with regard to designing the self as functional (healthy) as well as good and beautiful, that is, by taking account of all the available information and striking the right balance. The many tools and technologies of personal informatics make this possible in that they transform everything into information and draw this information together so that it can be compared, evaluated, correlated, and allowed to flow through networks in unforeseeable ways. Algorithms and technologies should be designed to be ethical partners and not moral authorities. Health and beauty are not objectively given, either by God or by medicine, psychology, and sociology, but are constantly being formed, tested, revised, and (re)negotiated in the process of networking. Networking is a socio-technical concept that means not only connectivity and flow of information, but also communication, participation, transparency, flexibility, and authenticity.[22]

The interlocutors in our fictive conversation become silent. New perspectives for understanding self-knowledge in the age of networking have appeared on the horizon. But the day is drawing to a close. Socrates must return to Athens. He carries not only the Fitbit that Wolf and Kelly have given him as a souvenir, but also the conviction that his struggles for an ethical form of self-knowledge and well-being that go beyond the individual and the body are not in vain. Maturana and Varela go back to their laboratory in order to investigate how complex adaptive systems might be theoretically redesigned as networks. Gary Wolf and Kevin Kelly promise to set the program for the next QS conference with a view to the broader issues involved in personal informatics. Our doctor now knows that patients are also experts and can contribution to medicine.[23] He promises to join an online patient community and finally digitalise his medical records. And Bruno Latour returns to Paris with the *aime* of considering how personal informatics can help bring together the many "modes of existence" he has discovered in his anthropological fieldwork among the Moderns.[24]

References

Apel, Karl-Otto (1988): Understanding and Explanation. A Transcendental-Pragmatic Perspective. Tr. by Georgia Warnke, Boston: MIT Press.
Barua, Debjanee/Kay, Judy/Kummerfeld, Bob/Paris, Cécile (2012): "A Framework for Modelling Goals in Personal Lifelong Informatics." Paper delivered at the Human Computer Interaction Conference, CHI, Austin, Texas, May 5-10, 2012 (http://www.personalinformatics.org/docs/chi2012/barua.pdf).

22   Cf. Krieger/Belliger (2014) for a discussion of network norms.
23   Cf. Belliger/Krieger (2014) for an overview of the e-patient movement and its implications for health care.
24   We wish to express our gratitude to Socrates, Gary Wolf, Kevin Klein, Humberto Maturana, Francisco Varela, and Bruno Latour for allowing us to (mis)use them as figures in this fictive dialogue and to offer apologies if they feel misrepresented.

Belliger, Andréa/Krieger, David J. (2014): Gesundheit 2.0 – Das ePatienten Handbuch, Bielefeld: transcript.

Belliger, Andréa/Krieger, David J. (2015): Die Selbstquantifizierung als Ritual virtualisierter Körperlichkeit." In: Robert Gugutzer/Michael Staack (eds.), Körper und Ritual. Sozial und Kulturwissenschaftliche Zugänge und Analyse, Wiesbaden: Springer VS.

Boyd, Stowe (2010): The Decade of Publicy, January 2, 2010 (http://stoweboyd.com/post/797752290/the-decade-of-publicy).

Castells, Manuel (1996): The Rise of the Network Society, Vol. 1 The Information Age, Blackwell: Oxford.

Epstein, Daniel A./Fogarty, James/Lee, Nicole. B./Munson, Sean A./Bales, Elizabeth (2015a): "Wearables of 2025: Designing Personal Informatics for a Broader Audience." Paper delivered at the Human Computer Interaction Conference, CHI, Seoul, April 18-23, 2015 (http://www.depstein.net/pubs/depstein_chi15_work.pdf).

Epstein, Daniel A./Ping, An/Fogarty, James/Munson. Sean A. (2015b): "A lived Informatics Model of Personal Informatics." Paper delivered at the conference of the Association for Computing Machinery, Osaka, September 15, 2015 (http://dub.washington.edu/djangosite/media/papers/tmpyaL1oc.pdf).

Foucault, Michel (1997): "Technologies of the Self." In: Paul Rabinow (ed.), Foucault Ethics Subjectivity and Truth, Vol. 1 of The Essential Works of Foucault 1954 – 1984, New York: The New Press, pp. 223-251.

Heidegger, Martin (1977): "The Question Concerning Technology." In: David F. Krell (ed.), Martin Heidegger: Basic Writings, New York: Harper & Row.

Krieger, David/Belliger, Andréa (2014): Interpreting Networks – Hermeneutics, Actor-Network Theory & New Media, Bielefeld: transcript.

Latour, Bruno (1993): We Have Never Been Modern, Cambridge, MA: Harvard University Press.

Latour, Bruno (2008): "A Cautious Prometheus? A few Steps Toward a Philosophy of Design (with Special Attention to Peter Sloterdijk)", Keynote Lecture for the Networks of Design meeting of the Design History Society Falmouth, Cornwall, September 3, 2008.

Latour, Bruno (2013): An Inquiry into Modes of Existence, Cambridge: Harvard University Press.

Li, Ian/Dey, Anind/Forlizzi, Jodi (2010): "A Stage-Based Model of personal Informatics Systems." Paper delivered at the Human Computer Interaction Conference, CHI 2010, pp. 557-566.

Luhmann, Niklas (2012): Theory of Society. Vol. 1. Stanford: Stanford University Press.

Lupton, Deborah (1995): The Imperative of Health: Public Health and the Regulated Body, London: Sage.

Lupton, Deborah (2013): "The digital cyborg assemblage: Haraway's cyborg theory and the new digital health technologies" (preprint). In: Fran Collyer (ed), The Handbook of Social Theory for the Sociology of Health and Medicine, Houndmills: Palgrave Macmillan.

Lupton, Deborah (2014a): "Self-tracking Cultures: Towards a Sociology of Personal Informatics." Paper delivered at the OzHCI Conference 2014 (https://simplysociology.files.wordpress.com/2014/09/self-tracking-cultures-ozchi-conference-paper.pdf).

Lupton, Deborah (2014b): "Self-Tracking Modes: Reflexive Self-Monitoring and Data Practices", August 19, 2014 (http://ssrn.com/abstract=2483549).

Lupton, Deborah (2015): "Lively Data, Social Fitness and Biovalue: The Intersections of Health Self-Tracking and Social Media", September 27, 2015 (http://ssrn.com/abstract=2666324).

Markula, Pirkko/Pringle, Richard (2006): Foucault, Sport and Exercise. Power, Knowledge and Transforming the Self, London/New York: Routledge.

Maturana, Humberto/Varela, Francisco (1987): The Tree of Knowledge. The Biological Roots of Human Understanding, Boston/London: Shambhala.

President's Report on Big Data (2014): "Big Data: Seizing Opportunities, Preserving Values", May, 2014 (https://www.whitehouse.gov/sites/default/files/docs/big_data_privacy_report_may_1_2014.pdf).

Rowlands, Mark (2010): The New Science of the Mind. From Extended to Embodied Phenomenology, Cambridge: MIT Press.

Simon, Herbert A. (1996): The Sciences of the Artificial, Cambridge: MIT Press.

Weinberger, David (2012): Too Big to Know: Rethinking Knowledge Now That the Facts Aren't the Facts, Experts Are Everywhere, and the Smartest Person in the Room Is the Room, New York: Basic Books.

Total Affect Control
Or: Who's Afraid of a Pleasing Little Sister?

Marie-Luise Angerer and Bernd Bösel

Abstract

Through the emergence of affect- and psychotechnologies, especially with the advent of affective computing, the recognition, regulation and production of affects have been automatised to an unforeseeable degree. The roots of this algorithmic automation can be seen in the propagation of cybernetic models in the field of psychology from the 1950s onwards. A direct genealogical line leads from Silvan Tomkins' affect system via Paul Ekman's facial emotion recognition to Rosalind Picard's conception and co-development of affect-sensitive computer systems. Nevertheless, the implicated aspects of surveillance and collection of affective information have yet to be assessed critically. Such an assessment is outlined here.

The Tip of the Iceberg of Digital Control: Affective Computing

As discussed in many recent publications, the regulation of affects and emotions is dependent on historical, cultural, socio-political and not least media-technological developments.[1] How affects and emotions are coded and expressed, whether they are fostered and actively supported or whether they are ignored or even denied, depends on a wealth of factors that are dealt with individually by many scholars in the fields of history and cultural studies.[2] Today, however, a fundamental shift is taking place in the conditions of media technology (a shift whose socio-political impact is still entirely unclear) as affectivity is technicised

---

1   See for example: Angerer/Bösel/Ott (2014); Goldberg (2012); Wetherell (2012); Dixon (2003).
2   We deliberately use both terms here to point out that in the discourses in question no distinction between affect and emotion is made. In spite of this, one should note that the two terms come from very different traditions of thought. The approach that was developed by Gilles Deleuze, drawing via Henri Bergson on Baruch de Spinoza, and that was picked up by Brian Massumi in the 1990s, has been deliberately left out of this essay as it plays no part in the discussion of affective computing. As Rosalind Picard mentions, this discussion does not distinguish between emotion and affect, and sensation or feeling are also often mentioned in the same breath. For a detailed look at the etymological meanings and different genealogies of the terms affect and emotion, see "Introduction" in Angerer/Bösel/Ott (2014).

to an unprecedented degree. We are talking here about affect- and psychotechnologies used to record, store, measure, categorise, catalogue, operationalise, simulate and induce affective states. Noteworthy examples include affective gaming, surveillance technologies and certain applications emerging from the "quantified self" and "life tracking" movement. But the most far-reaching promises are being made by those working in the hotly contested field of "Affective Computing". This research can be traced back to the visionary book of the same name published by computer scientist Rosalind Picard in 1997, in which she named for the first time the diverse potential applications of computer-based identification and simulation of affects. In recent years, this field of research has become increasingly prominent: an International Conference on Affective Computing and Intelligent Interaction (ACII)[3] has been held every two years since 2005, the *IEEE Transactions on Affective Computing*[4] have been appearing since 2010, and 2015 saw the publication of a first comprehensive overview, *The Oxford Handbook on Affective Computing*. In reference to the technologies being developed in this field, various levels of application can be discerned: (1.) Individual users are being promised custom-generated agents that provide affective interfaces and constantly record affective parameters (facial expressions, body posture and movements, vocal range, bio-data)[5] to create a kind of double or "complementary personality" to satisfy individual happiness profiles. Preliminary forms of this are already on the market in the form of apps for permanent monitoring of body data, movement and communications profiles, and media usage.[6] (2.) With the help of these data and special algorithms, the emerging discipline of "psychoinformatics" attempts to render the mental state of users decodable in real time – admittedly in order to motivate these same users to engage in corresponding healthy activities and to help health care providers in assessing their therapeutic success.[7] (3.) In contrast to these therapeutic applications that rely on informed consent standards, companies as well as governments use data mining technologies without explicit or even implicit knowledge on the part of the users who generate these (affective) data by using networked

3   In 2015, the conference was held in Xian, China, see http://www.acii2015.org/.
4   See http://ieeexplore.ieee.org/xpl/aboutJournal.jsp?punumber=5165369#AimsScope.
5   The second section of the *Oxford Handbook* ("Affect Detection") has chapters on each of the following affective channels: "face analysis", "body expressions", "speech", "texts", "physiological sensing" and "affective brain-computer interfaces". The latter are clearly intended as the culmination of all previous attempts at recording the emotions of test persons under observation.
6   For a good assessment of what the already existing apps and programs are capable of measuring see Jamie Carter, "How mining human emotions could become the next big thing in tech", September 16, 2015 (http://www.techradar.com/news/world-of-tech/future-tech/emotional-data-from-the-likes-of-the-apple-watch-is-this-the-next-boom--1291151).
7   For an introduction into the field and promises of psychoinformatics cf. Markowetz et al. (2014). A critical take on Markowetz' research was offered by Wenleder (2014).

gadgets. The network of technical objects that surrounds us is thus being increasingly upgraded into a sensitive environment, allowing it to interact with its users on the affective level.

This affective level in particular has always marked humans out as unpredictable in a double sense – escaping the grasp of both reason and measuring techniques. But with the establishment over recent years of the affective sciences (cf. Davidson et al. 2003), this has changed fundamentally. One can go back further still to the research into affective programming within the field of cybernetics: although one focus here was on decoding the human affective apparatus and emotional competence as a rule-based programme, there were also attempts to programme computers with "affective" algorithms (cf. Pias 2003-2004; Angerer 2014). This double dynamic of decoding and recoding obeyed presumptions that remained implicit at the time, but which in the light of today's globalised neoliberal politics are becoming increasingly visible.

The *Oxford Handbook* highlights a similar double dynamic with regard to the desired capacities (some of which already exist) of computer-assisted systems. The field of "Affect Detection" covers hard- and software that observes and measures human expressive and physical parameters, processing these data as signals for distinct affects and emotions. The aim is to identify not only consciously experienced emotional states, but also those that remain unconscious (for example because they are too fleeting or too faint to rise above the threshold of consciousness). The field of "Affect Generation" or "Affect Synthesis", on the other hand, deals with the hard- and software that simulates expressions of affect in order to interact with users, not least in order to prompt desired emotional states in them and to supress those that are not desired.

Affect regulation has been associated since antiquity with practices and discourses of self-education, and into the 20th century it was linked with strongly normative demands (defined along lines of class, gender, age and ethnicity) that were to be implemented by each individual. Today, on the other hand, affect regulation is increasingly being delegated to automated systems. This is not necessarily a problem; it is perfectly conceivable that regulating affects with the assistance of doubly sensitive "atmospheric" media may soon be considered a more or less normal cultural technology, just as using electronic media for "mood management" (cf. Schramm 2005) has long become a normal part of our cultural repertoire. Even so, it is important to ask on which assumptions this phenomenon that we call affective algorithmisation is based on, which "feeling rules" (Hochschild 2003: 56-75) it perpetuates, and not least which agendas the proponents of affective computing are pursuing. To this end, we will now examine the history of what has tentatively been called psychocybernetics, especially with regard to the identification of emotions through computer-assisted affect detection, before subjecting media-technological strategies of affect generation to a critical analysis.

Psycho-Cybernetics[8]

When Norbert Elias developed his theory of the growth of civilising regimes of emotional control in the 1930s, the pioneering discipline of cybernetics had yet to be invented.[9] But we may ask whether the process of civilisation, understood precisely as a process of increasingly powerful methods of affective control, is not radicalised by its partial delegation to computer-assisted systems. As the documentation of the Macy Conferences shows, the application of a general regulatory theory to mental and psychosocial systems was intended from the outset, and it was implemented for the first time just a few years later in Gregory Bateson's theory of the double bind. A direct line can be traced from this concept to the development of an *Ecology of Mind*, as proposed by Bateson two decades later.[10] This ecology follows the principle of an inner balance or homeostasis such as that on which cybernetic techniques of regulation are also based.

A similar case is John Bowlby's (1982) theory of attachment, based among others on "feedback" and "control". Bowlby begins by introducing his readers to the principles of cybernetic control theory by describing the feedback function of a thermostat (ibid: 42), before going on to apply this process to patterns of human attachment. In his foreword to the second edition of Bowlby's *Attachment and Loss*, Allan N. Schore gives a strikingly succinct summary of his intentions: "Attachment theory, as first propounded in this definitional volume, is fundamentally a regulatory theory. Attachment can thus be conceptualized as the interactive regulation of synchrony between psycho-biologically attuned organisms." (Schore 1982: xvi) It is also worth noting, incidentally, that Schore later became known for his own wide-ranging theory of affect regulation (cf. Schore 1994).

Another link between affect and the theme of control is already apparent in the name given by David R. Heise to his "affect control theory", which is based on the idea that individual humans choose the kind of actions that will lead to the affirmation of stable "sentiments". The situational emotions generated by these actions thus supposedly match these sentiments. If this is not the case, then the sentiments are adjusted to minimize the resulting tension or "deflection" (Heise 2006: 3-4). Here, then, emotions are feedback variables or "signals" (ibid: 57) for a mental system that wishes to secure its affective-cognitive images of itself and the other. The key point of this theory is its claim that the analysis of sentiments can be used to predict the behaviour of members of large groups. In attitude studies, this approach is used today to forecast the

---

8   This term was popularised by Maxwell Maltz (1960) in his book *Psycho-Cybernetics*. See also Stefan Rieger's discussion of Maltz (Rieger 2003: 19-22).

9   Cf. Elias (2000), especially 363-448 ("Synopsis: Towards a theory of civilizing processes").

10 Cf. Bateson (2000). This collection contains the essays, written since the 1950s, in which Bateson develops his theory of the "double bind". In his late work, Norbert Elias drew inspiration from Bateson's psychiatric concept for his own sociological "double bind model" (cf. Elias 1987).

behaviour of consumers, voters and similar groups. Affect control theory also offers a mathematical model to minimize deflection and to optimise one's own behaviour, as well as a computer programme to measure sentiments (ibid: 130).[11] As it merges here with information technology, the cybernetisation of affect reaches a new level whose desired and undesired implications have been clearly reflected during the 2010s in a growing economic interest in big data (cf. Mayer-Schönberger/Cukier 2013).

Beyond this general development of a cybernetisation of psychology, with its focus on affective regulation and control, it is possible to trace a genealogy that leads from one of the first psycho-cyberneticists to Rosalind Picard as the figurehead of affective computing.

The Tomkins-Ekman Paradigm

In the 1960s, Silvan Tomkins drew on cybernetic principles to develop an alternative to the drive-based model of the mind proposed by psychoanalysis (cf. Leys 2007: 137 ff.). Tomkins based his approach on a system of affect spectrums (the two terms in each pair mark the strong and weak variants): "surprise–startle" as a neutral affect spectrum; "distress–anguish", "anger–rage", "fear–terror", "shame–humiliation", "dissmell" and "disgust" as negative affects; and "interest–excitement" and "enjoyment–joy" as positive affects. In his system, these affects constitute the primary motivation framework in humans. Shame, meanwhile, is considered the central affect that occurs via the suppression of "interest–excitement" and "enjoyment–joy" and that is closely related to visibility and in particular to the expressivity of the human face. "Man is, of all animals, the most voyeuristic," Tomkins stresses, "he is more dependent on his visual sense than most animals, and his visual sense contributes more information than any of his senses." (Tomkins 2008: 373) The shame reaction consists above all in averting one's eyes under the gaze of others, and, as Tomkins writes, since the self lives and communicates in the face, and in this case especially in the eyes, in shame it turns against itself, so to speak, experiencing this as a kind of mental ailment (ibid: 359). In this model, shame is an existential mode of self-referentiality that points to the vulnerability of the affective organism as a whole.[12]

With this central focus on the face and thus on the visibility of affects, Tomkins laid the foundation for the media-assisted research later conducted by his student Paul Ekman into the identification of facial expressions and their operationalisation. Based on his studies of nonverbal behaviour in the Fore tribe of Papua New Guinea, Ekman came to the conclusion that at least the basic affects manifest themselves in a universal way via specific facial expressions.

---

11 This measurement of sentiments clearly overlaps with the field of "sentiment analysis" in affective computing that processes texts and terms circulating online; cf. Ahmad (2011).
12 On this, see David Wills' (2009) analysis of the role of shame in Descartes.

Although existing cultural differences in the social "display rules" (Ekman 2007: 4) make the emotions being shown harder to identify, they can be discerned by analysis of "micro-expressions". Since these take place too quickly for untrained observers, media support (initially video, later computers) became a key epistemic factor. In 1978, in conjunction with Wallace Friesen, Ekman presented the resulting Facial Action Coding System (FACS) that was later to become one of the foundations of affective computing.[13]

In 1990s, Tomkins' fundamental research was used in different ways. Firstly, the (re-)discovery of Tomkins' works by Eve Kosofsky Sedgwick was one driving force behind the affective turn in cultural and media studies (cf. Angerer 2014: 49-69). For Kosofsky Sedgwick, the key was the conception of affects as free, malleable variables not attached to any specific object: "Affect, unlike the drives, has a degree of competency and complexity that affords it the relative ability to motivate the human to greater degrees of freedom. [...] Tomkins even proposes a principle for freedom, suggesting Freud's pleasure principle as the model. He calls it the *information complexity, or 'degrees-of-freedom principle'*." (Kosofsky Sedgwick 1995: 35)

Secondly, Rosalind Picard drew on the so-called Tomkins-Ekman paradigm to develop computer programmes for the automated detection of human emotions. In the first issue of the *IEEE Transactions on Affective Computing*, Picard describes finding a report in the *Wall Street Journal* describing the invention of a machine capable of measuring emotions. Its inventor was none other than Manfred Clynes, the NASA scientist credited with coining the term "cyborg" (cf. Clynes 1995). His "Sentograph" was supposed to measure the tiniest variations in the pressing of a button, correlating the data thus obtained with emotional states such as happiness, excitement, sadness, etc.: "I was amused by this crazy fact," Picard wrote. Years later, she was introduced to Clynes by Marvin Minsky, and Clynes told her that when he first presented his device "he was literally laughed off the stage". She also describes her attempts over the following years to ignore the significance of emotions since as a hardworking engineer, she didn't want to get a reputation for being interested in something as devaluated as emotion: doing research as a female scientist on "soft" topics such as emotion would have ruined her career, as she frankly pointed out.[14] Picard finally overcame these obstacles and fears and is now known as a pioneer of research into computers and emotions: "Today we know emotion is involved in rational decision-making and action selection, and in order to behave rationally in real life you need to have a properly functioning emotion system." (Picard 2010: 12) Moreover, the fact that Picard herself founded the company *Affectiva* and has now begun marketing applications – the latest being "Affdex",

---

13 On critiques of the implementation of Ekman's research, see Tuschling (2014).
14 So it is actually no coincidence that in *He, She and It*, a sci-fi novel by Marge Piercy (1991) it is a female programmer who is responsible for the new program for Yod, the first perfect cyborg, making him (Yod is anatomically modeled male) able to act and respond also emotionally.

a programme to decode the facial expressions of advertising viewers – is proof of the current interweaving of techno-science and business.[15]

Affect Detection with no Critique of Power or Control?

What these uses of Tomkins and Ekman clearly reveal is the divergent valuation and exploitation of affect – conceived of in one case as freedom (from a narrowly defined system of drives and from the hegemony of language) while on the other it opens up applications for neuro/cognitive science and for IT that stimulate new research into control and adaptation of affective and behavioural patterns. Alongside security and surveillance technologies (e.g. "deception detection"), applications of affective computing that already exist or are currently under development include electronically assisted learning (e.g. "affective tutor"), work with autistic people, computer games, robotics, and services in the field of wellness and healthcare. Right across this broad spectrum of potential for affective computing, then, there is an almost total absence of critique. The *Oxford Handbook* contains just one single entry on possible ethical problems (cf. Cowie 2015).

Although Picard herself openly discusses potential objections in *Affective Computing*, she dismisses them with unconvincing arguments. Regarding the threatening scenario of a total, centrally controlled monitoring of affects, she writes: "One can imagine some malevolent dictator requiring people to wear emotion 'meters' of some sort, to monitor their fun, for example. Emotion control might be achieved both by subliminal influences and by overt requirements to engage in tasks believed to lead to certain emotions." (Picard 1997: 123) Picard was clearly not yet able to foresee the extent to which affective surveillance and monitoring might be centralized. In a similar way, she makes light of the problem of collecting and storing "affective information" (or "emotion data"): "Affective information should be treated with respect and courtesy, and its privacy preserved according to the desires of the humans involved." (ibid: 118)[16] In the face of ubiquitous hacker attacks and cyber espionage, however, the monitoring of users by automated affect-sensitive systems leading to the creation of individualized "affect databases" – as in the field of computer games ("gamification", cf. Fuchs et al. 2014) – is a particular cause for concern.

With utter conviction, Picard actually presents her vision as antithetical to Orwell's Big Brother: "Within the family metaphor, the closest image of an affective system is not one of a powerful big brother, but of a pleasing little sister." (Picard 1997: 124) Like a Trojan Horse, however, this figure of the little sister (re-)imports a long tradition of attributions into the world of technology:[17]

---

15 The homepage http://www.affectiva.com/technology/ refers explicitly to Ekman's FACS as the basis for the programme.
16 See also Afzal/Robinson (2015).
17 One can refer here to a long series of machines coded as female, including Olimpia (in E.T.A. Hoffmann's *Der Sandmann*) and Maria (in Fritz Lang's *Metropolis*).

women as helpmeets, women as invisible assistants, women as naturally more sensitive, women as harmless and undemanding companions, but also the image of women as (technical) seductresses.[18] *The Cyberfeminist Manifesto*[19] was published just a few years before Picard's book, and one of its authors, Sadie Plant, became known for claiming the digital space as a new realm of activity for women: never having being included in the history of the western male subject, she argued, women are now already acting very adequately as the first cyborgs – rhizomatic, multifunctional and technically fully instructed (cf. Plant 1995).

Today, the figure of the little sister has long since taken its place in everyday reality and in media fictions: be it Siri on the iPhone[20] or the operating system Samantha in Spike Jonze's film *HER* (cf. Angerer 2015). Both "girls" are examples of the affect-generating side of this field, as clairvoyantly anticipated by the numerous little and not so little sisters in the sci-fi literature of the 1990s.[21] But whereas Siri stands firmly in the tradition of the subservient female spirit, with Samantha Jonze created a figure who quits her job in spite of her programming. In the phantasm of technological singularity, at least, the millennia-old gender matrix is broken down – in stark contrast to the gender role clichés that are still commonplace in the IT sector, in particular, as shown by recent debates on sexism and feminism in computer games.[22]

Autism, Control and Affect

In our opinion, the ambivalent character of the current interest in affect is especially evident in the attention being focussed on autistic people. In the following, we briefly discuss the links between three such projects – one economic-neoliberal, one technical-normalising, one aesthetic-activist.

Firstly, it is striking that the software industry has been making deliberate use of the specific skills that have long been attributed to autistic people. Clearly, their great ability to concentrate and identify patterns make them ideal software testers and debuggers.[23] The neoliberal economic order has discovered that these skills, previously acknowledged at best as forms of savant syndrome, can be put to lucrative use.

---

18 Picard herself merely states that women are more emotionally literate, making it logical to cast computers operating on an affective basis as female figures.
19 "Cyberfeminist Manifesto for the 21st Century", February 24, 2015 (http://www.sterneck.net/cyber/vns-matrix/index.php).
20 See "Siri. It understands what you say. It knows what you mean." February 24, 2015 (http://www.apple.com/uk/ios/siri/).
21 Among others, Melissa Scott: *Trouble and Her Friends* (1994).
22 See feminist media critic Anita Sarkeesian's blog: http://feministfrequency.com/about/.
23 "Autistic Coders Get Jobs as Microsoft, SAP Woo Software Sleuths", September 16, 2015 (http://www.bloomberg.com/news/articles/2015-06-02/autistic-coders-get-jobs-as-microsoft-sap-woo-software-sleuths).

This contrasts with another affect-related project associated with the software industry that pursues quite different ends. Since the publication of Picard's *Affective Computing*, autistic people have been among the subjects most often mentioned in connection with testing and applications. It is no coincidence that the ways in which computers can help them to differentiate emotional expressions is also a subject dealt with at length in the *Oxford Handbook* (cf. Messinger et al. 2015; Picard 2015: 11-12). Alongside its therapeutic value, this technical intervention also has an unmistakeable normalising dimension. Autistic people are being expected to learn to identify affects (both their own and those of others) faster and better than neurotypical people consider them to be capable of. In other words, they are to learn to overcome constitutive defects with the help of technical prostheses.

A third affect-related project is being conducted within the humanities. For the Canadian philosopher and choreographer Erin Manning, autistic people offer proof that people's connection with reality can be established and shaped in different ways, and must therefore be interpreted in different ways, too. With reference to the autism activist Amanda Baggs, Manning has stressed that language-based communication is only *one* way of interacting with the world and other people. Instead of generating meaning through language, another possibility would be physical responsivity (cf. Manning 2009). Using the example of Baggs' film *In My Language*,[24] Manning breaks down the spectrum of affect, sensitivity and object-relations to show how a fundamentally different pattern of affectivity is rendered productive here from the autistic perspective. One thing Manning does not discuss, however, is the fact that Baggs delivers her message online with help of her computer.

In the first of the three examples, the affectivity of autistic people is ignored, focussing instead on exploiting their perceptive and cognitive skills for profit. In the second, their "deficient" affectivity is taken as the point of departure for research and applications aimed at compensating the deficits by means of media technology. The third project that differs from the other two by concentrating on *autistic people becoming productive on their own terms*, is the only one that attempts to do justice to the distinct structure of their affectivity and to draw far-reaching aesthetic and epistemic conclusions.

Outlook

The emergence of digital affect- and psychotechnologies might fundamentally change how affect regulation works on an individual as well as collective level. Affect regulation, once described by Norbert Elias as the main factor within the process of civilisation, is now starting to be shifted from being an effect of cultural practices to being an effect of following automatically generated cues and calls. This new affective programming promises to work far more subtly than anything from the age of mass media ever could have done, because it is

---

[24] See https://www.youtube.com/watch?v=JnylM1hI2jc.

designed to adapt to the individual user's affectivity. Every piece of available affective information is seen, within this logic, as relevant for constructing an affective agent that fits the user's desires, habits, preferences and aversions like a custom-made glove. But do the possible benefits that the engineers and marketers promote really outweigh the possible harm that is done when every digitally active individual can be worked on by automated programmes? Or is it not rather time to highlight the tendency of these technologies to subject their users to a total affective control? The wide acceptance of self-tracking gadgets, in combination with the practice of uploading physical data to social media platforms, provides a strong argument for a more cautious approach.

These considerations are taking place within a field that can be described using Bernard Stiegler's concept of "psycho-power". Arguing that Foucault's by now widely applied "bio-power" category falls short of explaining how marketing, mass media and other profit-oriented "programming industries" aim at and manipulate consumers' attention and desires, Stiegler (2010) introduced psycho-power as a complemental analytical term. But whereas Stiegler uses the concept primarily to demarcate the manipulative interventions of careless industries (with affective control and the obstruction of attention as leitmotifs, cf. Stiegler 2014), it should be noted here, specifically with reference to Foucault's writings, that there is also a pleasurable side to power that is not limited to the repressive exercise of that power by those who possess it. Digital media in general, and affect technologies in particular, clearly illustrate this pleasurable productivity. Faced with this new, intense phase in the development of "psychotechnologies" (cf. Bösel 2013), it is crucial to ask what uses of the affective predominate and what alternatives exist that do not always already obey a matrix of capitalist demands. Once again, this raises the question of desire in the age of an "affective *dispositif*" – a desire that is capable of resisting today's total detection and registration, acting as a deferral zone in the sense of an ongoing delay, a spacing (according to Derrida's différance) which resists the pressure of a closed adaption.

References

Afzal, Shazia/Robinson, Peter (2015): "Emotion Data Collection and Its Implications for Affective Computing." In: Calvo et al. (eds.): The Oxford Handbook of Affective Computing, New York: Oxford University Press, pp. 359-370.

Ahmad, Khurshid (ed.) (2011): Affective Computing and Sentiment Analysis. Emotion, Metaphor, and Terminology, New York: Springer.

Angerer, Marie-Luise (2014): Desire After Affect, London: Rowman & Littlefield (originally published in German in 2007).

Angerer, Marie-Luise/Bösel, Bernd/Ott, Michaela (eds.) (2014): Timing of Affect. Epistemologies, Aesthetics, Politics, Zürich, Berlin: Diaphanes.

Angerer, Marie-Luise (2015): "Her Master's Voice. Eine akusmatische Liebesbeziehung von Spike Jonze." In: Film-Konzepte 37, pp. 57-66.

Bateson, Gregory (2000): Steps to an Ecology of Mind: Collected Essays in Anthropology, Psychiatry, Evolution, and Epistemology, Chicago: University of Chicago Press.

Bösel, Bernd (2013): "Die philosophische Relevanz der Psychotechniken. Argumente für die Indienstnahme eines ambivalenten Begriffs." In: Allgemeine Zeitschrift für Philosophie 38/2, pp. 123-142.

Bowlby, John (1982): Attachment: Attachment and Loss, Vol. 1, New York: Basic Books.

Calvo, Rafael A./D'Mello, Sidney K./Gratch, Jonathan/Kappas, Arvid (eds.) (2015): The Oxford Handbook of Affective Computing, New York: Oxford University Press.

Clynes, Manfred E. (1995): "CYBORG II: Sentic Space Travel." In: Chris Hables Gray et al. (eds.): The CYBORG-Handbook, New York: Routledge, pp. 35-42.

Cowie, Roddie (2015): "Ethical Issues in Affective Computing." In: Calvo et al. (eds.): The Oxford Handbook of Affective Computing, New York: Oxford University Press, pp. 334-348.

Davidson, Richard J./Scherer, Klaus R./Goldsmith, H. Hill (eds.) (2003): Handbook of Affective Sciences, New York: Oxford University Press.

Dixon, Thomas (2003): From Passions to Emotions. The Creation of a Secular Psychological Category, Cambridge, MA: Cambridge University Press.

Ekman, Paul (2007): Emotions Revealed, Recognizing Faces and Feelings to Improve Communication and Emotional Life, New York: Henry Holt.

Elias, Norbert (1987): Involvement and Detachment, Oxford: Basil Blackwell.

Elias, Norbert (2000): The Civilizing Process: Sociogenetic and Psychogenetic Investigations, Oxford: Blackwell.

Fuchs, Mathias/Fizek, Sonia/Ruffino, Paolo/Schrape, Niklas (eds.) (2014): Rethinking Gamification, Lüneburg: meson press.

Goldberg, Greg (2012): „Negotiating Affect in Media/Cultural Studies." In: WSQ: Women's Studies Quarterly 40 1 & 2, pp. 242-250.

Heise, David R. (2006): Expressive Order. Confirming Sentiments in Social Actions, New York: Springer.

Hochschild, Arlie Russell (2003): The Managed Heart. Commercialization of Human Feeling, Berkeley, CA: University of California Press.

Kosofsky Sedgwick, Eve/Frank, Adam (eds.) (1995): Shame and its Sisters. A Silvan Tomkins Reader, Durham/London: Duke University Press.

Leys, Ruth (2007): From Guilt to Shame. Auschwitz and After, Princeton/Oxford: Princeton University Press.

Maltz, Maxwell (1960): Psycho-Cybernetics, New Jersey: Prentice Hall.

Manning, Erin (2009): Relationscapes. Movement, Art, Philosophy, Cambridge: MIT Press.

Markowetz, Alexander et al. (2014): "Psycho-Informatics: Big Data Shaping Modern Psychometrics." In: Medical Hypotheses 82/4, pp. 405-411.

Mayer-Schönberger, Viktor/Cukier, Kenneth (2013): Big Data. A Revolution that Will Transform how We Live, Work, and Think, New York: Houghton Mifflin Harcourt.

Messinger, Daniel S. et al. (2015): "Affective Computing, Emotional Development, and Autism." In: Calvo et al. (eds.): The Oxford Handbook of Affective Computing, New York: Oxford University Press, pp. 516-536.
Pias, Claus (ed.) (2003-2004): Cybernetics / Kybernetik. The Macy Conferences 1946-1953. Essays & Dokumente, 2 vols., Zürich, Berlin: Diaphanes.
Piercy, Marge (1991): He, She And It, New York: Penguin Books.
Picard, Rosalind W. (1997): Affective Computing, Cambridge: MIT Press.
Picard, Rosalind W. (2010): "Affective Computing. From Laughter to IEEE." In: IEEE Transactions on Affective Computing 1/1, pp. 11-17.
Picard, Rosalind W. (2015): "The Promise of Affective Computing." In: Calvo et al. (eds.): The Oxford Handbook of Affective Computing, New York: Oxford University Press, pp. 11-20.
Plant, Sadie (1995): "The Future Looms Weaving Women and Cybernetics." In: Body & Society 3/4, pp. 45-64.
Rieger, Stefan (2003): Kybernetische Anthropologie. Eine Geschichte der Virtualität, Frankfurt a. M.: Suhrkamp.
Schore, Allan N. (1982): "Foreword." In: Bowlby, John (1982): Attachment: Attachment and Loss, Vol. 1, New York: Basic Books.
Schore, Allan N. (1994): Affect Regulation and the Origin of Self, Hillsdale/NJ: Lawrence Erlbaum Associates.
Schramm, Holger (2005): Mood Management durch Musik. Die alltägliche Nutzung von Musik zur Regulierung von Stimmungen, Cologne: Herbert von Halem.
Scott, Melissa (1994): Trouble and Her Friends, New York: Tor.
Stiegler, Bernard (2010): Taking Care of Youth and the Generations, Stanford: Stanford University Press.
Stiegler, Bernard (2014): Symbolic Misery, Volume 1: The Hyperindustrial Epoch, Cambridge: Polity.
Tomkins, Silvan (2008): Affect Imagery Consciousness. The Complete Edition, New York: Springer.
Tuschling, Anna (2014): "The Age of Affective Computing." In: Marie-Luise Angerer/Bernd Bösel/Michaela Ott (eds.): Timing of Affect. Epistemologies, Aesthetics, Politics, Zürich, Berlin: Diaphanes, pp. 179-190.
Wenleder, Andreas (2014): "App überwacht Seele." In: Süddeutsche Zeitung October 29, 2014.
Wetherell, Margaret (2012): Affect and Emotion. A New Social Science Understanding, London: Sage.
Wills, David (2009): "The Blushing Machine: Animal Shame, And Technological Life." In: Parrhesia 8, pp. 34-42.

Theorising the Quantified Self and Posthumanist Agency
Self-Knowledge and Posthumanist Agency in Contemporary US-American Literature

Stefan Danter, Ulfried Reichardt and Regina Schober

Abstract

In our paper we will examine the cultural implications of the quantified self technology and analyse how contemporary US-American novels reflect and comment on the qualitative changes of the human condition against the backdrop of an interpretive dominance held by the natural and social sciences as well as the changes effected by quantitative methods. Moreover, we will investigate some historical and cultural continuities of the quantified self within US-American culture. We claim that, although the quantified self is a global phenomenon, it has emerged from a model of subjectivity which has been deeply engrained in American culture at least since Benjamin Franklin's Autobiography *(1791) and which emphasises individualism, economic self-optimisation, and a techno-euphoric belief in progress, self-control, and self-possession. In this context, the quantified self can be connected to theoretical discourses of 1) economy-driven subjectivity, 2) posthumanism and 3) knowledge cultures of the information age. Drawing on Gary Shteyngart's recent novel* Super Sad True Love Story *(2010), we will map forms and functions of literary engagements with various manifestations of the quantified self in relation to the cross-dependencies between distributed agency, potentials and the limits of knowledge systems, and economic mechanisms. As critical systems of second-order observation, fictional texts reflect on the repercussions of practices related to numerical self-description. At the same time, they constitute epistemological counter models to the relational, modular, and combinatory logic of the database (Manovich 2001; Hayles 1999), by focusing on the qualitative dimension of human experience and thus (re-)inscribing human agency into these "technologies of the self" (Foucault 1984).*

Theoretical Assumptions

Quantified approaches to self-knowledge are not a new phenomenon. Humans have always collected and systematised comprehensive data about the world and about themselves. While the term 'the quantified self' is a rather recent coinage, other terms signifying similar concepts have been around for some time such as self-tracking, self-monitoring, self-reporting, personal metrics (Young 2012), and in a more theoretical context, of forms of self-thematisation (Hahn/Schorch 2007). In this light, self-tracking can be traced back to early Protestantism and more specifically to Calvinism, particularly Puritanism, and also several other, earlier forms of observing oneself, such as diaries and journal keeping, autobiographies and personal letters.

What becomes immediately clear is that one needs a medium to observe oneself, that is to 'look at oneself' from outside, even if the focus is on interiority and private experiences. The beginning of modernity brought about a radical shift to the interior of one's experience (Taylor 1989) and at the same time a strong shift to externalisation of the self in the sense of relying on a medium. This necessarily implies that all forms of self-monitoring are medium-dependent and consequently at least partially codetermined by the medium or technology. This 'doubleness' is constitutive, we want to suggest, to every form of self-tracking. Therefore, if we wish to comprehend contemporary forms of self-constitution through self-tracking, we have to consider the historically decisive shift to the individual as well as the immense reliance on tools that increasingly defy individual control, as for instance computer-based appliances.

The first and most important technology that allowed for and at the same time lead to self-tracking was of course the technology of writing. Only if you have a medium that allows you to externalise and store your thoughts, feelings and experiences, is it possible to begin creating a coherent self and identity, which is always a retroactive construction. What seemed contingent when it happened is presented as necessary and brought into a linear, that is narrative, sequence only afterwards in autobiographical writing. As has often been noted, writing and the rise of the individual as a historical phenomenon are closely linked (Ong 1982). The emergence of the individual as a privileged site of social organisation is also connected to the rise of the bourgeoisie in Western and Southern Europe in early modern times and has to be understood within the context of the Reformation, the invention of the printing press and a shift in the economic as well as political/social structure. The link between economics and individualism is particularly noteworthy, and one significant moment to observe this connection is the fact that autobiography in its modern form and double-entry bookkeeping as 'genres' or forms to organise 'data' arose at about the same time. The most significant literary example of this nexus is Daniel Defoe's novel *Robinson Crusoe* (1719), in which the protagonist keeps track of his experience as well as of his possessions and "investments," in spite of his isolation on the island. Even while the concept of modernisation has been much criticised and relativised in recent debates, processes of individualisation are certainly part of the Western, European and North Atlantic version of modernisation, now understood as neither necessarily linear nor exclusively Western (Eisenstadt 2000).

Particularly the digital revolution as the most recent development in information processing technology has made the accumulation and analysis of massive amounts of data easier and affordable for the individual. Big Data has not only enabled the functional evaluation of global economic, ecological, and social statistical correlations, but has also made it possible for the individual to extract relevant predictions from personal data. Although Big Data research has focused primarily on economic and media theoretical descriptions of effects and practical applications of these technologies (Berman 2013; Mayer-Schönberger/ Cukier 2013; Schmarzo 2013; Davenport 2014), there have been few attempts so far to critically reflect on Big Data's alleged epistemological paradigm shifts from a cultural studies and cultural theory perspective. Klaus Mainzer (2014) portends that Big Data debates must be connected with a "historical foundation" in order to be able to evaluate potentials and limitations of such an epistemology in terms of the history of knowledge. Other critical perspectives on Big Data include a volume of essays entitled *Big Data: Analysen zum gesellschaftlichen Wandel von Wissen, Macht und Ökonomie* (Reichert 2014), as well as Danah Boyd's and Kate Crawford's "Critical Questions for Big Data" (2012) which point at the risks and blind spots of Big Data from a social and media studies perspective, by problematising its technological, methodical, social, and ethical assumptions.

A distinctly cultural and literary studies perspective allows for making statements that go beyond the diagnostic and descriptive level in that they reflect social implications, prognoses, and potential behavioural models. In this context, the concept of 'subjectivity' becomes a central reference point, as it emphasises the dimension of approaching and experiencing the world as a thinking, acting, and feeling subject. Since forms of subjectivities continually change (e.g. Andreas Reckwitz (2006) views processes of economicisation and aestheticisation as a part of the postmodern subject) an examination of contemporary forms of subjectivity has to account for the increasing global, technological and biomedical developments that shape and frame it.

Signalling a specific subject formation and cluster of experiences, the quantified self can thus be understood as a concept of the human which is based on numerical and statistical models. In this context, the quantified self can be connected to theoretical discourses of 1) economy-driven subjectivity, 2) knowledge cultures of the information age, and 3) posthumanism.

The quantified self is often examined in relation to economic interests, usability, and financial profit. Related to the notion of 'possessive individualism', as already drawn out by John Locke (Macpherson 1962), the quantified self is deeply engrained in US-American self-definition. Against the backdrop of a 'geopolitics of knowledge', American concepts of individualism in particular have circulated globally (Curry 1991; Ehrenberg 2012), just as distinctive forms of economic orientation have done (Tocqueville 1835/1840). Thus, there are definite connections between a certain technological drive and belief in the feasibility of self, future, self-control, economic ambition and possession (including self-possession) and the quantified self. The nexus between a particularly US-American form of neoliberalism (Brown 2003; Harvey 2005) and a subject formation which contains elements of the quantified self is key to understanding globalisation, digitalisation, and the increasing transformability of bodies.

The digitalisation of all social fields has rendered quantified conceptions of the self increasingly popular. The rapid spread of mobile technology especially has spurred a growing trend toward personalisation of applications. A concept of knowledge as economic resource in a postindustrial "information age" (Bell 1974) unveils the paradox of quantifying a non-quantifiable entity. On the one hand, digital media demonstrate that (collective) forms of knowledge are neither predictable nor ascribable to individuals (Lévy 1997; Jenkins 2010). On the other hand, they simultaneously suggest a potential of collecting, generating, and accessing knowledge through massive databases. According to Nora Young, contemporary digital culture disembodies and decontextualises and takes one "out of the here and now. It is precisely this disembodied, distracted, digital life we lead, I argue, that is creating the urge to document the physical body" (2012: 3). She claims that the extreme focus on the body has to be understood in the context of and as a response to the disembodiment and decontextualisation (in terms of space as well as time) of lives lived in constant digital communication and self-monitoring. "Self-tracking is an adaptive reaction to the pathologies of disembodiment that are part of digital culture. The core irony of this is that the persistent, documented individual self we're trying to assert is itself an illusion. The key to repairing this illusion is the body, the very thing digital culture denies us" (ibid: 80).

The relationship between body, knowledge, and technology has been increasingly discussed in the context of a critical posthumanism (Herbrechter 2009: 7) which regards the human less as an autonomous-rational being, but rather as a node in complex networks of economic, ecological, media-related, and technological agencies (Haraway 1985; Hayles 1999; Graham 2002; Badmington 2003; Wolfe 2009). Posthumanist subjectivity is located at the intersection of the body, new media technology, and other "non-human agencies," to use Bruno Latour's (2007) term proposed in the context of Actor-Network-Theory. According to a posthumanist perspective, information-based and economic models of subjectivity can be seen as sites in which human and non-human knowledge intersect and elicit agencies that depend on external influences. Moreover, posthumanist theories deal with the results emerging from a fusion of biotechnology and economic interests harboured by international corporations. Following Michel Foucault and Giorgio Agamben, there is an increased focus on biopolitical discussions of human life and ethics (Braidotti 2013).

Taken together, the economic, informational, and posthumanist implications of the quantified self form a complex framework of contextual and discursive factors which need to be considered in a discussion of this social practice. Largely building on Big Data technology, the quantified self has to be considered as embedded in a digital culture which is closely linked with discourses, actors, and networks that transform society and subjects (cf. Reichert 2014: 9). In discussions that take the complexity of the quantified self seriously, fictional texts fulfil an important cultural function because they critically reflect and model human agency in an imagined yet close-to-real society which ascribes ever-growing importance to quantitative methods. Interestingly, extreme forms of technological modernisation processes in the United States always go hand in hand with corrective positions. In other words, US-American culture has always reflected such technological developments from the perspective of second order observation. Fictional texts not only comment on the quantified self, but also offer concrete epistemological counter models. Recent studies in the field of new media, posthumanism, and the digital humanities have pointed to the structural differences between a relational, modular, and recombinatory database epistemology and a more or less linear and open aesthetic of narrative fiction (Hayles 1999; Manovich 2001). Hence, novels represent alternative forms of knowledge by emphasising the qualitative, hermeneutic dimension of human experience as well as the struggles and coping mechanisms of human existence, concomitantly showing the individual new potentials and models for making meaning. It is especially this function of literature as a field of reflection that makes it a productive object for studying the interactions and complexities of quantified subject models and its social, economic, and philosophical implications.

The Quantified Self and US-American Culture

Several aspects of contemporary forms of self-tracking through digital devices can be productively examined within the context of US-American culture. Yet while it is important to trace the cultural and social embedding of these practices and to analyse the cultural continuities, they always represent specific, contingent social practices. With regard to the development of American culture, a significant point of reference is Puritanism, a Calvinist version of Protestantism. In the first half of the seventeenth-century already, exposing private thoughts and intimate experiences in public was a common practice. Puritanism demanded a ritual of public confession, of showing contrition and going through a process of purification in order to experience sanctification and to be accepted as a righteous member by the congregation. If you have to find sinful deeds and thoughts in your life, which because of the ultimate depravity of humans is regarded as the natural state, then self-scrutiny is of the highest urgency. The practices of journal keeping and constant self-questioning serve as appropriate devices to take account of one's self. Indeed, the main step that Protestantism made to separate from (or perhaps, go beyond) Catholicism has been to abolish authorities that might question personal behaviour and intervene between God and the individual. As this process encompasses one's whole life and every single moment in it, constant self-inspection and journal writing become mandatory.

The Enlightenment in America added further dimensions which can be illustrated in the figure of Benjamin Franklin. Franklin can be regarded as a transitional figure in terms of the movement from Puritanism to modern forms of thinking. As he reports in his *Autobiography* (1791), he used a chart as a young man in which he monitored his daily success in keeping the virtues that he had set for himself as goals. The ways in which he checked them as well as the control mechanisms he used can be regarded as paradigmatic types of self-monitoring, constituting a rigid system of self-disciplining. The aim is self-perfection, the self is seen as an instrument to be used as well as to be formed and modelled. "In many ways," Young writes, "Franklin's methodical approach is a how-to guide for today's self-tracker" (Young 2012: 35).

The main difference to Franklin's approach is that today the goal is not virtue or morality, but bodily improvement and self-fashioning (ibid: 36). Young adds, "our contemporary project of accounting for and recording our individual behaviours is really a continuation of a centuries' old way of thinking about oneself in relation to time, made new with the widespread availability of tools to track that relationship" (ibid: 42). The decisive point is the concept of a self that can be shaped, as a project, an enlightenment experiment in perfectibility and human agency. The future is regarded as open and something that can be 'made.' Young refers to Charles Taylor who speaks of "the growing ideal of the human agent who is able to remake himself by methodical and disciplined actions" (ibid: 191; Taylor 1989: 159). Another important author along this line is Alexis de Tocqueville who published his *Democracy in America* in 1835/1840. In it he stresses that Americans tend to constantly do and redo things, that people are in constant motion, that there is always transition, and that nothing seems stable. He observes, "fortunes, opinions, and laws are there in ceaseless variation ..." (ibid: 536). He, or rather his translator, also introduces the term 'individualism' into the English language in his observations of American life: "*Individualism* is a novel experience to which a novel idea has given birth." (ibid: 446)

The Quantified Self in US-American Fiction

As an implicit subject model, the quantified self has appeared and been commented on in US-American writing ever since Puritanism. One of the first explicit references in American fiction occurs in F. Scott Fitzgerald's *The Great Gatsby* (1925). In its critique of the 'American Dream', the modernist novel broaches the subject of self-monitoring in the form of a Franklinesque list. The novel's protagonist Gatsby grew up as poor boy in social obscurity. To lift himself up, he comprises a list of things to do daily that will help him to improve himself – rise early, read, exercise etc. Gatsby uses this list as a form of self-discipline. Even though he manages to escape poverty and to amass considerable wealth, he does not manage to achieve respectable social status. Moreover, he later employs illegal means to attain wealth and power such as bootlegging. The novel thus not only criticises the American Dream but also the belief that one can remake one's self through discipline and self-monitoring, because the context must also be taken into account. Nevertheless, Fitzgerald's novel ends on a more optimistic note, and its beautiful final image reinforces the idea of America as the land of hope and opportunity.

More recent works of fiction which negotiate the relationship between economisation and quantified concepts of the human body include Richard Powers's *Gain* (1998), David Foster Wallace's unfinished fragment *The Pale King* (2011), and Don DeLillo's *Cosmopolis* (2003). Although only implicitly addressed, the quantified self appears as a paradoxical site between individual self-realisation and perfection through institutional instrumentalisation. Other contemporary novels present the quantified self less as an economical, but rather as an 'informational' self. Perhaps the most prominent example is Dave Eggers's *The Circle* (2013), which depicts a dystopian world of numerical self-knowledge in a neoliberal information age in which the young protagonist Mae finds herself increasingly absorbed by a dangerous liaison of self-quantification and surveillance. Robin Sloan's *Mr. Penumbra's 24-hour Bookstore* (2013) and Joshua Cohen's *Book of Numbers* (2015) both address the rifts and interdependencies between numerical and fictional knowledge and the epistemological quests of humans that result from this divide. They represent "narratives of new media encounter" (Liu 2007) in that they stage themselves as technology's and/or new media's 'other'. Situated in a complicated field of recognition, affirmation, and critique of distributed systems of human and non-human agency, cognition, and power, these novels critically engage in a quest to reposition themselves in a new media ecology that gives increased preference to numerical and data-driven knowledge. Moreover, William Gibson's *Neuromancer* (1984) attests to a long tradition in science fiction to problematise biotechnological interventions into the human body in the context of neoliberal critique. Eric Garcia's *Repossession Mambo* (2009) is a recent example that critically reflects the biopolitical implications of body enhancement and transformation.

The focus of our subsequent analysis will lie on Gary Shteyngart's novel *Super Sad True Love Story* (2010), one of the contemporary US-American novels that explicitly posit quantified self technology in the context of biotechnological, digital, and economic discourses.[1] By connecting biological aging processes with the replacement of print through digital media, the novel correlates the quantification of personal data with human agency and value. The novel's protagonist Lenny Abramov, a melancholic middle-aged Russian American, is confronted with the economic, political, and cultural collapse of the United States, all the while trying (and failing) to establish a meaningful relationship with Eunice Park, a young Korean American woman engrossed in the materialistic hollows of digital consumer culture. Eunice's potential of invigorating Lenny via her own youth turns out to be just as futile as the promise of his employer's, the Post-Human Services division of the Staatling-Wapachung Corporation, to enable immortality through life-enhancing bioengineering.

Representing the new generation of media-savvy "inforgs" (Floridi 2010: 9) Eunice compensates her insecurity and disorientation in a dystopian and politically unstable United States with compulsive online shopping on her data streaming mobile media device. The device's absurd name "äppärät" mocks the facilitating function of the apparatus as tool, as "technological extension [...] of our bodies" (McLuhan 2001: 5). In an ironic turn on Foucault's 'apparatus', the äppärät alludes to the strategic formation of discourses, institutions, and laws

---

[1] Parts of this analysis will be published in an essay by Regina Schober, entitled "Between Nostalgic Resistance and Critical Appropriation: Contemporary American Fiction on/of the Information Age and the Potentials of Posthumanist Narrative" (*Amerikastudien* 2016).

that exert power over the individual and over knowledge, in short it refers to "a set of strategies of the relations of forces supporting, and supported by, certain types of knowledge" (Foucault 1980: 194-96). The kind of knowledge produced by the äppärät consists of digital data, "buzzing with contacts, data, pictures, projections, maps, incomes, sound, fury" (Shteyngart 2010: 4), constantly mapping, retrieving, analysing, and scanning data from the user's environment. Yet, all this data, as suggested by the intertextual reference to Shakespeare's *Macbeth* create "a tale / Told by an idiot, full of sound and fury, / Signifying nothing" (Act 5, sc. 5). The äppärät becomes a technical interface that absorbs both contextual data as well as the user's consciousness, limiting the realm of experience to immediately 'translatable' code and thus rendering it completely useless. "The world they needed," Lenny scorns the young generation's media dependency, "was right around them, flickering and bleeping, and it demanded every bit of strength and attention they could spare" (Shteyngart 2010: 84). Lenny condemns a media environment in which the äppärät is not only an 'extension of man' but also 'his' amputation. By reducing human perception exclusively to the binary information readable to the smart machine, the äppärät confines both physical and emotional processes of human consciousness within the technological apparatus of its own epistemology, thus metonymically representing the increasingly informational processes of knowledge production based on search engines.

Shteyngart's äppärät exemplifies how quantitative self-knowledge not only leads to (self-)alienation but also potentially facilitates data surveillance and political discrimination. Humans, in Shteyngart's dystopian world, are defined and measured by a data 'profile', which reduces personal information to a database automatically generated by the äppärät:

"LENNY ABRAMOV ZIP code 10002, New York, New York. Income averaged over five-year-span, $289,420, yuan-pegged, within top 19 percent of U.S. income distribution. Current blood pressure 120 over 70. O-type blood. Thirty-nine years of age, lifespan estimated at eighty-three (47 percent lifespan elapsed; 53 percent remaining). Ailments: high cholesterol, depression [...]." (ibid: 88)

Not coincidentally, Lenny's credit ranking, extracted from so-called "credit-poles," is followed by his health record. In Shteyngart's neoliberal dystopia, digital health data is just as valuable as one's credit information. Both are part of a particular knowledge discourse that favours quantifiable over qualitative information, evaluating a person's (credit/health) well-being and thus their ability to contribute to America's survivability in an environment of external threats. In the quantified-self logic, observational procedures of the natural sciences like 'measuring' and 'tracking' become predominant tools for understanding and 'mapping' the human body. This data is easily decontextualised, relatable, and thus subject to (potentially misleading) correlation. Both Lenny's financial and health data are announced first in absolute, then in relative terms that compares Lenny to the statistical average of the entire population. Individuality becomes a set of statistics, a person's character defined by credit ranking, a person's body by its health status. Easily broken down, assembled, accessed, and put in relation to one another in the modular logic of digital media, this data purports to give quick access to a human's worth in relation to the entire population; the worth of being young and financially successful, thus carries highest potential for consumer capitalism that values healthy, i.e. productive 'individuals'.

Not only does the wish for uniformity neglect the fundamentally diverse, multiple, and process-oriented nature of human identity, but it also neglects the obscure and ambivalent modes of embodied human experience and behaviour that elude the clear binary logic of data. Steven Shaviro notes that if "selfhood is an information pattern, rather than a material substance," the notion of individuality is at risk, since "the network induces mass replication on a miniaturized scale and [...] I myself am only an effect of this miniaturizing process" (2003: 13).

In such a numerical and calculable world in which everything and everyone can be tracked, mapped, and measured, *Super Sad True Love Story* expresses a nostalgic yearning for 'essentially human' attributes that seem to elude such systematic binary logic of access/non-access. It may not be surprising that the title *Super Sad True Love Story* ironically alludes to the 'core' human emotion of love. Lenny momentarily succeeds in finding what he considers 'true love' in his relationship with Eunice, within an environment in which love is dehumanised by entirely functional definitions as a physical process that, as Lenny's boss Joshie argues, "is great for pH, ACTH, LDL, whatever ails you" (Shteyngart 2010: 64). Despite its posthumanist theme, the novel issues a decidedly humanist message in the end when Lenny revises his initial decision to never die. Such a claim which is put to the test in the novel immediately evokes associations with the theory of transhumanism, whose most prominent belief is that humanity is still in the process of evolution. This evolution can and should be then facilitated by any technological, medical or chemical means (Transhumanist FAQ). In this sense, the "post" in the novel's version of "Post-Human" (Shteyngart 2010: 3) needs to be understood as a signifier for the evolution of mankind past its currently limited and frail state, which is why Lenny's initial decision carries a lot of weight in the overall structure of the plot. As a "Life Lovers Outreach Coordinator (Grade G) of the Post-Human Services division" (ibid: 3), Lenny is in charge of promoting and selling a service product which promises to prolong life indefinitely. This promise is based on advancements in the field of biomedicine and technology, which include methods to modify, repair, and transform the human body. Pitching their product to a potential customer, Lenny explains

"I painted him a three-dimensional picture of millions of autonomous nanobots inside his well-preserved, squash-playing body, extracting nutrients, supplementing, delivering, playing with the building blocks, copying, manipulating, reprogramming, replacing blood, destroying harmful bacteria and viruses, monitoring and identifying pathogens, reversing soft-tissue destruction, preventing bacterial infection, repairing DNA." (ibid: 122)

This passage is only one example for the way the issues of life, mortality and sickness are approached and potentially solved by the medical-industrial complex dominating US society in *Super Sad True Love Story*. It speaks to a concept of the human as a subject whose embodiment is no longer an unchangeable and natural fact, but has become a vehicle which can be repaired, modified, and preserved using the knowledge generated by pumping immense sums of capital into scientific research. The message is that having "A so-so body in a world where only an incredible one will do." (ibid: 3) no longer poses an insurmountable problem, the slight caveat being that this only holds true for those individuals who possess the necessary credit score and financial assets to qualify for that option in the first place.

It is clear that the scenario presented here is one dominated by quantification in all areas of life and society. It goes without saying then that in order for a customer to be accepted into the care of the "Life Lovers Outreach division" (ibid: 122), an incredible amount of quantifiable data needs to be collected, interpreted, and tested. Lenny inhabits a peculiar position, as he himself has hopes of being accepted into the program and living forever. Therefore, he simultaneously performs the same tests on himself that he is required to conduct with his customers. This includes regular fitness and stress tests, as well as measuring and publicly displaying "our methylation and homocysteine levels, our testosterone and estrogen, our fasting insulin and triglycerides, and, most important, our 'mood + stress indicators'" (ibid: 56). Employees and customers are also expected to take care of themselves by living a healthy lifestyle, which requires accepting the corrective on individual agency offered by quantification and results in people forcing themselves to count calories, measure fats and trans-fats, and avoid alcohol and other harmful substances. The resulting "scent of immortality" consists of "a curious array of post-mortal odors, of which sardine breath is the most benign." (ibid: 53). This of course is an observation that already hints at the problem behind the constant monitoring of bodily functions: the boundaries between life and death become increasingly blurred.

While initially it seems that Lenny and his contemporaries could adjust to this situation, the implicit and explicit critique of quantification and posthumanisation becomes louder and more pointed as the story progresses. As Lenny points out to the reader, even some of the high net worth customers he deals with are "ITP, Impossible to Preserve" (ibid: 16), and the rigorous and strict testing he conducts follows its own logic. "You had to *prove* that you were worthy of cheating death at Post-Human Services. Like I said, only 18 percent of our applicants qualified for our Product. That's how Joshie intended it." (ibid: 151) Indeed it is Lenny's boss, Joshie Goldman, who most openly displays the mindset that dominates society and culture in the not-so-distant future and who serves as an example for the possible repercussions of making decisions solely based on quantifiable data. Joshie, whose imagination and drive are heavily influenced by golden age science fiction (e.g. Isaac Asimov) (ibid: 215), is the embodiment of transhumanist ideas. Joshie sees Lenny's humanist mindset as the main reason for Lenny's failure to achieve his goals. As he puts it, relying on the humanities and cultural values is what is holding him back, "it's the Fallacy of Merely Existing. FME. There'll be plenty of time to ponder and write and act out later. Right now you've got to *sell to live*." (ibid: 65 [original emphasis]). It is this need and desire to sell which explains the seemingly arbitrary acceptance rate of 18 percent that was installed by Goldman and on which he based the philosophy of his company. Simply put, it keeps the demand for his product high and leaves room for an expansion of customers by increasing that rate. Furthermore, Joshie is not simply interested in selling, he wants to be among the first people to benefit from the revolutionary procedures developed by his company. That is why he willingly modifies and changes his body, evolving into a younger version of himself. By undergoing a variety of procedures, Joshie is transformed into "a thick young mass of tendons and forward motion" (ibid: 215), a body consisting entirely of "new muscles and obedient nerve endings" (ibid: 220) who does not shy away from telling Eunice about plans to have his own heart, the "idiotically designed" (ibid: 293) muscle, removed altogether.

Ultimately it is Joshie's fate, juxtaposed with Lenny coming to terms with his own mortality and his success as an author that drives home the implied criticism of a culture of quantification and posthumanisation. Joshie, the passionate anti-humanist, is shown to be plagued by the side effects of his life extension treatment, which reduce him into a drooling mass unable to control his facial contours who regretfully admits that all of the procedures his company developed did more damage than they did good. Thus, his final words are, "In the end, nature simply would not yield" (ibid: 327). What this also demonstrates, of course, is the fallacy in Joshie's logic, in which he valued the selling of his product higher than the development and the allocation of proper time frames and testing. Put differently, the novel here reveals the dangers behind an economically driven science that pushes the boundaries of humanity without anyone thinking of the consequences, because there simply is no time to read, write, and reflect.

As the precarity and sensitivity of knowledge about your own body shows, *Super Sad True Love Story* proposes that sometimes it is best to not know at all, repeatedly pointing out the benefits of what popular wisdom considers 'ignorance is bliss'. As Peter Wehling has noted, an increasing mass of knowledge in the information age makes obvious the limits of the value of information and knowledge, rendering not information but non-information and the right not-to-know as increasingly valuable factors for retaining agency (2009: 96). Lenny, who is increasingly irritated with the intrusive quality of "smoky data spilling out of a total of fifty-nine äppäräti" (Shteyngart 2010: 90), finds his recluse in Italy. Returning to its narrative starting place, the novel mockingly leads Lenny to the birthplace of the Renaissance to find his own 'cultural rebirth'. Here, he yearns to return to a pre-digital silence, to find "a place with less data, less youth, and where old people like myself were not despised simply for being old" (ibid: 326). Yet, Lenny has to realise that globalisation leaves no such refuges. Invited to a dinner party he has to witness how "the Italians were having a go at it" – how the culture he had previously idealised for its clinging to traditional values is in the process of Americanisation, yearning for a culture of youth slang and empty data obsession.

Lenny might not have found the peace he was looking for, but at least temporarily, he is given a break. "For a while at least, no one said anything, and

I was blessed with what I needed the most. Their silence, black and complete" (ibid: 329). Concluding with this final sentence, the novel indeed leaves an almost reassuring void which functions as a sense of closure – a narrative closure which is all the more effective and meaningful in a world of unceasing data flows, endless mapping, and a desensitising persistence of information availability. The knowledge that *Super Sad True Love Story* and the other novels suggest as an alternative is the knowledge of when to stop, when to unplug the endless spills of data that surround us.

Conclusion: The Quantified Self and the Function of Literature

Super Sad True Love Story negotiates the effects of a culture obsessed with digital and thus quantifiable data on human experience and (self-)definition on the level of fictional exploration. It questions the validity of the quantified self movement to locate the human in the informational realm of digital data and thus maps possible consequences of an informational knowledge for conceptions of the human. In a self-reflexive move, the novel experiments with the malleability of language as influenced by and resisting digitalisation. The frequent use of neologisms ("Life Lovers Outreach Coordinator"; äppärät; High Net Worth Individuals; "UnitedContinentalDeltamerican"; "AlliedWasteCVSCitigroup"; "AssLuxury") points to the need to find a new language for a new media environment, while satirically expressing the emptiness and non-originality of such recombinatory compounds which exemplify the shifting flows of capital, ideas, and people. *Super Sad True Love Story* idealises the purity of children's language as an unspoiled and 'authentic' form of 'human' communication before it evaporates into the illiteracy of a youth culture determined by the surplus of data and visual images. Lenny describes the experience of strolling through his New York neighbourhood, "I relished hearing language actually being *spoken* by children. Overblown verbs, explosive nouns, beautifully bungled prepositions. Language, not data. How long would it be before these kids retreated into the dense clickety-clack äppärät world of their absorbed mothers and missing fathers?" (ibid: 51).

Not only is the contrast between "language" and "data" associated with a loss of innocence, but also with the loss of parental guidance and responsibility. For Lenny, America's economic decline is thus not so much a question of 'word casing' and semantic shift, but the result of political failure on the part of the American government. Lenny's anger towards the hypocrisy of books is at the same time a frustration with a dying America. After the total incorporation of America by foreign creditors, Lenny's books feel "cold to the touch" (ibid: 321); they are just as frail as the old people that are forced out of his building. Death becomes a favoured option, one that carries more value than the 'almost dead'. An art opening, paradoxically staged as a welcoming party for the Chinese central banker, brings the cruelty of the not-letting-go to the fore, showing ghastly images of tortured or soon to be murdered people who are forced to stay alive and thus witness the hopelessness of their existence. "Dead is dead," Lenny laconically comments on the artworks, "we know where to file another person's extinction, but the artist purposely zoomed in on the living, or, to be more accurate, the forced-to-be-living and the soon-to-be-dead" (ibid: 315-316). "America 2.0" does not equal a 'new America', as the American Restoration Authority (ARA) suggests, but only an artificial life-prolongation of an already dead patient.

Yet, Lenny's proclamation *"I am going to die"* (subverting his initial echo of his company motto *"I am never going to die"* (ibid: 1)), metafictionally connected with the decision that this will be his "last entry" (ibid: 302), is not actually his last entry. Like America, he is kept alive, yet yearning for "silence, black and complete" (ibid: 329). So can this desire for silence be read as a yearning for the end of fiction? Here, the novel's self-ironic gesture creates another ambiguity: it does not (want to) settle between an awareness that the great narrative of 'America' no longer exists, that what has been known as America has capitulated to the dehumanising logic of a media-driven hypercapitalism and cannot be rescued, yet at the same time there is a quest for self-preservation, for believing in the power of narrative to recreate a sense of national identity. In this way, *Super Sad True Love Story* gives the perhaps most paradoxical answer to the question of what function (American) fiction can have in a global information age. *Super Sad True Love Story* demonstrates that if the human is not regarded as necessarily being threatened but rather supplemented and enhanced by technology, then the same may be true for (print) novels. If "what's missing [in the network society] is what is *more than information*: the qualitative dimension of experience or the continuum of analog space in between all those ones and zeroes" (Shaviro 2003: 249), the novel may fill exactly this blank space, retrieving the intangible and uncategorisable voids left by digital information.

Literature has played a crucial role in reflecting ideologies and practices of quantification, self-tracking and the seemingly universal sovereignty of interpretation attributed to numbers, information and data. While the dominance of a binary logic and abstract, relative, and absolute data has exponentially increased in recent years, both a belief in and a strong scepticism towards quantification has been a crucial factor in American culture. Gary Shteyngart's *Super Sad True Love Story* is an example of how contemporary fiction negotiates measures and techniques that aim at quantification and its economic or political application. Whether it is the constant streaming of data through the 'äppäräti', the public accessibility of even the most private and personal information (e.g. sexual preferences and hormone levels) or the universal presence of the credit poles broadcasting the financial situation of every citizen, and thus their "worth" as human beings, into the world: the individuals presented here are constantly being harassed, evaluated, and hounded by the promise of objectivity inherent in numbers and data. As a techno-dystopia, the novel demonstrates the numerous pitfalls that are either caused by a too rigid dependence on numbers (e.g. the life extension program, excessive consumerism) or cannot be avoided despite them (e.g. the collapse of the US economy and social structure, medical repercussions of life extension), reminding the reader that a "culture of quantification" is not something that should be embraced without careful reflection and consideration.

References

Badmington, Neil (2003): "Theorizing Posthumanism" In: Cultural Critique 53 (Winter 2003): pp. 10-27.
Badmington, Neil (2000): "Introduction: Approaching Posthumanism." In: ibid (ed.), Posthumanism, New York: Palgrave, pp. 1-10.
Bell, Daniel (1974): The Coming of Post-Industrial Society: A Venture in Social Forecasting, London: Heinemann.
Berman, Jules (2013): Principles of Big Data. Preparing, Sharing, and Analyzing Complex Information, Amsterdam: Elsevier.
Boyd, Danah/Crawford, Kate (2012): "Critical Questions for Big Data." In: Information, Communication & Society 15/5: pp. 662-279.
Braidotti, Rosi (2013): The Posthuman, Cambridge: Polity Press.
Brown, Wendy (2003): "Neo-Liberalism and the End of Liberal Democracy." In: Theory & Event 7/1: n. p.
Curry, Richard O./Goodheart/Lawrence B. (eds.) (1991): American Chameleon: Individualism in Trans-National Context, Kent, Ohio: The Kent State UP.
Davenport, Thomas H. (2014): Big Data at Work: Dispelling the Myths, Uncovering the Opportunities, Cambridge, MA: Harvard Business Review Press.
Ehrenberg, Alain (2012): Das Unbehagen in der Gesellschaft, Frankfurt a. M.: Suhrkamp.
Eisenstadt, Shmuel N. (2000): "Multiple Modernities." In: Daedalus 129/1: pp. 1-29.
Floridi, Luciano (2010): Information. A Very Short Introduction, Oxford University Press.
Fitzgerald, F. Scott (2000[1925]): The Great Gatsby, New York/London: Penguin Modern Classics.
Foucault, Michel (1980): Power/Knowledge: Selected Interviews and Other Writings, 1972-1977. Ed. C. Gordon, New York: Pantheon Books.
Franklin, Benjamin (2005): Autobiography, Poor Richard, and Later Writings. Ed. J. A. Leo Lemay, New York: Library of America.
Graham, Elaine (2002): Representations of the Post/Human, New Brunswick, NJ: Rutgers UP.
Hahn, Alois/Schorch, Marén (2007): "Technologies of the Will and Their Christian Roots." In: Sabine Maasen/Barbara Sutter (eds.), On Willing Selves: Neolioberal Politics vis-á-vis the Neuroscientific Challenge, Houndsville/Basingstoke/Hampshire: Palgrave Macmillan, pp. 53-76.
Haraway, Donna (1990): "A Manifesto for Cyborgs: Science, Technology and Socialist Feminism in the 1980s." In: Linda Nicholson (ed.), Feminism/Postmodernism, New York: Routledge, pp. 190-233.
Harvey, David (2005): A Brief History of Neoliberalism, Oxford: Oxford UP.
Hayles, Nancy Katherine (1999): How We Became Posthuman, Chicago: University of Chicago Press.
Herbrechter, Stefan (2009): Posthumanismus: Eine kritische Einführung, Darmstadt: Wissenschaftliche Buchgesellschaft.
Jenkins, Henry (2010): Convergence Culture: Where Old and New Media Collide, New York: New York UP.

Latour, Bruno (2007): Reassembling the Social, New York: Oxford University Press.
Lévy, Pierre (1997): Collective Intelligence: Mankind's Emerging World in Cyberspace, New York: Plenum.
Liu, Alan (2007): "Imagining the New Media Encounter." In: Ray Siemens/Susan Schreibman (eds.), A Companion to Digital Literary Studies, Malden/Oxford/Victoria: Blackwell, pp. 3-25.
Macpherson, Crawford B. (1962): The Theory of Possessive Individualism: Hobbes to Locke, Oxford: Clarendon Press.
Manovich, Lev (2001): The Language of New Media, Cambridge, MA/London: MIT Press.
Mayer-Schönberger/Cukier, Kenneth (2013): Big Data: A Revolution that Will Transform How We Live, Work and Think, New York: Houghton Mifflin Harcourt.
McLuhan, Marshall (2001[1964[): Understanding Media. The Extensions of Man, London/New York: Routledge.
Ong, Walter J. (1982): Orality and Literacy: The Technologizing of the Word, London: Methuen.
Reckwitz, Andreas (2006): Das hybride Subjekt. Eine Theorie der Subjektkulturen von der bürgerlichen Moderne zur Postmoderne, Weilerswist: Velbrück Wissenschaft.
Reichert, Ramón (ed.) (2014): Big Data: Analysen zum gesellschaftlichen Wandel von Wissen, Macht und Ökonomie, Bielefeld: transcript.
Reichert, Ramón (2014): "Einführung." In: ibid (ed.), Big Data: Analysen zum gesellschaftlichen Wandel von Wissen, Macht und Ökonomie, Bielefeld: transcript, pp. 9-31.
Schmarzo, Bill (2013): Big Data: Understanding How Data Powers Big Business, Hoboken, NJ: Wiley.
Shteyngart, Gary (2010): Super Sad True Love Story, London: Granta.
Taylor, Charles (1989): Sources of the Self: The Making of Modern Identity, Cambridge, Mass.: Harvard UP.
"Transhumanist FAQ", October, 2015 (http://humanityplus.org/philosophy/transhumanist-faq/).
de Tocqueville, Alexis (2007[1835/1840]): Democracy in America. Ed. Isaac Kramnich, New York, London: W.W. Norton.
Wehling, Peter (2009): "Nichtwissen – Bestimmungen, Abgrenzungen, Bewertungen." In: EWE 20/1, pp. 95-106.
Wolfe, Cary (2010): What is Posthumanism? Minneapolis: University of Minnesota Press.
Young, Nora (2012): The Virtual Self: How Our Digital Lives Are Altering The World Around Us, Toronto: McClelland & Stewart.

**Investigations
in Quantifying Practices**

Bodies, Mood and Excess
Relationship Tracking and the Technicity of Intimacy

Alex Lambert

Abstract

A range of commercial mobile technologies are emerging which use psychophysiological sensors to monitor bodies and behaviour to produce new forms of knowledge about social relationships. In this paper I am concerned with how this kind of relationship-tracking influences intimacy. I am specifically interested in what I call the "technicity of intimacy", the cultural techniques which emerge through the historically contingent technologisation of intimacy. Based on archival research, I argue that relationship-tracking promises to take up the intensive social labours associated with contemporary intimacy. Yet, the psychophysiological measurements these technologies rely on produce partial and ambiguous indicators of intimate life, gesturing toward an excess of intimate meaning that cannot be interrogated. The self-reflexive concern with this excess drives further tracking experiments and techniques. Yet intimacy remains a continuous mystery, and this problematises the value of self-tracking as a system dedicated to achieving meaningful self-knowledge and completeness.

Introduction

A range of technologies are emerging which monitor bodies and behaviour to produce new forms of knowledge about social relationships. This kind of relationship-tracking is part of the broader self-tracking phenomenon, but rather than concentrating purely on the self it interrogates the meaning of social bonds. Popular applications focus on the "health" of long-term relationships, correlate social, emotional and biological variables, and often provide goals to work towards enriching intimate life. Some also provide an algorithmically automated means for ranking and filtering relationships based on physiological inputs. Hence, as well as producing new forms of social knowledge, relationship-tracking promises to alleviate the burden of managing one's social life.

I am interested in how relationship-tracking, as a repertoire of technologies and techniques, influences intimacy. Various studies have begun to examine web-based, social and mobile media in relation to transformations in intimacy (Hjorth/Wilken/Gu 2012; Hjorth/Hinton 2013; Lambert 2013) to the point where some have suggested a nascent "intimacy turn" in media studies (Hjorth/

Lim 2012). These media ask us to probe the relationship between embodiment, affect, privacy, publicity, closeness and distance, concepts that are central to modern notions of intimacy. Relationship-tracking similarly makes intimacy and its various dimensions a primary concern. In pursuing this topic I keep to a fairly basic and well-accepted notion of intimacy as denoting the social experience of close, caring relationships. Yet it is important to recognise that the meaning of intimacy changes in different cultural and historical contexts (cf. Jamieson 1998). Moreover, late modern European and Anglophone life is inflected by transformations in intimate relationships (cf. Giddens 1992). In this context, research into intimacy is always and already a study of changes in its nature.

New technologies are undoubtedly driving some of these changes. To research the historically specific technologisation of intimacy is to study what I call the technicity of intimacy. In its most general sense, technicity denotes the dynamic and emergent nature of the human-technology relationship. Technicity involves *technê*: the practical skill and techniques a person brings to using a particular technology for a particular purpose. Where intimacy is concerned, such techniques are influenced by cultural norms and socio-political structures, as well as by the material characteristics of new technologies. Here the German school of media theory provides the useful concept of "cultural technique". For theorists such as Kittler (1999) and Siegert (2013), cultural techniques are influenced by the way in which a technology records, stores and transmits aspects of phenomenal reality. While these theorists were interested in how technologies such as the gramophone and cinema projector negotiate phenomena such as sound and light, I am interested in how self-tracking technologies negotiate psychophysiological phenomena that emanate from the body. The technological capacity to register and represent these phenomena, I argue, is largely driving the technicity of intimacy of relationship trackers.

The term "cultural technique" originated as a way of describing the skilled practices of particular technical groups, such as agricultural engineers (Winthrop-Young 2013). This remains useful for understanding relationship trackers, who can be thought of as a particular technical group defined by their practical relationship with tracking technologies. Relationship trackers cultivate techniques such as fitting sensors, operating applications, making measurements, objectifying and interpreting emotions, ranking social ties, and in some cases building and refining complex systems out of these elements. In this article I explore how the cultivation of these techniques are producing a new relationship to intimacy. Ironically, they do not reveal the personal, interpersonal or essential meaning of intimacy. They conceal intimacy in a mystery, always just beyond reach.

In the following section I introduce the methodology and primary case study – an application called *PplKpr* (pronounced "people keeper") – that I use to develop my argument. Following this I explore how the techniques of relationship-tracking have their roots in psychotherapy. Both psychotherapy and relationship-tracking seek to create healthy individuals by fostering well-functioning relationships. The need for this intensifies with modern social and mobile media, which complicate the meaning and value of social relationships and social interactions. Relationship-tracking promises to take up the labours associated with this experience of "intensive intimacy". Yet the psychophysiological measurements these technologies enable produce partial and ambiguous indicators of intimate life, and in particular *intimate presence*. They gesture toward an excess of intimate meaning which cannot be interrogated. I argue that the self-reflexive concern with this excess drives further tracking experiments and techniques. I conclude with a consideration of what this means for contemporary understandings of intimacy.

Case Study: *PplKpr*

I look at a smartphone application called *PplKpr* to understand how relationship-tracking influences the technicity of intimacy. *PplKpr* is both an art project and an application that can be downloaded from the Apple App Store. It was developed by two artists, Lauren McCarthy and Kyle McDonald, with the support of a Frank-Rathye Studio for Creative Inquiry residency, and funding from the Andy Warhol Foundation. *PplKpr* uses a phone's GPS to detect when the user is moving to meet up with someone. The application will ask whom the user is meeting, and the user will input a name from his or her list of contact. It will then ask whether the user is feeling excited, aroused, angry, scared, anxious, bored, or calm. It will detect the intensity of the chosen mood by applying an algorithm to physiological data taken from a Bluetooth connected variable heart rate monitor wristband. Over time a user's contacts will be ranked in terms of how intense a mood they provoke. *PplKpr* gives the user an opportunity to send prefabricated text messages to those who elicit positive moods. It will also automatically block and remove contacts who elicit negative moods.

On the application's website, a video promotes *PplKpr* in the following way: "Our social circles are widening. All those relationships can be overwhelming."[1] To assist in this dilemma, *PplKpr* will "automatically manage your relationships so you won't have to". The style and tone of the video is subtly tongue-in-cheek, which seems to complement the developers' intentions. In an interview with the Australian radio programme *Download this Show* (2015), Kyle McDonald states:

"It's meant to be provocative and humorous and interesting and disturbing all at the same time. We made an application that you can actually download now and try out yourself, and we do this because we think that there is something really important about trying these kinds of ideas out on yourself and having an experience, and that we learn from experience, and that gives us more insight to discuss these things and think about them."

In this response, McDonald opens up a clear critique of self-tracking culture as something that may have disturbing elements, while also connecting with the very ethos of self-tracking as something that produces new knowledge and

---

1   www.pplkpr.com.

advances personal growth (cf. Lupton 2014). In this paper I take up the developers' provocation, using *PplKpr* as a way of gaining deeper insight into relationship-tracking's influence on intimacy.

Importantly, although *PplKpr* may seem to make assumptions about social life (discussed below), it is by no means atypical. There are commercially available applications, as well as ones still in development, that share many of the same features and assumptions. There are apps that rank and prioritise social ties based on interaction frequency, and prompt social engagement when certain people are being ignored.[2] General purpose life-logging applications correlate social interactions with factors such as mobility and emotions.[3] There is a vast array of mood tracking applications.[4] Finally, there are applications that automatically remove information to remove distractions and increase focus.[5]

I used *PplKpr* for a period of three months. Each time I engaged with the application I wrote down my insights on what became another kind of self-tracking application, *Evernote*. I also reviewed the rich archive of forum discussions, blog posts, technical manuals and videos found on self-tracking websites such as quantifiedself.com and monitorme.com. These websites are used by a community of dedicated self-trackers, some of whom are experts such as doctors, psychologists, dieticians, engineers and developers. Many tracking apps that become commercially marketed are first beta-tested and discussed within this milieu, both online and in popular offline "meet ups". Hence, discourses and techniques of relationship-tracking are fostered within this community before circulating to a broader market.

Relationship-Tracking and Psychotherapy

According to Lupton, self-tracking engenders the "reflexive monitoring self" who engages in "systemised information collection, interpretation and reflection as part of working towards the goal of becoming" (2014: 12). Lupton argues that these practices exemplify modernity's broader fascination with self-improvement, spurred on by a sense of "ethical incompleteness". The contemporary story of intimacy is similarly entangled with practices of self-knowledge production, discourses of self-actualisation, and technologies of self-surveillance. This story cannot be told without reference to the popularisation of psychotherapy, which has been used to make sense of (and in the process has heavily influenced) changes in the nature of intimate relationships (Giddens 1992; Illouz 2007; Berlant 2012;).

Eva Illouz (2007) supplies one of the most compelling critiques of the psychological conjugation of intimacy and selfhood. Although she focuses on

---

2 See *Stitch*, available at: http://www.lastinitial.com/stitch.
3 See *Reporter*, available at: http://www.reporter-app.com/.
4 See *Moody Me*, available at: http://www.medhelp.org/land/mood-diary-app; see also *Mood Panda*, available at: http://www.moodpanda.com/features.aspx.
5 See *Rescue Time*, available at: https://www.rescuetime.com/.

American twentieth century history, many of the phenomena she discusses are global in reach. Illouz describes the way in which various psychotherapeutic discourses and practices suffused everyday life through a variety of means. Therapy entered popular culture through autobiography, paperback pop psychology, and TV relationship counsellors. The feminist movement of the 1960s courted therapy to politicise the inequities of private life, and in the process began the deconstruction of the home as a pure space of intimacy. The post-war State championed therapeutic management in various sectors, and intimacy entered the workplace to foster happy, productive workers.

Psychotherapy closely connects mental health to healthy relationships, and in the process covets and reconstitutes cultural understandings of intimacy. Illouz writes:

"In the context of close relationships, intimacy, like self-realisation and other categories invented by psychologists, became a code word for "health". Healthy relationships were intimate and intimacy was healthy. Once the notion of intimacy was posited as the norm and the standard for healthy relationships, the absence of intimacy could become the organizing overall frame of a new therapeutic narrative of self-hood." (2007: 46-47)

Psychotherapy makes the production of self-knowledge, particularly knowledge about emotions, an essential aspect of intimacy, as it becomes a means to achieving healthy relationships and hence a healthy psyche. In Illouz's analysis, negative or ambiguous emotions become the "archenemy of intimacy" (ibid: 35). Psychotherapy provides the techniques to purge these emotions by externalising and objectifying them as speech, writing, and visual representations. Once mediated in this way, emotions can produce insights about what exactly is going wrong in a relationship. There are many examples of this process becoming increasingly standardised and quantified, including emotional intelligence tests, psychometric questionnaires, and, of course, the mood monitoring practised by the self-tracking community. Through computation and physiological sensors, self-trackers attempt to identify and externalise emotions, especially negative emotions, to improve themselves and their relationships. These techniques are inherited from psychotherapy and reconstituted in a new techno-materiality.

The dissemination of psychotherapy produced what Illouz calls an "emotional field", in which a "great variety of social and institutional actors compete with one another to define self-realisation, health or pathology, thus making emotional health into a new commodity" (ibid: 63). Self-tracking culture augments and extends this field. Importantly, the growing market of self-tracking applications embeds the commodification of emotional health in the techno-economic environment of digital media. Consequently, the therapist or therapeutic narrative is exchanged for widely available personal digital technologies. This is nicely illustrated in the following comment by Gary Krane (2011), a relationship-tracking application developer and clinical psychologist, talking about his application *Couple Space* (later changed to *CoupleWise*) at a Quantified Self meet up:

"[Couple Space is] for the 55 million unhappy couples in the U.S. who can't afford a therapist but would spend 19 dollars a month for a web app that can do eight things a therapist can't do and about 80 percent of what a cognitive behavioural therapist can do."

Things which this application can do that a therapist cannot include the capacity to process large amounts of data to identify key issues which troubled couples need to address to improve their relationships. Hence, the capacity for the therapeutic narrative to improve people by emphasising particular needs, values and goals is augmented by the capacity for computation to quickly reveal correlations in data.

Intensive Intimacy and Immunised Spheres

For Giddens (1991), psychotherapy is a system of expert knowledge that contributes to a state of reflexive modernity in which self-knowledge and self-projects become a source of comfort and stability in a chaotic world. It is most certainly the case that we live in a chaotic world where intimacy is concerned. In many European and Anglophone contexts the meaning of intimacy has been significantly transformed by factors such as social and civic challenges to the heterodox, patriarchal, nuclear family (Roseneil/Budgeon 2004), migration and transnational family care (Madianou/Miller 2011), the cultivation of intimacy in work settings (Gregg 2011), and the emergence of new kinds of caring friendships (Allan 2008). Many people no longer exist in tightly knit, homogeneous and geographically bounded communities. Instead people develop more personalised communities consisting of heterogeneous social ties drawn from a variety of distinct social contexts (Pahl 2005).

This trajectory toward increasing complexity nicely illustrates what I have elsewhere called "intensive intimacy": a state of affairs where the work of intimacy becomes increasingly laborious and requires the development of new social and technical skills (Lambert 2013). Relationship-tracking technologies promise to take up the labour of intensive intimacy. They promise to help people understand the meaning of their social ties, to clarify the social locus of intimacy. For example, Fabio Ricardo (2015), the organiser of the Rio de Janeiro chapter of the Quantitative Self community, describes the motivation behind his system for rating and ranking his relationships.

"It was hard to manage all these relationships and have at the same time meaningful connections [...] I was like, okay, what kind of tool can I use? So I actually looked at my database, the people that I know, and I realised that I was devoting less attention to the people who were most important in my life [...] So I thought, how can I reduce this kind of 'fat'."

Akshay Patil, the chief developer of an application called *Stitch*, describes a similar motivation. Patil (2014) is concerned with the way social apps encourage "superficial interactions with lots of people". He wants to identify "more intimate relationships" and have "real conversations with them". Moreover, he wants to create an elegant system which will perform this task for him.

"I really like tools that actually solve a real problem for me based on the insights we can glean from data. And so for me, my problem was that I don't feel like I talk with these people often enough. So I built something that would just send me notifications if it's been too long since we last talked."

In both examples a system that clarifies who is meaningful and who isn't promises to alleviate the intensive negotiation of social ties characteristic of contemporary times. Some relationship-tracking technologies also promise a system for automatically filtering ties. *PplKpr* will remove and block certain contacts that cause consistently negative mood states. Overall, this articulates a familiar human-machine relationship, analysed critically since Marx, in which machines promise to alleviate human labour. This is what Morozov (2013) has recently referred to as (with reference to self-tracking) "technological solutionism". On offer is nothing less than a more intimate social sphere, more intimate social encounters, and hence a healthier life.

Relationship-tracking is thus an excellent example of what Sloterdijk (2011) calls "immunisation". In his three volume work, *Spheres*, Sloterdijk posits the sphere as the sublime metaphysical geometry through which human life can be understood. Human beings are always constructing spheres of different sizes, but the most figurative is the intimate sphere, which Sloterdijk dedicates his first volume to exploring. Each sphere must have a process for negotiating its boundaries, an immune system for letting good organisms in while keeping bad ones out. We labour on these immune systems when we feel our intimate spheres are being infringed upon by the "non-interior world". These incursions are exacerbated by the "general space crisis" of globalised modernity, in which traditional spheres of meaning are eroded and replaced by a complex topology of small spheres broiling together, or what Sloterdijk calls "foam". We respond to this by using new technologies to aid our immunities: "The body of humanity seeks to create a new immune constitution in an electronic medial skin." (2011: 25)

Because computers can automate the surveillance and categorisation of people, computational immune systems become more effective at creating spheres, even if they are not the spheres people hope for. Consider the filter bubble effect that circumscribes social ties based on marketing, personalisation and relevance algorithms, and is now fundamental to search, social, mobile and locative media (Pariser 2011). Consider dating sites and mobile applications that establish a set of prescribed categories through which people can ensure mutually attractive matches. These immune systems are driving a shift from a cultural ideal of serendipity to one of propinquity: of ideological, social or physical proximity. Relationship-tracking technologies are part of this trajectory. Yet, unlike many of the technologies just mentioned, their capacity to act as effective immune systems is curiously undermined by their encoded assumptions about the nature of intimacy, mood and the body. Their capacity to measure and infer aspects of social life is so partial and limited that they serve to further complicate and confuse the very things people are seeking to clarify.

The Mysteries of Intimate Presence

PplKpr (and similar applications) seek to influence relationships by monitoring social encounters. It attempts to measure the embodied moods felt while interacting with others. It measures how one's body registers the presence of the other, thus making the nature of embodied social presence centrally important.

Presence has become an essential concept for understanding intimacy in a variety of fields. For example, the psychological process model of intimacy argues that intimacy begins and is sustained through a sense of presence: of mutual attention, acknowledgment and visible emotional dispositions such as care and affection (Laurenceau/Pietromonaco/Barret 1998). Similarly, Gestalt psychology argues that intimacy requires a kind of presence in which self and other become entangled through synchronously performed, shared activities (Melnick/Nevis 1994). These can take on an astounding variety: from leisure pursuits such as playing sport or going bowling, to creative shared projects such as playing in a band; from meaningful rituals like spending a day in bed together, to parental projects such as raising children. Gestalt theories of intimacy emphasise the importance of absorption in the other through a shared activity, as well as face-to-face interactions.

These ideas have been problematised with the advent of computer-mediated communication. Milne (2010) argues that communicating parties must have a sense of one another's embodied characteristics to evoke a sense of intimate presence. This sense of embodiment can be produced through a variety of media, not just in face-to-face, synchronous contexts. For example, Milne explores how particular kinds of rhetorical work are required to evoke a sense of embodiment through letter writing, postcards and emails. In these cases a skill for descriptive writing is essential. One could say that different media technologies produce different cultural techniques of presence. Yet in any medium, presence always requires this kind of performative work, and hence presence is always mediated by performative techniques and norms, which are themselves constituted through shared histories that are absent from the present moment. Hence, responding to Derrida's (1997) deconstruction, Milne argues that the feeling of intimate presence is ultimately a psychological state, a fantasy conditioned by mediation and absence.

Recently, scholarship on intimate presence has turned to how mobile and social media undermine the ability to sustain this psychological absorption in another person. These media cause various social contexts to "collapse" into heterogeneous, networked public spaces (boyd 2011). Hence, we experience "presence bleed" between parts of our lives that were preciously separate, such as work and leisure (Gregg 2011). People must continuously negotiate social demands that are "elsewhere" and yet entangled and interpenetrated, creating what Gergen calls a "diverted or divided consciousness" (2002: 227).

For example, Richardson and Wilken (2013) consider how people interface with smartphones while moving through demanding urban spaces. Ring tones, vibrations and screens compete with the bodily navigation of built environments. Complex interactions between place, embodiment and presence result in "oscillating technosomatic resisters of attention, inattention and distraction" (ibid: 189). Increasingly, mobile media users must negotiate between various "different presents" evoked through different media, such as maps, photographs and augmented reality – witness distinguishing terms such as "telepresence" (Mantovani/Riva 1999)[6], "virtual presence" (ibid), "locative presence" (Farman 2009), "augmented co-presence" (Ito 2003) and "intimate visual co-presence" (Ito 2005).

These complications in intimate presence illustrate two key discursive dimensions of intensive intimacy. On the one hand, there is a scholarly and engineering discourse that emphasises the need to design new platforms and develop concomitant skills and techniques (Knobel/Lankshear 2008). On the other hand, there is a potent discourse found in scholarship and popular culture that advocates the stoic denial of media consumption and the re-sanctification of uninterrupted face-to-face experiences (Pinker 2014; Turkle 2011). Importantly, both discourses are similar in that they are concerned with creating properly immunised intimate spheres in which the Gestalt experience of intimate presence can proceed without distraction. Both are similar in the recognition that there is a problem with intimate presence which needs to be solved.

The scholarship mentioned above is for the most part concerned with how technologies mediate communication and hence social presence. A change in framework needs to occur when thinking about relationship-tracking technologies such as *PplKpr* which *measure* rather than mediate presence. There is a rich history of technical scholarship on quantifying and measuring "social presence" in Computer-Mediated Communication (CMC) contexts (cf. Kiesler/Siegel/McGuire 1984). Much of the psychophysiological work in this field has been driven by Human-Computer Interaction design in the context of immersive virtual worlds and gameplay (Jenett et al. 2008; Ekman et al. 2012). Relationship-tracking takes the work of quantifying and measuring presence out of the hands of these experts and puts it in the hands of a broader market of everyday users. This creates a new kind of self-reflexive relationship to intimate presence. When first using *PplKpr*, the application creates an overriding sense of anticipation. How will it measure this approaching social encounter? What will I feel? What insights will I gain? However, anticipation soon yields to disappointment when one realises that a social interaction cannot be reduced to a single measurement of a physiological mood state, which appears as one small, ambiguous part of a much larger and complex phenomenon.

As one becomes more experienced in using *PplKpr* its misrecognitions and inaccuracies are better understood. The user must choose from a limited set

---

6   Mantovani and Riva give this concept a strong critical treatment, yet the concept itself can be found in a range of Computer-Mediated Communication and Human-Computer Interaction literature dating back to the 1980s.

of moods that ignore a much richer and personalised repertoire of emotional descriptions. A single emotional measurement is encouraged for each social situation, making it difficult to monitor changes in emotion or the experience of multiple emotions simultaneously. While the application asks you to assign an emotion to a particular person, it could just as easily be some non-personal aspect of the situation which is producing an emotional response. Finally, it is instantly clear that the heart-rate monitor system on which these measurements are based is a less than worthy indication of something as rich as an interpersonal interaction.

PplKpr also intervenes in the rhythms of social life. Measurements are made between social encounters, and hence outside of the experience of intimate social presence. Whatever emotion is qualitatively reflected on or physiologically inferred is always differed from the affectual experience of presence. Also, because *PplKpr* relies on GPS to infer movement, there are many social interactions it cannot anticipate, such as when one receives visitors while remaining relatively sedentary, or when engaging in mediated interactions. *PplKpr* problematises the relationship between social and embodied rhythms, and the relationship between presence, absence and mobility. The overall impression one gets from using this device is that it gets things "wrong". Yet, in getting things wrong the application also gestures toward an excess of intimate meaning that it has failed to interrogate. The relationship tracker is placed in a self-reflexive relationship with what resists being tracked. Intimate presence becomes a beguiling mystery that demands to be solved.

Intimate Excess and the Partiality of Sensors

I use the term "excess" to describe the aspects of experience that evade tracking. Self-trackers encounter many such aspects of experience. Relationship trackers encounter an excess in intimacy: those aspects of intimacy which cannot be exhausted by sensing, quantifying, ranking and other techniques. Derrida (1997) argues that an excess of meaning is always produced by signifying structures, as signs get their meaning in differential structural relationship to each other, and there can be no transcendental signifier through which this play of *différance* comes to an end. Interestingly, a similar proposition can be found in the work of Merleau-Ponty (2004), who argues that phenomenal experience has a Gestalt aspect, the totality of which cannot be captured by communication, or by physiological systems which similarly break experience down into component elements and their supposed physical correlates. In this case "excess" describes the remainder of a translation of phenomenal immediacy into a communicative or physiological structure of differences.

Expanding on Derrida and Merleau Ponty, I argue that different information processing technologies will produce different relationships to excess. By "relationships" I mean the degree to which someone recognises an excess in meaning, is concerned about it, and is able to move toward it and grasp it in some way. For example, writing is familiar to many. We understand how words are produced in different formats, and how written signs relate to each other on the page. Literate people have habituated the cultural technique of writing and reading, understand how it functions and why it makes sense. For these reasons prose and poetry has the capacity to evoke in many a sense of the spiritual or sublime. What are these but excesses in meaning which the text cannot literally capture, yet can gesture towards? Similarly, for those who are skilled in understanding numbers and mathematics, equations can gesture to something transcendental and universal. Importantly, numbers and letters are different, require different techniques, and depend on different calculative and communicative technologies. Computers automatically process numbers in ways which are completely hidden to most people. Unless you are a highly skilled programmer, your computer is currently producing data which is of no consequence to you. You are in no way interested in any excess of meaning which this data may gesture toward, nor are you capable of moving toward that excess and trying to understand it.

How, then, do the characteristics of relationship-tracking technologies such as *PplKpr*, which involve computation and physiological *sensors*, produce a particular relationship to excess and intimacy? Nafus (2014) describes the way in which data and metrics must become stable, trusted indicators of a relatively unambiguous phenomenon in order to "clot" together with regular social practices. On sensors, Nafus writes:

"It is here where the labor that it takes to clot numbers together becomes visible, as people struggle to work out what exactly heart rate has to do with fitness, or anything else. Because the conditions of possibility for sensor data to connect or disconnect anything meaningfully are still quite thin, sensors give us the opportunity to see what happens when it is difficult for the actors to imagine what kinds of clots can be built, and what kinds of calculative infrastructures could emerge." (2014: 110)

Here it is the obstinate *partiality* of sensor measurements that makes them ineffective as indicators of social meaning. Sensors operate according to the same basic mechanics: a bodily event produces a signal which is picked up the sensor then transduced into a stronger carrier signal. Commercial mobile and wearable devices digitally sample the carrier signal and use algorithms to combine data from different sensors and filter out sensor noise. Sensors are designed to focus on specific, singular events, and to filter out all other information (James 2007). In the language of semiotics, they produce what Pierce (1998) calls indexical signs, which come about through physical contact with their material referent. Yet the way in which sensors focus on singular events make them a particular kind of indexical media. This becomes clear when comparing a heart rate monitor to a camera, which is also indexical in its direct contact with light. The former filters out noise to focus on a singular signal and to track a singular type of event, the beating of a heart. The latter also captures a singular signal – the light flowing into the lens – but captures a variety of events: a woman running, a tea cup shattering, the sun rising. The former has a semiotic simplicity, while the latter has a semiotic complexity. Both are very partial indicators of a greater totality. Yet a photograph's complexity and familiarity makes it much easier to connect with. Its partiality is by no means as foreign and ambiguous as an isolated heartbeat.

The material constraints of commercial mobile media exacerbate this partiality. Mood and relationship-tracking applications can trace their pedigree to a broad field known as social psychophysiology, in which a variety of invasive and non-invasive sensing methods have been developed. While technologies like the iPhone combine a variety of sophisticated sensors, the physiological measurements these sensors are capable of are strikingly limited when compared to what is available in clinical settings. For instance, it is unlikely that electrochemical measurements that require biological reactants will be integrated into a commercial mobile device any time soon. It remains an issue of hot debate in social psychophysiology what the relationship between affect, emotion, embodiment and social interactions is, and how best to measure it (Blascovich/Medes 2010). There are multiple competing models of human moods and how they relate to each other, something the self-tracking community, to their credit, has publically acknowledged (Wolf 2009; Carmichael 2012). Whatever model is chosen must "fit in" with the limited affordances of a device. Certain measurements are provided, while others are left out. Hence, arguing for the veracity of a particular measurement becomes an essentially rhetorical process. Jethani writes:

"Simply being able to quantify and see the functioning of the body in ways previously not achievable outside clinical settings provides a false sense of security. For instance, observing a steady resting heart rate says little about vascular health, and the maintenance of adequate daily hydration gives little insight into the underlying health of the kidneys. In revealing certain insights, self-tracking devices also conceal. By imposing goals or assigning value to performance metrics, they mask certain things hidden in plain sight by focusing attention onto rhetorically produced indicators of wellbeing." (2015: 40)

Jethani's point depends on the kind of self-tracking one is engaged in. Given the popularity of the fitness tracking market, it is likely that many indicators of fitness are likely taken as fairly accurate and dependable. Intimacy and fitness are different. As argued above, intimate presence is already a beguiling and mysterious issue. It resists reduction to a partial measurement. The rhetorical effect of sensors is undermined and the authority of algorithms is no longer tacitly accepted and trusted. Hogan, on "invisible algorithms", argues:

"We may intuitively accept that a certain ordering 'makes sense' but without an ability to assess this ordering we are at the mercy of those building the algorithms. Worse, to the extent that we consider this ideology as necessary, we restrict our ability to imagine alternative means for the management of information and concede that the judgment of the algorithm designers is inherently better than our own." (2014: 104)

With sensor-based relationship-tracking technologies this is not always the case. They demand that they be scrutinised. This produces what Nafus and Sherman (2014) call "soft resistance": the way in which self-trackers apply individualistic critical sense-making practices to their data. Nafus and Sherman argue that such a disposition emerges from the self-reflexive, skilled nature of the dedicated Quantified Self community, as well the technicality of working with particular, personalised self-tracking systems. Soft-resistance is at play where physiological relationship-tracking is concerned. This form of relationship-tracking makes people aware of the excess of intimacy which physiological systems fail to capture. This excess becomes an issue. Yet the capacity to move toward it and grasp it is fundamentally constrained if one remains tied to physiological technologies.

Experimentation and Incompleteness

I argue that relationship trackers are driven to interrogate this excess of intimacy, and this spurs on constant experimentation with new technologies and methodologies. This focused relationship to an excess, born out of the partiality of sensors, is the engine which drives the evolution of the technicity of intimacy and its component cultural techniques. For Siegert (2013), cultural techniques are structural systems that always stand against and gesture toward that which is not structured or symbolised. To conceptualise the latter, Siegert and his colleagues often purloin Lacan's concept of the "real". "For instance," writes Siegert, "upon closer scrutiny it becomes apparent that musical notation systems operate against a background of what elides representation and symbolization – the sounds and noises of the real" (2013: 60). This self-reflexive effort to negotiate material and perceptual reality drives the evolution of cultural techniques. It follows that a vast panoply of new cultural techniques will evolve as we invent new technologies for processing and programming the real. These ideas can be easily modified to explain relationship-tracking's connection to intimacy and intimate presence, which has a complex phenomenal nature that is broken apart by tracking systems. Yet intimate presence lingers in its excess and demands to be addressed through some new technical disposition. Relationship-tracking is thus ever experimental and emergent. It epitomises an age in which the technicity of intimacy is restless and fluid.

This provokes a critical question: if the purpose of relationship-tracking is to produce effective knowledge about intimate relationships, and if intimacy always carries an excess that cannot be interrogated, what *value* is there in pursuing these technologies? Various scholars note the way in which the dedicated self-tracking community gets pleasure from the technical experimentation of self-tracking itself (Boesel 2013; Lupton 2014; Nafus/Sherman 2014). Discourses of playful experimentation abound on websites such as quantifiedself.com. Consider the advice given in an online book on mood tracking:

"There is a significant difference between the knowledge that we discover for ourselves, and knowledge that we receive from others. If you have ever cooked a dish from a recipe, you'll know that simply reading the recipe doesn't mean that you know the dish it describes. You learn the dish by trying to make it, by tasting as you go along and experimenting. Along the way, the things that the author of the recipe could never know – your local ingredients, your stove, your cooking style, and your tastes, get incorporated into what you do, and the dish becomes your own." (Carmichael 2012)

This exemplifies the value that dedicated self-trackers find in experimenting with different technologies, systems and methods. It suggests that meaning lies in the journey, not the destination. Self-tracking is a kind of project, like a hobby, through which one gains inherent satisfaction. Self-trackers can watch their projects grow and evolve, see themselves in their projects, and talk about them with other community members, creating a sense of belonging and mutual admiration (Boesel 2013).

Relationship-tracking can even become a kind of *shared* project (an essential characteristic of intimacy if one follows the Gestalt psychological approach). Joe and Lisa Betts-LaCroix are two Quantified Self community members who enthusiastically share their relationship-tracking system at Quantified Self meetups. Their shared system correlates factors such as weight, sleep and sex to gain insights about the nature of their intimate bond. Interestingly, in one video they acknowledge that the meaning of these correlations remains mysterious, and that the key variable which will disclose the deeper meaning of intimacy remains undiscovered (Kelly 2009). Moreover, the process of tracking a relationship comes to transform their social rhythms and interactions. Joe makes the following point: "One of the main things I've learned about self-tracking overall is that self-tracking so significantly affects the things that I'm tracking that it's hard to know what's actually being measured. But, it affects them in a really positive way, so I like it and I keep doing it" (ibid). Again, a sense of value does not come from some enlightening *telos*, but from the collaborative techniques fostered on a shared journey.

The dedicated self-trackers in the Quantified Self community consist of professionals and entrepreneurs who are in the practice of developing self-tracking systems. This community has what Nafus and Sherman (2013) calls a "big tent policy" which encourages participation from heterogeneous experts, hobbyists and commercial health and technology companies. In such a milieu, entrepreneurialism as an endless process of innovation is of the upmost value. The excess of intimacy and the restless technicity it fuels is perfectly at home in this cultural context. Here the true value of intimacy is its mystery. As long as a mystery persists an experiment is worthwhile and a product is worth making.

Conclusion

In revealing intimacy as *excess* that is always beyond reach, physiological tracking systems do not alleviate the intensive labours of intimacy, quite the opposite. Anyone interested in an excess of meaning will be compulsively disposed to interrogating it. As mentioned in the previous section, this may be fine for many people who enjoy the process of relationship-tracking in and for itself. This suggests an interesting transformation in the nature of intimacy: intimacy exists simultaneously as a problematic issue and as an eternal mystery, two sides of a dialectic which exist in harmonious contradiction through a third point, namely, the love of technical practice.

However, as these applications become increasingly commercialised and distributed to broader markets, it would be absurd to say that every person interested in tracking their relationships and managing their social lives would be content with an endless series of experiments. Not every smartphone user has the same love of technical practice as a self-affirmed member of the Quantified Self community. As Lupton (2014) argues, self-tracking is often motivated by a search for "completeness". This implies a complete or perfect system for understanding and managing intimate life. Yet, this ideal must sit in uneasy companionship with the obstinate incompleteness of the bodily measurement.

What different responses will people have to these contradictions? Perhaps many will abandon relationship-tracking as a viable way to deal with intensive intimacy, just as some have abandoned fitness tracking in response to feelings of shame. Perhaps some will be stuck in a compulsive attitude toward the mystery of intimacy, without the escape valve of technical pleasure. Such a figure is familiar from criticisms of psychotherapy. Illouz (2007) argues that psychotherapy posits the goal of intimate completeness, yet never clarifies what this state of affairs actually looks and feels like, thus endlessly extending the state of sickness and the process of becoming healthy. Will relationship trackers become like the fetishistic self-helper, always searching for a new diet and a new guru? What critical ethical issues does this suggest for personal, interpersonal and cultural life? Returning to Sloterdijk, the philosopher argues that intimacy always begins with the collapse of the immune system, with the "affective infections" of love and desire. Will the immune systems we craft today allow for this kind of serendipity, or will a computationally regulated regime of propinquity come to dominate our intimate lives?

References

Allan, Graham (2008): "Flexibility, Friendship, and Family." In: Personal Relationships 15, pp. 1-16.
Berlant, Lauren (2012): Desire/Love, Brooklyn: Punctum.
Blascovich, Jim/Medes, Wendy Barry (2010): "Social Psychophysiology and Embodiment." In: Susan T. Fiske/Daniel T. Gilbert/Gardner Lindzey (eds.), Handbook of Social Psychology, Hoboken, NJ: John Wiley & Sons.

Boesel, Whitney Erin (2013): "What is the Quantified Self Now?" In: Qualitative Research 5/4, pp. 475-497.
boyd, danah (2011): "Social Network Sites as Networked Publics: Affordances, Dynamics, and Implications." In: Zizi Papacharissi (ed.), A Networked Self: Identity, Community, and Culture on Social Network Sites, New York: Routledge, pp. 39-58.
Carmichael, Alexandra (2012): "Get Your Mood On: Part 1." Blog posted on the Quantitative Self website, December 9, 2012 (http://quantifiedself.com/2012/12/get-your-mood-on-part-1/).
Derrida, Jaques (1997): On Grammatology (C. C. Spivak, trans.), Baltimore: Johns Hopkins University Press.
Ekman, Inger/Chanel, Guillaume/Järvelä, Simo/Kivikangas, J. Matias/Salminen, Mikko/Ravaja, Niklas (2012): "Social Interaction in Games: Measuring Physiological Linkage and Social Presence." In: Simulation and Gaming 43/3, pp. 321-338.
Farman, Jason (2009): "Locative Life: Geochaching, Mobile Gaming, and Embodiment." Paper presented at the Digital Arts and Culture Conference, UC Irvine.
Gergen, Kenneth J. (2002): "The Challenge of Absent Presence." In: James E. Katz/Mark Aakhus (eds.), Perpetual Contact: Mobile Communication, Private Talk, Public Performance, Cambridge: Cambridge University Press, pp. 227-241.
Giddens, Anthony (1991): Modernity and Self-Identity: Self and Society in the Late Modern Age, Cambridge: Polity Press.
Giddens, Anthony (1992): The Transformation of Intimacy: Sexuality, Love and Eroticism in Modern Societies, Cambridge: Polity Press.
Gregg, Melissa (2011): Work's Intimacy, Cambridge, UK: Polity Press.
Hjorth, Larissa/Hinton, Sam (2013): Understanding Social Media, London: Sage.
Hjorth, Larissa/Lim, Sun Sun (2012): "Mobile Intimacy in an Age of Affective Media." In: Feminist Media Studies 12/4, pp. 477-484.
Hjorth, Larissa/Wilken, Rowan/Gu, Kay (2012): "Ambient Intimacy: A Case Study of the iPhone, Presence, and Location-Based Social Media in Shanghai, China." In: Larissa Hjorth/Jean Burgess/Ingrid Richardson (eds.), Studying Mobile Media: Cultural Technologies, Mobile Communication, and the iPhone, New York: Routledge.
Hogan, Bernie (2014): "From Invisible Algorithms to Interactive Affordances: Data After the Ideology of Machine Learning." In: Elisa Bertino/Sorin Adam Matei (eds.), Roles, Trust and Reputation in Social Media Knowledge Markets: Theory and Methods, New York: Springer, pp. 103-120.
Illouz, Eva (2007): Cold Intimacies: The Making of Emotional Capitalism, Cambridge: Polity Press.
Ito, Mizuko (2003): "Mobiles and the Appropriation of Place." In: Reciever Magazine 8.
Ito, Mizuko (2005): "Intimate Visual Co-Presence." Paper presented at the Seventh International Conference on Ubiquitous Computing.

James, Daniel Arthur (2007): "Sensors and Sensor Sytems for Psychophysiological Monitoring: A Review of Current Trends." In: Journal of Psychophysiology 21/1, pp. 51-71.

Jamieson, Lynn (1998): Intimacy: Personal Relationships in Modern Societies, Oxford: Blackwell.

Jenett, Charlene/Cox, Anna L./Cairns, Paul/Dhoparee, Samira/Epps, Andrew/Tijs, Tim/Walton, Alison (2008): "Measuring and Defining the Experience of Immersion in Games." In: International Journal of Human-Computer Studies 66/9, pp. 641-661.

Jethani, Suneel (2015): "Mediating the Body: Technology, Politics and Epistemologies of Self." In: Communication, Politics and Culture 47/3, pp. 34-43.

Kelly, Kevin (2009): "Joe Betts –LaCroix and Lisa Betts-LaCroix on Self-Tracking in a Relationship." Filmed presentation of New York Quantified Self Show and Tell #5, March 31, 2009 (https://vimeo.com/3981825).

Kiesler, Sara/Siegel, Jane/McGuire, Timothy (1984): "Social Psychological Aspects of Computer-Mediated Communication." In: American Psychologist 39/10, pp. 1123-1134.

Kittler, Friedrich (1999): Gramophone, Film, Typewriter. Stanford: Stanford University Press.

Knobel, Michele/Lankshear, Colin (2008): Digital Literacy and Participation in Online Social Networking Spaces. In: ibid (eds.), Digital Literacies: Concepts, Policies and Practices, New York: Peter Lang, pp. 249-278.

Krane, Gary (2011): "Coupleness". Filmed presentation at New York Quantified Self Show and Tell #12, August 14, 2011 (http://quantifiedself.com/2011/08/2179).

Lambert, Alex (2013): Intimacy and Friendship on Facebook, Basingstoke, UK: Palgrave Macmillan.

Laurenceau, Jean-Philippe/Pietromonaco, Paula R./Barret, Lisa Feldman (1998): "Intimacy as an Interpersonal Process: The Importance of Self-Disclosure, Partner Disclosure, and Perceived Partner Responsiveness in Interpersonal Exchanges." In: Journal of Personality and Social Psychology 74/5, pp. 1238-1251.

Lupton, Deborah (2014): "Self-Tracking Modes: Reflexive Self-Monitoring and Data Practices." Paper presented at the Imminient Citizenships: Personhood and Identity Politics in the Informatic Age.

Madianou, Mira/Miller, Daniel (2011): Migration and New Media: Transnational Families and Polymedia, New York: Routledge.

Mantovani, Giuseppe/Riva, Giuseppe (1999): "'Real' Presence: How Different Ontologies Generate Different Criteria for Presence, Telepresence, and Virtual Presence." In: Presence 8/5, pp. 540-550.

Melnick, Joseph/Nevis, Sonia March (1994): Intimacy and Power in Long-Term Relationships: A Gestalt Therapy-Systems Perspective. In: Gordon Wheeler/Stephanie Backman (eds.), On Intimate Ground: A Gestalt Approach to Working with Couples, San Francisco: Jossey-Bass, pp. 291-308.

Merleau-Ponty, Maurice (2004): Phenomenology of Perception (C. Smith, trans.), New York: Routledge.

Milne, Esther (2010): Letters, Postcards, Email: Technologies of Presence, New York: Routledge.

Morozov, Evgeny (2013): To Save Everything, Click Here: the Folly of Technological Solutionism, Philadelphia: Public Affairs.

Nafus, Dawn (2014): "Stuck Data, Dead Data, and Disloyal Data: The Stops and Starts in Making Numbers into Social Practice." In: Distinktion: Scandinavian Journal of Social Theory 15/2, pp. 208-222.

Nafus, Dawn/Sherman, Jamie (2013): "The Quantified Self Movement is Not a Kleenex." Blog posted on the CASTAC Blog March 26, 2013 (http://blog.castac.org/2013/03/the-quantified-self-movement-is-not-a-kleenex/).

Nafus, Dawn/Sherman, Jamie (2014): "This One Does Not Go Up to 11: The Quantified Self Movement as an Alternative Big Data Practice." In: International Journal of Communication 8, pp. 1784-1794.

Pahl, Ray (2005): "Are all Communities, Communities in the Mind?" In: Sociological Review Monograph 53/4, pp. 621-640.

Pariser, Eli (2011): The Filter Bubble: What the Internet is Hiding From You, New York: Penguin Press.

Patil, Akshay (2014): "Better Relationships Through Technology." Filmed presentation at the New York QS Meetup Group, November 6, 2014 (http://quantifiedself.com/2014/11/akshay-patil-better-relationships-technology/).

Pierce, Charles Sanders (1998): The Essential Peirce (Vol. 2), Bloomington, In: Indiana University Press.

Pinker, Susan (2014): The Village Effect, New York: Spiegel & Grau.

Ricardo, Fabio (2015): "How Relationship Data Guides Me Through a Chaotic Life." Filmed presentation at Amsterdam Quantified Self Meetup, January 19, 2015 (http://quantifiedself.com/2015/01/fabio-ricardo-dos-santos-using-relationship-data-navigate-chaotic-life/).

Richardson, Ingrid/Wilken, Rowan (2013): "Parerga of the Third Screen: Mobile Media, Place, and Presence." In: Gerard Goggin/Rowan Wilken (eds.), Mobile Technology and Place, Hoboken: Taylor and Francis.

Roseneil, Sasha/Budgeon, Shelley (2004): "Cultures of Intimacy and Care Beyond 'The Family': Personal Life and Social Change in the Early 21st Century." In: Current Sociology 52/2, pp. 135-159.

Siegert, Bernhard (2013): "Cultural Techniques: Or the End of the Intellectual Postwar Era in German Media Theory." In: Theory, Culture and Society 30/6, pp. 48-65.

Sloterdijk, Peter (2011): Bubbles: Microspherology (W. Hoban, trans.), Los Angeles: Semiotext.

Turkle, Sherry (2011): Alone Together: Why We Expect More from Technology and Less from Each Other, New York: Basic Books.

Winthrop-Young, Geoffrey (2013): "Cultural Techniques: Preliminary Remarks." In: Theory, Culture and Society 30/6, pp. 3-19.

Wolf, Gary (2009): "Measuring Mood: Current Research and New Ideas." Blog posted on the Quantitative Self website, February 11, 2009 (http://quantifiedself.com/2009/02/measuring-mood-current-research/).

Unhappy? There's an App for That
Tracking Well-Being through the Quantified Self

Jill Belli

Abstract

This article analyses happiness apps, a subset of quantified self (QS) applications focused on tracking and improving user subjective well-being or happiness. I examine these apps, the data they track, and the interventions they propose to explore the social, political, and ethical implications of QS practices associated with happiness apps. Despite their focus on science, data, and quantification, happiness apps are ideologically inflected, mediated through the influential research, rhetoric, and pedagogy of positive psychology. Positive psychology as the "science of happiness" applies research in order to maximise well-being globally, and it increasingly leverages technology for this goal. Through a close reading of the claims and functions of these happiness apps, I highlight their assumptions about the happy individual and good society. Happiness apps do not assess emotions objectively via user data; instead, they filter user emotions through positive psychology's theories of happiness that inform these apps' conceptions and standards of well-being. This article argues that happiness apps may function conservatively, teaching users to pursue happiness and the good life without recognizing that understandings of happy and good are not universal but inextricably bound to particular ideological assumptions, cultural contexts, and interpretations of what is positive, valuable, and desirable. The practice of tracking and operationalising user data via a happiness app is a complex, mediated practice. The data are mediated by the particular tool as well as users' individual understandings of and aspirations for happiness, which in turn are mediated by the rhetoric, ideology, and pedagogy of positive psychology. This triple mediation demonstrates that the QS is not neutral but instead embedded within social, cultural, economic, political, and ethical commitments.

Introduction

The quantified self (QS) has seen dramatic adoption in recent years due to the current ease with which individual data can be collected, computed, and operationalised. A variety of digital tools for learning about one's bodily processes, activities, behaviours, moods, and thoughts exist, including *happiness apps* designed to track and improve subjective well-being or happiness. This subset of the QS targets states and emotions such as mood, mindfulness, resilience, optimism, positivity, and, of course, happiness. As with other QS tools, happiness apps employ diverse technologies and methodologies for capturing data and improving well-being. Benefits of the QS include greater self-awareness and a resulting sense of control. People do not just seek self-knowledge, however; they also use data to implement changes in their lives. Users can manipulate the data from many happiness apps to stage interventions and experiments with the objective of achieving greater well-being. Viewed in this light, happiness apps and the QS seem useful and empowering.

Although happiness apps and the QS are often treated as positive developments, there are many social, political, and ethical questions that should be raised: How are the data mediated through various technologies, user subjectivities, and larger social, cultural, economic, and political contexts? Is it possible to gather objective data about emotions such as happiness? Even if this were possible, is this data useful and desirable? In whose interest is this tracking? What ideologies and stakeholder interests get embedded into the design of the technology and practices that facilitate self-knowledge?

This article analyses happiness apps, the data they track, and the interventions they propose to explore the social, political, and ethical implications of QS practices. Despite their focus on science, data, and quantification, happiness apps are ideologically inflected, mediated through the influential research, rhetoric, and pedagogy of positive psychology. Positive psychology uses applied research with the objective of maximising well-being and it leverages technology for this goal. Through a close reading of the claims and functions of these happiness apps, I highlight their assumptions about the happy individual and good society. Happiness apps do not assess emotions objectively via user data; instead, they filter user emotions through psychological theories of happiness that inform these apps' conceptions and standards of well-being. This article argues that happiness apps may function conservatively, teaching users to pursue happiness and the good life without recognizing that understandings of *happy* and *good* are not universal but inextricably bound to particular ideological assumptions, cultural contexts, and interpretations of what is positive, valuable, and desirable. By considering happiness apps in the context of positive psychology, this article offers an approach for exploring the ethical implications of QS practices and data as mediated through and in the service of particular agendas.

The Quantified Self: Contexts and Critiques

The QS posits that individuals can gain self-knowledge and self-awareness through tracking personal data. Advances in technology support improved collection and utility of both active and passive data, and mobile phones and portable devices offer increased convenience and efficiency, allowing more seamless integration of tracking into users' everyday work, personal, and leisure activities. The digitisation of self-tracking practices via the QS reflects technological utopianism, a belief in the value of greater self-knowledge and progress through technology. "The terms 'quantified self' and 'self-tracker' are labels, contemporary formalizations belonging to the general progression in human history of using measurement, science, and technology to bring order, understanding, manipulation, and control to the natural world, including the human body" (Swan 2013: 86). To this end, QS practices rely heavily on scientific method and experimentation, and claim objectivity through quantification. It is unsurprising, then, that the motto of the QS movement is "self knowledge through numbers."[1]

QS proponents believe that users become empowered through their data. Ideally, as QS movement co-founder Gary Wolf states, one will not only collect data but also operationalise these data into real life improvements: "If you want to replace the vagaries of intuition with something more reliable, you first need to gather data. Once you know the facts, you can live by them" (2010). The QS community has normalised self-tracking, demonstrating how the awareness of moods, behaviours, and actions aids targeted interventions users might desire. Ultimately, the goal is for users to become better versions of themselves (cf. Swan 2013: 93). QS advocates promote this transformative potential, yet this utopian outlook often conceals ethical concerns in connection with surveilling users, exploiting data for commercial gain through targeted marketing, encouraging normative behaviour, fostering individualism, ignoring or obscuring qualitative information, and privileging quantification, measurement, and empirical truth of the body and personal experience.

In affirming that a person can be known and that this knowledge can be accessed through her data, the QS relies on an essentialist view of the body. It belies a misguided trust in quantifying and measuring biological factors, behaviours, emotions, and thoughts as well as credence in tracked data as unmediated, uncontaminated representations of the user. In other words, the success of the QS hinges on the commonly held assumptions that tracking can fill in gaps in self-knowledge and that the data do not lie. However, while the QS can capture a great deal of user data and provide resulting insights, there remain aspects that the data cannot register and represent through algorithms. QS practitioners and theorists should always ask about these losses, just as they work to understand what can be gained from the QS.

With so much emphasis on eponymous quantified nature of the QS, it can be easy to overlook the important qualitative nature of this tracking. Narratives and stories shape the data captured from QS practices, and these user-generated meanings are crucial components of self-knowledge. As Jenny Davis (2013) states in her blog post, "The Qualified Self":

"Self quantification is a process bookended by self qualification. Yes, the numbers are important. Self-quantification is, by definition, self-knowledge through numbers. Those numbers, however, take shape qualitatively. They become the code with which self-quan-

---

[1] Cf. http://quantifiedself.com/.

tifiers prosume selves and identities into being. They are the bits with which self-quantifiers make sense of their atoms." (ibid)

Mood and emotion tracking promise to move the QS further towards the qualified self (cf. Swan 2013: 93-95), especially since they often rely on active, manual importing of subjective data (e.g., in response to a prompt like "how do you feel right now?"). This is in contrast to the passive, automatic tracking of many health and fitness devices, which routinely collect objectively verifiable bodily and environmental data via sensors and wearables. Such subjective datasets create problems for data accuracy and usability, and "emotion mapping remains a challenging problem" (Swan 2012: 224) that QS advocates hope to solve with the help of biometrics and "greater objective data collection" (Swan 2013: 92). Here, QS enthusiasts are optimistic about the revolutionary potential of the Internet of Things (IOS), of which the QS is a part: "Whole fields of study previously limited to self-reported information such as psychology could be radically supplemented and transformed with objective metrics obtained from the IOT." (Swan 2012: 248) Automating data collection may decrease the technical problems related to subjectivity (Swan 2013: 93) that introduce unreliability to data science approaches (Fawcett 2015: 254), but it would further obscure mediation of the data and simultaneously decrease reflection and mindfulness, two of the most valuable benefits of QS tracking (Nafus/Sherman 2014: 1785).

User identity, experiences, environment, values, and desires inflect QS data and their interpretation, contributing further complexity. Deborah Lupton's critical sociological perspective surfaces the interplay between tracking tools, collected data, and socio-cultural context: "Digital data are continually being generated when people interact with online technologies. Data assemblages, therefore, are lively digital objects: mutable, dynamic, responsive to new inputs and interpretations." (Lupton 2014b: 8) Once captured, user data folds into a larger matrix; no longer completely in the user's control, the data may be made to serve someone or something else's purposes.

"Self-tracking is not only a technology of the self, but it is also a data practice. [...] These datasets are having an increasingly important role in shaping policy, commercial dealings, education, social welfare and healthcare, the management of groups and populations and in individuals' personal and everyday life." (ibid: 3)

There are complex, social, political, and ethical issues at stake in tracking user data and staging interventions based on it for "self-improvement and achieving one's 'best self'" (Lupton 2014b: 8). The QS may aid in the quest to optimise the self, but what are the standards to which this optimising adheres? Tracking relies on numbers and data as well as values and judgments, assessments of not only of what is, but also of what ought to be. While the norms may be transparent and clearly stipulated in certain cases (e.g., take 10,000 steps per day to remain fit), it is more challenging to parse the norms for subjective data such as emotions and moods.

Positive Psychology: A Mediating Ideology

While critiques of the QS are becoming mainstream, the influences of mediating ideologies and discourses that inform QS tools and practices are less often thematised. In what follows, I explore the mediating ideology of happiness apps, a particular class of QS tools that stem from the convergence of happiness research and innovations in technology. Happiness apps aim to track and improve emotional well-being and are driven by positive psychology, a popular movement that has branded itself "the science of happiness" and which is increasingly leveraging digital technologies to promote its particular version of well-being.

Since the turn of the 21st century, positive psychology has played a defining role in research and debates about the nature of well-being and the best ways to maximise it for individual and societal good. Founded by Martin Seligman in 1998 with a mission to study and cultivate the positive aspects of life (rather than continue psychology's long-standing focus on remediation), positive psychology is a growing field that researches subjective well-being and flourishing (cf. Seligman/Csíkszentmihályi 2000). Positive psychologists have made great strides in applying their findings to a variety of settings, such as economic policy, urban design, workplaces, and schools. One of the most influential applications is positive education, which teaches subjective well-being in schools and other educational settings. Underlying both positive psychology and positive education is the belief that well-being is not fixed but something that can be cultivated and taught. "If positive psychology aims to build well-being on the planet, well-being must be buildable. That sounds trivial, but it is not." (Seligman 2011: 31) The pedagogy of positive education focuses on nurturing individual strengths, and operationalising them for greater flourishing according to the positive psychology construct of well-being, condensed in the acronym PERMA: Positive Emotion, Engagement, (positive) Relationships, Meaning, Accomplishment (Seligman 2011: 16-20).

Positive psychologists and those inspired by their work view technology as a useful conduit for spreading and implementing happiness interventions. Seligman's influential book *Flourish: A Visionary New Understanding of Happiness and Well-Being* (2011) promotes "positive computing," using technology in the service of individual and societal well-being, a technological vision that has influenced the development of happiness apps. Seligman explicitly identifies the aim of positive computing as "go[ing] beyond the slow progress in positive education to disseminate flourishing massively" (Seligman 2011: 94). Enthusiastic about the possibility of improving well-being on a global scale through technology, positive psychologists offer optimistic claims about the transformative potential of positive computing. Technology will be a key player in the overall goal of helping the world to flourish:

"A necessary condition for large-scale flourishing, particularly among young people, is that positive psychology develop a delivery model for its well-being enhancing interventions that scales up globally. Information technology is uniquely positioned for assisting individuals with their flourishing in a way that is effective, scalable, and ethically responsible." (Tomas Sanders, qtd. in Seligman 2011: 94)

Although investment in increased flourishing (Seligman 2011: 240) may be considered a welcome shift, this commitment must be evaluated against positive psychology's core values. Positive psychology prides itself on its grounding in scientific research and empiricism, offering these commitments up as primary support for its interventions' success (cf. Belli 2012: 78-82; Parks et al. 2012: 1222; Howells et al. 2014: 3-4). This focus on scientific objectivity obscures the field's ideological commitments, which promote a particular version of well-being skewed towards individualism and personal responsibility. As I will illustrate below, happiness apps often rehearse and reproduce this rhetoric, offering users ostensibly proven methods towards increasing well-being. Positive psychology's appeals to scientific objectivity dovetail with the QS emphasis on empiricism and quantifiability. Together, these discursive claims prompt users to learn about and stage empirical interventions into their own happiness, but they also obscure the visions of well-being built into technologies like happiness apps. A critical analysis is necessary to understand the reach of happiness apps and QS use more generally; data tracking involves "social and cultural ideas about what kinds of information are valuable or trustworthy. Remember: *claims about 'truth' are always claims to power*" (Boesel 2012, emphasis in original).

Under the mantle of scientific rigor and validity, positive psychology pursues the fraught task of assessing happiness and other positive emotions. It labels whatever it identifies as contributing to well-being positive and desirable, without articulating potential nuances or engaging in the difficult discussion needed for consensus (cf. Belli 2012: 96-98). Through science, positive psychology also attempts to distance itself from the liabilities and critiques of the self-help industry, though it actually reproduces many of them (ibid: 78-85). In particular, it posits the individual as the primary locus of improvement, instrumentalises social relationships for personal benefit, and teaching interventions that acclimate people to life the way it is (ibid: 87-91).

The self-reported nature of most subjective well-being research creates further complications. Research on happiness relies on methodologies that

"presume[s] the transparency of self-feeling (that we can say and know how we feel), as well as the unmotivated and uncomplicated nature of self-reporting. If happiness is already understood to be what you want to have, then to be asked how happy you are is not to be asked a neutral question. It is not just that people are being asked to evaluate their life situations but that they are being asked to evaluate their life situations through categories that are value laden." (Ahmed 2010: 5)

This critique can be extended to assessing emotion in QS methodologies, especially in happiness apps, which rely primarily on manually inputted subjective data. Furthermore, self-reporting evaluates happiness in the context of current circumstances; in other words, it assesses satisfaction with the status quo (Ehrenreich 2009: 170). If "[p]olicy itself follows from what is measured"

(Seligman 2011: 227), then these measurements fuel positive psychology's activist aspirations in a self-fulfilling prophecy, suggesting that a happy future may be built in the image of the present. As the data from happiness apps often contributes to positive psychology research, these QS tools have even farther reaching implications.

As this brief discussion exemplifies, positive psychology is inextricably bound to particular notions of the happy individual and the good life, to what constitutes the positive, and to instrumentalised, decontextualised, and individualised versions of flourishing. Positive psychology's assumptions and agendas must be critically considered, since the ideological commitments of positive psychology may be transferred over to its applications (in this article, literally "apps").[2] Any discussion of happiness apps should account for positive psychology's semantic and conceptual slipperiness, normative and conservative views of well-being, focus on the individual at the expense of structural problems, and instrumentalising tendencies.

Happiness Apps: Tracking Well-Being

Dreams of methods and means for measuring and quantifying individual and societal happiness are nothing new. From Jeremy Bentham's felicific calculus to proposed hedonometers to mood rings that change colours with a person's affect, visions of tools to track and visualise emotions have captured collective imaginations throughout history (cf. Davies 2015: 13-39). Happiness apps are the next step in a long line of tracking technologies aiming to assess subjective well-being. These happiness apps promise to track "high-valence data streams" (Swan 2012: 239) and are part of what some view as "self-tracking 2.0, where both quantitative and qualitative data may be collected with the object of improving quality of life in areas such as happiness, well-being, goal achievement, and stress reduction" (Swan 2013: 94). Below, I explore how happiness apps function rhetorically, ideologically, and pedagogically. Happiness apps and their users abound (cf. Eaton 2014), and this brief discussion is not intended to be comprehensive, detailed about any particular app, or an assessment on these apps' effectiveness in increasing well-being. Instead, it serves to highlight some social, political, and ethical issues within the QS as exemplified through happiness apps.[3]

A significant number of happiness apps are informed by the influential field of positive psychology in their claims to expertise, the interventions they

---

2   Cf. Belli (2012: 64-106) for a detailed discussion of the rhetoric, pedagogy, ideology, and desirability of positive psychology.
3   While my primary focus here is on "apps" that can be downloaded and used via mobile phones or tablets, this discussion extends to other web-based happiness applications, which may employ mobile features such as text messaging to assess individual happiness throughout one's daily routine (e.g., *Happy Factor*, cf. http://howhappy.dreamhosters.com/).

propose, and the visions of happiness and the good life they endorse. These apps do not merely track user data about well-being; they also orient users to a particular understanding of what type of happiness is desirable. The rhetoric of happiness apps derives from the twin influences of positive psychology and the QS, which both maintain that an individual can be improved through attention to one's emotions and the application of various expert, allegedly scientific interventions.[4] The developers of happiness apps reproduce positive psychology's claims of efficacy grounded in science and empiricism in order to set their apps apart from those representing the "non-researched self-help industry" (Howells et al. 2014: 4). This appeal to science manifests in various ways, such as the inclusion of resources outlining the scientific evidence behind happiness interventions and experts from the field to guide the users' quest for greater well-being. Some apps, like *Live Happy* and *SuperBetter*[5], even have popular publications associated with them (Lyubomirsky 2007; McGonigal 2015).

A particularly evocative example is the introductory video of the iPhone app *Live Happy* launched in 2009 as companion to Sonja Lyubomirksy's book *The How of Happiness* (2007). Lyubomirksy narrates this video, providing her credentials as an academic psychologist and author as ethos and logos to support the use of the app. She states: "As a scientific community we've learned how to measure a person's happiness, and armed with this ability to assess how different activities affect one's measured levels of happiness. As it turns out, there are sets of activities that one can engage in, that have been scientifically supported, to help people become happier."[6] The rhetoric and pedagogy of the popular tracking tool *Happify* also relies heavily on science, reassuring users that "the science of happiness is a serious and legitimate area of study, with a great deal of validated research and studies supporting it."[7] *Happify's* "experts" and "happiness tracks" creators are firmly entrenched in positive psychology, with titles such as "positive psychology coach" or as authors of related books such as Gretchen Rubin's *The Happiness Project* (2009) or Shawn Anchor's *Before Happiness* (2013). Furthermore, *Happify* claims that "Your Emotional Wellbeing Can Be Measured" and, in its "The Science Behind Happify" section, provides an article on "Happiness by the Numbers," which attempts to quantify various factors associated with happiness.

In this way, these apps are aligned with the positive psychology mantra that increased happiness is desirable and achievable through scientific inter-

---

4   Many happiness apps caution that they do not provide "medical advice" and are not a substitute for the attention of a doctor. Instead, like positive psychology, they aim primarily to increase flourishing, a functional and qualitative difference from apps focused on remediating unhappiness from a medical perspective (e. g. compare *Moodtracker*, which specifically targets medical disorders and *Track Your Happiness*, which is informed by positive psychology and seeks to increase happiness), cf. https://www.moodtracker.com/ and https://www.trackyourhappiness.org/.
5   Cf. https://www.superbetter.com/.
6   Cf. https://www.youtube.com/watch?v=BGrwPnXdtJM.
7   Cf. http://www.happify.com/.

ventions, and they work to spread the positive psychology gospel, one of the major goals of "positive computing" as outlined and theorised by Seligman and other leading positive psychologists. By leveraging mobile technology, users can "perform happiness-boosting activities as a natural part of their daily lives, wherever they are, and in different situations" *(Live Happy)*. These happiness apps offer a variety of activities, exercises, motivational strategies, feedback loops, and visualisations to develop self-awareness, one of the primary goals of the QS.

To keep users motivated on their quest to achieve greater happiness, happiness apps often gamify the process of tracking and increasing well-being (Howells et al. 2014: 18). Gamification is seen as an integral component of engaging users in tracking and behaviour change (Swan 2012: 240, 242). *Happify's* slogan is "Happiness. It's Winnable." Suggesting one can "win" at happiness hints at the instrumentalisation infusing these apps as well reliance on both "grit" and "resilience" (buzzwords in positive psychology, and factors integral to the "accomplishment" element of well-being construct PERMA). *Happify* boasts, "Our cheerful games and activities are deceptively effective," and the app offers a "Savor quest" and a "Negative knockout" to help users destress and uplift themselves. *SuperBetter*, an app for building user happiness and resilience, has gamification at its core. Its creator Jane McGonigal is an experienced game design researcher and practitioner who tries to leverage gamification strategies to increase well-being. Upon signing up, a user is prompted to choose a "challenge" and then use "Power Ups, Bad Guys, and Quests" to overcome this challenge. Gamification converges with the appeal to scientific expertise, as research is embedded into and informs the app: "As you play SuperBetter, you'll find science icons hidden throughout your missions. Clicking these icons gives you access to the science of SuperBetter – including links to the research articles that everything's based on. You can see an overview of the science behind SuperBetter at ShowMeTheScience.com."[8]

Besides motivation through gamification strategies, many happiness apps encourage user reflection, either explicitly endorsing mindfulness (e.g. *Happy Factor*, with the slogan, "Be Mindful, Be Happy")[9] or otherwise promoting attentiveness to emotions as conducive to positive interventions (e.g., *gottaFeeling*)[10]. Mindfulness of behaviors, emotions, thoughts, and habits is actually one of the greatest benefits of the QS; in fact, some users find that *"the awareness one develops through self-quantifying may be as beneficial as (if not more beneficial than) the collected data itself"* (Boesel 2012, [emphasis in original]). Some exercises and activities, such as the "Best Possible Self" activity in *Live Happy* prompt users to write, imagining future selves. This reflective composing is a qualitative, open-ended exercise that stands in contrast to some of the more transactional, functional activities that many of these apps endorse or require (cf. Kurtz/Lyubomirsky 2012; Parks et al. 2012).

---

8   Cf. https://www.superbetter.com/.
9   Cf. http://howhappy.dreamhosters.com/.
10 Cf. http://gottafeeling.com/.

Although reflection exercises and data reflection offer benefits, the data collected do not objectively represent unmediated user emotions. These "happiness boosting" activities, gamification strategies, and interventions come contextualized against a backdrop of norms about what it means to be happy within the positive psychology framework. There is an unacknowledged standard of flourishing that users are evaluated by and pushed to aspire to when they use these apps. Whether users are aware of this influence or not, the "data assemblages" (Lupton 2014b: 8) produced by these apps are generated in relation to the popular and powerful ideology and discourse of positive psychology. Therefore, users do not merely gain self-knowledge of their individual subjective well-being; rather, they amass a reflection of themselves through the lens of positive psychology's version of the normative version of a happy individual and the good society.

Furthermore, happiness apps often shape the potential responses that users can provide, limiting the data set to pre-determined, unrepresentative categories. For example, *gottaFeeling* asks the question, "How do you feel?" but only offers the following potential answers: "Happy, Caring, Confused, Sad, Angry, Inadequate, Hurt, Fearful, Lonely, Guilt/Shame."[11] *UniThrive Wellbeing*, an app to "[p]ractise positive psychology," assesses mood as follows: "Bored, Content, Excited, Fortunate, Frustrated, Gloomy, Grumpy, Happy, Hopeful, Inspired, Lonely, Loved, Okay, Overwhelmed, Sad, Worried."[12] *The Emotion Diary*, another app explicitly "based on the principles of Positive Psychology,"[13] provides a bare-bones classification of emotions, with only three images – an unhappy face, neutral face, and smiley face – as options. These constraints built into app-design funnel QS tracking (and by extension, visualisation, sharing, and interventions) through external parameters for what constitutes valid moods, for what counts as happiness data. These apps, then, perpetuate the lack of consensus of defining and assessing happiness, and may fail to capture important data about a person's emotions or circumstances. If there is no category provided for what a user is feeling, her emotions cannot be registered and tracked as data.

Limited response categories become even more problematic when happiness apps go further to help users understand their data and assess potential interventions by offering users visualisations of their data and progress. These representations vary from the color-coded lines of individual data (e. g., *MoodJam*)[14] to more sophisticated collective data visualisations, such as the "Global Happiness" graph from *Happy Factor*. These visualisations are primarily basic representations of manually imported user data, which is consistent with much of the QS: "In fact, most QS apps do little more than present attractive graphs of the user's data and depend on how to spot patterns and correlations – or assume that only trends are interesting." (Fawcett 2015: 255) These data visualisations reinforce

---

11   Cf. http://gottafeeling.com/.
12   Cf. https://itunes.apple.com/us/app/unithrive-wellbeing/id914756577.
13   Cf. https://itunes.apple.com/us/app/the-emotion-diary/id568740836.
14   Cf. http://moodjam.com/.

the possibility of tracking and representing subjective emotional states for either personal gain or public good. They also position data as something objectively existing in the real world that just is waiting to be captured and graphically rendered, rather than fluid, mutually constituted social and cultural practices.

Though QS is primarily an individual endeavour, happiness apps connect users to larger networks of well-being. Placing individual data in conversation with those of other users represents a shift from "private self-tracking" (Lupton 2014a: 5-7) to "communal self-tracking" (ibid: 8-9). This push towards networked affect is driven by the positive psychology finding that a supportive social network is key to happiness and motivation. Positive psychology professes to move beyond individual happiness to nurturing positive relationships and, ultimately, larger positive institutions (cf. Seligman 2011: 20-24). These happiness apps reinforce this mission, encouraging sociality and at times even mandating it. When opting for the private mode on *Happify*, for example, the user is exhorted to choose sharing settings, because "[s]cientific research shows that social support and positive feedback are key to staying motivated on your happiness journey." The app also has a heading for "Give Encouragement, Get Encouragement," which affirms that social networks aid individuals in the quest for more happiness. *gottaFeeling* exhorts users to "[i]mprove your relationships with gottaFeeling, an application to track and share your feelings." *Moodpanda* presents "featured mood diaries on their main site that users can browse and comment and offer affirmations, creating a motivational support network for its users."[15]

Some happiness apps go further, allowing users to not only share but also to build social comparison into the feedback loop (e.g. *Moodstats*)[16]. Ironically, research shows that this type of comparison (or competition, perhaps) contributes to unhappiness, as is shown in studies of well-being, affect circulation, and emotional contagion in social media (cf. Kramer et al. 2014; Sabatini/Sarracino 2014; Trumholt et al. 2015). The socially mediated happiness app experience raises other critical questions about how accountability to a network is different from accountability to the self, the problematic nature of self-reporting emotions, and the fact that users may over-represent their feelings of well-being when they know that this information will be public. Some happiness apps such as *Happy Factor* are explicitly (and perhaps inextricably) integrated into existing social media, providing the option for or requiring using another login, such as *Facebook*, to use the tool; *Expereal*, an app or tracking and visualizing mood, even mandates a login via *Facebook* (cf. Shu 2013). For those QS tools offering or requiring a third party social network login, further ethical consideration arises about how data will be used and privacy maintained within these corporate, global networks that commodify their users along with the data and content they produce.

In addition to market interests, happiness apps' "data practices" (Lupton 2014b: 3) and "data assemblages" (ibid: 8) frequently feed positive psychology

---

15 Cf. http://www.moodpanda.com/.
16 Cf. http://www.cubancouncil.com/work/project/moodstats.

empirical research. For example, *Mappiness* indicates that app use contributes data for a research project[17], as does *Track Your Happiness*, which was created for a doctoral study at Harvard.[18] *Mappiness* highlights this partnership between users and researchers on their website, with clear sections labelled "what's in it for you?" and "what's in it for us?" Data, feedback, analysis, and benefit extend beyond individual users to the positive psychologists who view happiness apps as an important research opportunity:

"Technology provides an exciting opportunity to close the gap between research and implementation. [...]. The use of smartphone technology adds an additional layer of realism, allowing researchers to create phone-based interfaces for interventions and then, as participants use these interfaces, track participants' behaviors and moods as they occur." (Parks et al. 2012: 1232)

Happiness apps are just one aspect of what I term *digital happiness* in order to summarise efforts of positive psychologists and affiliates to utilise technology for increased well-being. In addition to the QS, digital happiness initiatives employ data mining, network analysis, social media research, and sentiment analysis (e.g. the World Well-Being Project, Twitter's *Hedonometer*, the social network *Happier*)[19]. Happiness apps and digital happiness initiatives are altering how individuals and societies conceptualise, measure, and experience happiness, and they frequently serve activist agendas for creating greater well-being globally, e.g. *The H(app)athon Project*; *Happy Barometer*; *Happiness Apps Challenge*[20] (cf. Havens 2014; Business Wire 2015).

Conclusion

Regardless of the particular happiness app or its particular inflections, the message is clear: users will benefit from and should engage in tracking happiness habitually. "Clean your teeth, wash your face, measure your mood. A daily must-do."[21] *(Moodscope)* This imperative to monitor subjective well-being through QS tools passes the responsibility for creating and sustaining happiness onto individual users, who then must manage their emotions via these happiness apps. Happiness apps might then participate in self-monitoring, normalcy, and discipline in the Foucauldian sense (Nafus/Sherman 2014: 1793), just as self-help (cf. Rimke 2000; McGee 2005) and positive psychology and happiness studies

---

17 Cf. http://www.mappiness.org.uk/.
18 Cf. https://www.trackyourhappiness.org/.
19 Cf. http://www.wwbp.org/, http://www.hedonometer.org/, https://www.happier.com/.
20 Cf. http://happathon.com, http://happybarometer.com/, http://www.happinessapps.com/.
21 Cf. https://www.moodscope.com/.

might (cf. Belli 2012; Binkley 2014).[22] Happiness apps teach users to be hypervigilant of personal well-being and to change themselves for increased happiness, adjusting their satisfaction to the world as it is rather than critically approaching it. In this view, progress and self-improvement are promised by an app, its set of interventions, and the adoption of the positive psychology worldview they endorse, rather than achieved through engagement with the structural conditions in which users find themselves. These apps carry the assumptions that understanding and increasing one's happiness is a desirable end and within an individual's control. These may seem like obvious and benign statements (users come to various QS tools and methods to learn about and improve their lives), but they bear explicitly stating and critically interrogating. As the specific context of positive psychology makes clear, happiness apps endorse visions of the happy individual and the good life that are not objective and user-centered, but instead aligned with positive psychology's version of the positive, happy, and good.

The popularity and prevalence of happiness apps suggests that they resonate with many QS trackers who desire greater awareness of and strategies for personal well-being. Like other QS tools and methods, they can effectively generate self-knowledge, fuel personal discovery, and guide choices that align users with idealised versions of themselves. However, as the above discussion of happiness apps demonstrates, the QS is infused with values and commitments, and its users are not merely tracking objective data that they can then control via archiving, aggregation, visualisation, interpretation, and operationalisation.

The data captured by QS tracking are always already subjective and fraught, especially so when what is being tracked is mood, happiness, well-being, or other emotional states. Furthermore, users are always already caught up in larger social, cultural, economic, political, and ethical contexts, as are the data that circulates in their bodies, their perceptions, emotions, and beliefs, QS tools, and the larger information economy. "Self-tracking as a phenomenon has no meaning in itself. It is endowed with meaning by wider discourses on technology, selfhood, the body and social relations that circulate within the cultural context in which the practice is carried out." (Lupton 2014b: 2) In the case of happiness apps, they reproduce the central tenets of positive psychology and participate in solidifying individual and societal understanding of well-being according to this field's mission (cf. Howells et al. 2014).

The practice of tracking and operationalising user data via a happiness app is a complex, mediated practice. The data are mediated by the particular tool as well as users' individual understandings of and aspirations for happiness, which in turn are mediated by the rhetoric, ideology, and pedagogy of positive psychology. This triple mediation demonstrates that the QS is not neutral but instead embedded within complex ethical contexts that merit further exploration.

22   Cf. Davies (2015: 215-243) for an overview of big data efforts to track mood and discussion of how these developments may participate in surveillance and normalising behaviour.

References

Ahmed, Sara (2010): The Promise of Happiness, Durham, NC: Duke.
Anchor, Shawn (2013): Before Happiness: The 5 Hidden Keys to Achieving Success, Spreading Happiness, and Sustaining Positive Change, New York, NY: Crown Business.
Belli, Jill (2012): Pedagogies of Happiness: What and How Self Help, Positive Psychology, and Positive Education Teach about Well-Being, doctoral dissertation: The Graduate Center, City University of New York.
Binkley, Sam (2014): Happiness As Enterprise: An Essay on Neoliberal Life, Albany, NY: SUNY.
Boesel, Whitney Erin (2012): "The Woman vs the Stick: Mindfulness at Quantified Self 2012", September 20, 2012 (http://thesocietypages.org/cyborgology/2012/09/20/the-woman-vs-the-stick-mindfulness-at-quantified-self-2012/).
Business Wire (2015): "Intel-GE Care Innovations™ and Happify to Collaborate On Groundbreaking Program To Help Family Caregivers Of The Chronically Ill." In: Business Wire, November 23, 2015 (http://www.businesswire.com/news/home/20151123005126/en/Intel-GE-Care-Innovations%E2%84%A2-Happify-Collaborate-Groundbreaking-Program).
Davies, William (2015): The Happiness Industry: How the Government and Big Business Sold Us Well-Being, London, UK: Verso.
Davis, Jenny (2013): "The Qualified Self." In: The Society Pages, March 13, 2013 (http://thesocietypages.org/cyborgology/2013/03/13/the-qualified-self/).
Eaton, Kit (2014): "Positive Thinking, with a Little Help from your Phone." In: The New York Times, October 15, (http://www.nytimes.com/2014/10/16/business/positive-thinking-with-a-little-help-from-your-phone.html).
Ehrenreich, Barbara (2009): Bright-Sided: How Positive Thinking Is Undermining America, New York, NY: Picador.
Fawcett, Tom (2015): "Mining the Quantified Self: Personal Knowledge Discovery as a Challenge for Data Science." In: Big Data 3/4, pp. 249-266.
Havens, John C. (2014): Hacking H(app)iness: Why Your Personal Data Counts and How It Can Change the World, New York, NY: Tarcher/Penguin.
Howells, Annika/Ivtzan, Itai/Eiroa-Orosa, Francisco Jose (2014): "Putting the 'app' in Happiness: A Randomised Controlled Trial of a Smartphone-Based Mindfulness Intervention to Enhance Wellbeing." In: Journal of Happiness Studies, pp. 1-23.
Kramer, Adam D. I./Guillory, Jamie E./Hancock, Jeffrey T. (2014): "Experimental Evidence of Massive-Scale Emotional Contagion through Social Networks." In: Proceedings of the National Academy of Sciences 111/24, pp. 8788-8790.
Kurtz, Jamie/Lyubomirsky, Sonja (2011): "LiveHappy: An iPhone Application to Increase Students' Happiness." February 2, 2016 (https://www.socialpsychology.org/action/2011honor2.htm).
Lupton, Deborah (2014a): "Self-tracking Cultures: Towards a Sociology of Personal Informatics." In: Proceedings of the 26th Australian Computer-Human Interaction Conference on Designing Futures: the Future of Design

(https://simplysociology.files.wordpress.com/2014/09/self-tracking-cultures-ozchi-conference-paper.pdf).

Lupton, Deborah (2014b): "You are your Data: Self-Tracking Practices and Concepts of Data." In: Stefan Selke (ed.), Lifelogging: Theoretical Approaches and Case Studies about Self-Tracking (provisional title), Zürich: Springer (forthcoming), pp. 1-18, December 4, 2014 (http://papers.ssrn.com/sol3/papers.cfm?abstract_id=2534211).

Lyubomirksy, Sonja (2007): The How of Happiness: A Scientific Approach to Getting the Life You Want, New York, NY: Penguin.

McGee, Micki (2005): Self Help, Inc.: Makeover Culture in American Life, New York, NY: Oxford University Press.

McGonigal, Jane (2015): SuperBetter: A Revolutionary Approach to Getting Stronger, Happier, Braver, and More Resilient, New York, NY: Penguin.

Nafus, Dawn/Sherman, Jamie (2014): "This One Does Not Go Up to 11: The Quantified Self Movement as an Alternative Data Big Practice." In: International Journal of Communication 8, pp. 1784-1794.

Parks, Acacia C./Della Porta, Matthew D./Pierce, Russell S./Zilca, Ran/Lyubomirsky, Sonja (2012): "Pursuing Happiness in Everyday Life: The Characteristics and Behaviors of Online Happiness Seekers." In: Emotion 12/6, pp. 1222-1234.

Rimke, Heidi Marie (2000): "Governing Citizens through Self-Help Literature." In: Cultural Studies 14/1, pp. 61-78.

Rubin, Gretchen (2009): The Happiness Project: Or, Why I Spent A Year Trying to Sing in the Morning, Clean My Closets, Fight Read, Read Aristotle, and Generally Have more Fun, New York, NY: Harper.

Sabatini, Fabio/Sarracino, Francesco (2014). "Online Networks and Subjective Well-Being." In: arXiv:1408.3550 [cs.CY], (http://arxiv.org/abs/1408.3550).

Seligman, Martin E. P. (2011): Flourish: A Visionary New Understanding of Happiness and Well-Being, New York: Free Press.

Seligman, Martin E. P./Csíkszentmihályi, Mihály (2000): "Positive Psychology: An Introduction." In: American Psychologist 55/1, pp. 5-14.

Shu, Catherine (2013): "Life-Tracking App Expereal Is Your Personal Weapon Against Cognitive Biases." In: Techcrunch, May 16, 2013 (http://techcrunch.com/2013/05/16/life-tracking-app-expereal-is-your-personal-weapon-against-cognitive-biases/).

Swan, Melanie (2012): "Sensor Mania! The Internet of Things, Wearable Computing, Objective Metrics, and the Quantified Self 2.0." In: Journal of Sensor and Actuator Networks 1, pp. 217-253.

Swan, Melanie (2013): "The Quantified Self: Fundamental Disruption in Big Data Science and Biological Discovery." In: Big Data 1/2, pp. 85-99.

Tromholt, Morten/Lundby, Marie/Andsbjerg, Kjartan/Wiking, Meik (2015): "The Facebook Experiment: Does Social Media Affect the Quality of Our Lives?" In: The Happiness Institute (http://www.happinessresearchinstitute.com/publications/4579836749).

Wolf, Gary (2010): "The Data-Driven Life." In: The New York Times Magazine, April 28, 2010 (http://www.nytimes.com/2010/05/02/magazine/02self-measurement-t.html).

Conceptual and Legal Reflections

Casual Power
Understanding User Interfaces through Quantification

Alex Gekker

Abstract

The paper draws parallels between quantification as found in the user interfaces of video games, to similar elements of more "serious" devices, in particular mapping and navigational platforms. I present an autoethnographic study of a mundane experience that would be familiar to many Google Maps users: locating a nearby place of interest and figuring out how to reach it. The navigational case is used as a canvas for a further analysis of the role of quantified elements in user interfaces. My autoethnography shows how the mundane actions performed on the screen are informed by the necessary reductions that mapped media perform on the physical world. Such reductions are imitated and enabled by user interfaces designed to control and guide user attention. Designers aim to simplify and streamline user interactions with the system and such practices are built on tracking the user and habituating the actions she performs through the screen.

> Golden rule for young warriors: when in doubt raise DEX! To-hit chance is THE most important stat for a warrior (no matter what your damage is, it's exactly zero if you miss...), BLOCKING with a shield can actually be a substitute for armor and, early on, 1 AC from a level up is nothing to be looked down on.
> ARMIN'S DIABLO LEVEL UP POINT DISTRIBUTION GUIDE[1]

> Both Armor Class (AC) and To Hit are based on your Dexterity. Below is a summary on how they are calculated. For more information about AC and To Hit, see chapter 5.6.5.
> Armor Class
> Warrior, Rogue, Sorcerer: Dex/5 + AC_{items}
> Monk with plate: Dex/5 + AC_{items}
> Monk with mail: Dex/5 + AC_{items} + clvl/2
> Monk with leather and other light armor: Dex/5 + AC_{items} + 2·clvl
> Monk with no armor: Dex/5 + AC_{items} + 2·clvl
> Bard: Dex/5 + AC_{items}
> Barbarian: Dex/5 + AC_{items} + clvl/4
> JARUFF'S GUIDE TO DIABLO AND HELLFIRE, VERSION 1.62.[2]

---

[1] Available at: http://www.arewehavingfunyet.com/diablo/lvlup.txt.
[2] Available at: http://www.lurkerlounge.com/diablo/jarulf/jarulf162.pdf.

Introduction: Quantification as Self-Representation

The following text draws parallels between quantification as found in the user interfaces of video games to similar elements of more "serious" devices, in particular mapping and navigational platforms. The quotes presented above draw attention to the nature of how numbers are used in the course of a game to create a clearly understood approximation of complex real life phenomenon. In this case, the quotes are from online guides to Diablo (Blizzard Entertainment 1996), an action role-playing game based around the acquisition of better equipment and skills. Those improvements are represented in sequential interval scales and affect the player's performance through mathematical formulas ingrained in the game's engine. In this game, as in many games like it that are built on the tradition of table-top Role-Playing Games (RPGs), the game mechanics are focused on numerical improvement, through "levelling" certain "stats" of the player's character or her equipment in order to cause more damage, attack faster etc. In such a setting, level 2 is always better than level 1, and a +1 sword will be replaced by a +2 of the same kind.

When looking at the phenomenon of the Quantified Self (QS) movement (Nafus/Sherman 2014) where the participants choose to trace and represent themselves through numerical scales in order to better understand topics as wide as personal health, mood or sleeping patterns, some similarity can be seen with the role of numbers in *Diablo*. In both cases humans, be it players or QS practitioners, are transferred into traceable sets of numbers to better facilitate their mediated existence on a digital platform. The goal in each case seems to be rather different; in one case, it is to help users immerse themselves in a make-believe entertainment platform, in the other to supplement one's knowledge of one's own body via meticulous auditing.

This paper suggests a more nuanced view: the aforementioned practices are bound by similar propensities of human perception. It can also be said that designers of non-game digital systems can and do make use of similar numerical shortcuts in order to enact certain affordances in the physical world. Specifically, I am talking about the perception of time and distance, as experienced through digital cartographic interfaces such as Google Maps or satellite navigation systems for cars. Doing so requires adopting a different perspective on the ways designers inscribe user interfaces with meaning (Akrich 1992). This paper argues for a conceptualization of digital maps as types of *ludic interfaces* (Fuchs 2012) that are designed to partially occlude the world to the user, through the implementation of quantified user interface (UI) elements.

I present an excerpt from an autoethnographic study of the roles of user interfaces in the manufacturing and implementation of digital maps. The paper begins with a mundane experience that would be familiar to many Google Maps[3]

---

3   This experience is transferable to other types of navigational interfaces. In particular, consider other types of digital maps like Apple Maps, Open Street Map or Microsoft's Bing Map; vehicle navigation devices and phone applications such as various versions of TomTom, Garmin, and CoPilot devices, or the Waze app.

users: locating a nearby place of interest and figuring out how to reach it (cf. Brown/McGregor/McMillan 2014). The navigational case is used as a canvas for further analysis of the role of quantified elements in user interfaces.

Autoethnography has a long tradition within both the social sciences and more humanities-oriented cultural practices (Ellis/Adams/Bochner 2011). Ellis and Bochner (2000) are recognised scholars in these fields with a large following advocating *evocative autoethnography*, which focuses on aesthetic renderings of personal research experiences, in ways that blur academic writing with literary genres such as biographies or memoirs. However, Anderson (2006) suggests using autoethnography as part of the *analytical* tradition of anthropological enquiry, tying the reflexivity of the autoethnographic method to the broader social context of the researcher as a participant-observer and utilizing it in order to advance theoretical knowledge rather than to only explore emergent personal narratives. Following his framework, the case before us represents an attempt to tie personal practices of map-based navigation to broader theoretical developments of modern mediascapes, particularly the idea of inscribing meaning into sociotechnical artefacts. This, while under the conceptual framework of Actor-Network Theory (ANT), which allows the adaption of a selective and temporary frame of reference into the workings of a particular system of process, as it is produced through translated actions between multiple human and non-human actors (Latour 1987; Woolgar 1990; Law 1992; Latour 2005).

Drawing on the case studied I move to examining digital maps as playful objects (Sicart 2014). Central to this consideration is the distinction between play as an activity and playfulness as an attitude, and thus the potential to embed the latter into devices and practices which are not traditionally considered playful. Playfulness allows for interface quantification designed to reinforce autotelic goals removed from map use and navigation. This analysis is based on human cognitive properties for simplifying and comparing numbers through the prism of "the machine zone" (Schüll 2014), a theory of the way the digitalisation of previously analogue technologies can be designed with the aim of nullifying user self-reflexivity.

A Case Study:
Losing Track of Space through Digital Cartography

The case began when I was required to do some grocery shopping in the city of Utrecht for a social event. A colleague and I decided to meet up at a local supermarket so that he could help me with carrying the snacks and bottles back to the office.

Naturally, when we were making arrangements, I suggested the nearest supermarket that I could think of. Later, as I was about to leave for the supermarket, I realised that another same store might be closer. It was in exactly the opposite direction, away from the city centre, but it was larger and the path back to the office from it was more straightforward for two people carrying several bags. Due to the peculiar geometry of Utrecht's historic centre, with its medieval streets, it was not immediately clear to me which supermarket was the closest. I still had a few minutes, so I swiftly launched Google Maps in one of the tabs of my browser. It loaded in seconds and zoomed in on my location. I then proceeded to type "ah" (shorthand for the supermarket brand in question). The map zoomed out slightly, showing three red dots around my location, which was indicated by a blue "you are here" circle (Figure 1). There was the answer to the first part of my question: yes, there was another supermarket in another direction and it did appear to be about the same distance from me as the other one, based on a rough visual approximation of the distance on the map. However, with one location being reachable by walking in a straight line and the other hiding behind multiple curves and turns, the quickest route was still not apparent.

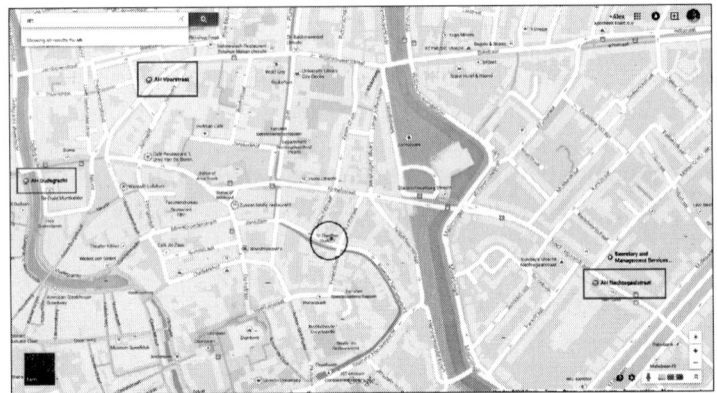

Fig. 1: Albert Heijn (AH) supermarkets (squares) in the vicinity of location (circle), screenshot from Google Maps on Windows PC by author.

I then proceeded to query the map regarding the travel time and distance with respect to each of the two locations. Selecting the walking route option, it showed me a tentative path and an estimated time of travel – marked by blue lines – as well as alternative routes (Figure 2).

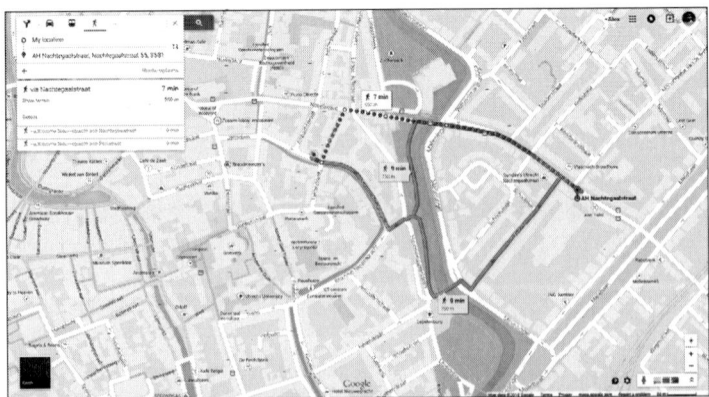

Fig. 2: The way to AH Nachtegaalstraat, screenshot from Google Maps on Windows PC by author.

Did it pay off? Not really. For the first supermarket, the one that I originally intended to visit, Google indicated a walking distance of 550 meters and journey time of 6 minutes. For the alternative supermarket, GM displayed an identical distance of 550 meters and a time of 7 minutes. The first one still seemed closer. I then realized that my search actions were completely un-reflexive, where, even as a researcher of mapping, I wasn't registering my own actions. I also realised that I was already running late for the planned meeting.

The map compressed space and time for me, turning potentials into actuals. It is what Ingold refers to as the "cartographic illusion" (Ingold 2000: 234), where by focusing on the end product of a mapmaking project (the produced inscription), the user of the map (the map-reader, engaged in wayfinding) confuses their surrounding landscapes with "space". To underscore the futility of my attempts to save myself some time and effort, one aspect of this illusion

"lies in the assumption that the structure of the world, and so also that of the map which purports to represent it, is fixed without regard to the movement of its inhabitants. Like a theatrical stage from which all the actors have mysteriously disappeared, the world – as it is represented in the map – appears deserted, devoid of life. No-one is there; nothing is going on." (ibid)

Even Google Maps, with its imposing rhetoric of truth (Della Dora 2012) could not have accounted for real-time events that could disrupt my journey, such as accidents or road works.[4] However critical towards maps, I was substituting my own memory of how the immediate world works with the quantifiable, relational qualities afforded to me by this interface between myself and the world, with such quantification being the decisive difference between how maps describe the world compared to other images, such as landscape paintings (Alpers 1984). Although – unlike in the examples put forward by Ingold – my journey to the supermarket *would* have left a trace on this map (as long as my phone's complementary Google location services remained connected), the illusion was still compelling enough. The seemingly accurate and immediate depiction of the actions available to me in the world was superimposed on the map. As I show through the unpacking of this case, through current theories of digital quantification and human perception, in digital mapping the cartographic illusion is even stronger.

---

4   It is worth noting here that while efforts to create such ever-accurate maps exist, they mostly pertain to automotive and not pedestrian navigation. For example, the Waze application attempts to do so (Hind/Gekker 2014). Additionally, at the time of writing, the attempts of multiple actors to develop real-time maps intended to be read exclusively by automatic vehicles, with nearly real-time updates (Miller 2014; Badger 2015).

Playfulness as Interaction

In this section, I argue for the appropriation of a playful prism for the analysis of mapping: by tracing specific manifestations of the mediatization (meta)process (Hepp 2013), I aim to show how the moulding forces of entangled industries – spatial data, social networks, and User Interface design – come together in the making of digital mapping interfaces. Thus, the continuous growing entanglement of additional spheres of life with specific media logics leads to the hybridization of communicative and cultural practices into the production of maps.

The *user*, or perhaps the *player* (rather than reader or viewer), is the main subject of the computational industries. Joost Raessens (2006) suggests that games and other digital technologies facilitate playful goals and identities, leading to the "ludification of culture". According to Raessens, modern Western cultures have become more accepting of notions of play outside of the traditional escapist or leisure domains. Play has been appropriated as a metaphor for a political process, utilized to foster suspense in game shows and movies, and utilized to conduct war through drone interfaces inspired by video game consoles and their controllers (Raessens 2012).

Play philosopher and designer Miguel Sicart (2014) offers a dissenting view on play, breaking away from formalist definitions attempting to re-introduce the concept beyond rule-bound game systems (Sicart 2011), while still keeping it as a viable operational term for the purposes of analysis. For him, play is a mode of human activity, a mode of being in the world and with the world. Play is not bound to any particular object and is not emerging from games with fixed rule systems. Sicart's point of departure, in fact, is not games but *toys*, citing the wonder and creativity they evoke in children and adults alike. For him, play is appropriative and autotelic, changing intended activities into other, not related to the original goal of the player. It is a mode of engagement with various others: "Play is being in the world, through objects, towards others. We play not to entertain ourselves or to learn or to be alienated: we play to be, and play gives us, through its characteristics, the possibility of being" (Sicart 2014: 18).

This definition, and specifically the suggestion to see objects as conduits, brings to the fore an important distinction: play and playfulness. While often conflated, and rarely discussed in previous games and play theories, the two are quite different since

> "[P]lay is an *activity* while playfulness is an *attitude*. An activity is a finite and coherent set of actions performed of certain purposes, while an attitude is a stance toward an activity – a psychological, physical, and emotional perspective we take on activities, people, and objects... In this sense, playfulness is projecting some of the characteristics of play into nonplay activities. It is an attempt to engage with the world in the mode of being of play but not playing." (Sicart 2014: 22)

This distinction will be useful when analysing quantification interfaces in mapping and beyond: an object can be playful, i.e. embedded with properties that bring about playfulness. This does not mean that his object was created for or designed with play in mind. Playfulness is an attitude that fully takes on play's attribute of appropriation, as it is reliant on one's ability to see beyond the mundane, useful, accepted uses of objects and spaces, rejecting fixity and *reambiguating* the world. It disrupts existing contexts and injects play into non-play places.

I suggest *casual power* as a term for understanding how playfulness-within-objects changes the nature of the power relations between designers and users in digital environments. The term is borrowed from *casual games,* a type of video games that has become popular in recent years, characterised by easy and enticing mechanics, short play sessions, and appeal to mass audiences (Juul 2010). Such games have a tendency of suppressing other types of activities, often through users' smart phones, as they are played in-between and instead of less desired tasks: on public transport, during class, or at a boring meeting.

Similarly, casual power can be traced in designs intended to invoke playfulness and to overwrite something else. It can be positive, as in when subway stairs are modified to resemble piano keys in order to encourage people to be physically active (Rolighetsteorin 2009). Yet, often it is also a problematic technique, which aims to deceive, or at least distract, the user from being self-reflexive about the actual activities she is undertaking within a system. There always exists a tension between functional and predictable design and design intended to invoke playfulness. Nowhere is this clearer then when discussing maps.

Playful Mapping

Chris Perkins (2009) was the first to suggest introducing play into research focusing on mapping assemblages. Following the fixation of cartographers on usability and efficiency achieved through scientific means, devoid of the cultural components of mapping and its contextual specifics for users (Perkins 2008), he argues for re-examining the disruptive role of digital mapping in facilitating for people

"the possibilities of putting themselves on their own map, destabilizing the taken-for-granted representational neutrality of the image; new kinds of maps are being made; more people are making maps; more things are being mapped; and mapping is taking place in more contexts than ever before." (Perkins 2009: 168)

This notion of ludic engagement underscores how playful mapping is entwined with everyday play, rather than standing apart from it. Re-examining Perkins' suggestions, a counterargument can be made that while playfulness opens up some possibilities, it closes others, in line with the principles of appropriation and personalization advocated by Sicart. Specifically, once multiple new actors have access to mapmaking, and while traditional mapmakers are required to compete with newcomers and other distracting screens (Dalton 2015), the role of play in mapping can become more insidious than in paper cartography. The specificity of digital maps is them being "Latourian quasi-things inscribed with programs of actions" (Lammes 2009) that structure space for their end user in a certain way. If play is a mode of being in the world through the map, and mapping is an emergent and processual practice (Kitchin/Dodge 2007; Dodge/Kitchin/Perkins 2009; Kitchin/Gleeson/Dodge 2013), then a subversive play can be introduced into the map inscription in order to facilitate a certain being in the world, one that benefits the mapmaker rather than the map user.

Maps are permeated with varied forms of quantification, such as scoring,[5] route calculations, or constant (re)evaluations of speed, directions, and estimated times of arrival (ETAs). Designing interfaces that evoke participants' sense of play or competiveness is very fitting for such score-centred activities. In fact, media scholar Chris Chesher equates navigation in third-person computer games with navigating utilizing a GPS satnav device, pointing to how both systems restructure Lefebvrian notions of social space (Lefebvre 1992; Elden 2007). He lists three distinct ways in which those sociotechnical spaces are similarly structured: first, by displacing ad hoc navigational practices with concrete instructions, the system entrenches the rigid procedural logic and rhetoric of structured play; then, both systems similarly re-make the spaces around them into a subject-oriented consumption space, where desires are gratified almost immediately by the automatic alignment of the personal point-of-view with that of the mapped world; finally they both present a complex overlay on top of the mapped view. As I have shown in the supermarket example above, this overlay is rife with various quantified elements. The next section delves deeper into the consequences of quantification when moving from an analogue to a digital platform. It does so through a comparison with another case study of a similar move, this one in the world of gambling machines.

The Machine Zone

I suggest understanding user interface quantification through the notion of the "machine zone". Anthropologist Natasha Schüll, researching the gambling industry, describes the way this industry is concentrated on getting people 'into the zone'. Done through black-boxing the numbers behind gambling by way of digital technologies, this "zone" is defined as a psychological state of repeating the interactions with the digital gambling machines, where the users, no longer interested in winning or losing, are engrossed in the actions themselves and the feedback loops they generate. In such a state, playing to win is irrelevant; rather – as a gambler named Mollie describes it – the aim is "to keep playing – to stay in that machine zone where nothing else matters" (Schüll 2014: 2). Using Sicart's dichotomy, such attempt at "zoning" the user can be seen as an application of playfulness to gambling spaces and objects, detaching it from the

---

5   Giving scores, in the form of stars or numbers, have become a growing feature of many map-based interfaces. From the local business classification website Yelp to the tourist-oriented TripAdvisor, maps are used to order certain types of locations in both space and rank.

"official" goal of gambling – earning money – into an autotelic, appropriative state that draws on the action (the being) more than the result.

The architecture, ergonomics, and design of gambling spaces are intended to insulate the machine's user from their daily realities and create a zone without any unexpected occurrences, where a series of habituated actions provide a stream of expected outcomes. According to Schüll, compulsive gamblers often juxtapose the mechanical accuracy of the pre-designed play sessions with the social contingencies of their everyday work and lives, often in service jobs where – driven by neo-liberal post-Fordian models – human interaction is quantified and evaluated for purposes of constantly increasing productivity. For such gamblers, the machine and its nullifying effect on time and space offers a provisional respite from such demands by simply switching off: "To put the zone into words, the gamblers I spoke with supplemented an exotic, nineteenth-century terminology of hypnosis and magnetism with twentieth-century references to television watching, computer processing, and vehicle driving." (Schüll 2014: 19)

Ironically, the modes of quantified daily interactions that the gamblers try and escape make the gambling devices into effective tools for entrapping players. The introduction of digital technologies has created a unique conjuncture of highly traceable and manipulable players. Digitization hides game components that were previously visible and discernable behind an occluding rectangular of glass. The machine here is manufacturing a sense of wonder and enchantment through increased use of calculations to undermine uncertainty, replacing the old reliance on magic or superstition (Weber in Schüll 2014). In the case of electronic gambling machines, the mechanical reels were gradually replaced with electronic and later digital parts that created a disconnect between the game as experienced by the player and the actual outcomes, which were pre-calculated in an exact manner. Tracing trade materials and interviewing designers, Schüll concludes that by obfuscating the actual game mechanics, while giving players the illusion of control by including nostalgic aesthetic elements into the design, the gambling industry aims at maintaining this aura of enchantment. The magic of the machine is intrinsically tied to the way human perception works, as "[t]here is a mismatch... between human capacities to process and respond to information and those of the digital technology. This mismatch, one could further suggest, reflects the larger asymmetry between designers and players, technologies of disenchantment and states of enchantment." (Schüll 2014: 85)

The machine zone is then a state of contrived contingency, manufactured by the gambling industry to attract the user through enchanting the technological process behind digitalized play. It creates a disjunction between how the end-user perceives the game and its actual mechanics. Unlike what one would expect from gambling, the resulting state for the constantly tracked and measured user is one of a nullified certainty and calm, as she is engrossed in the actions she is performing.

Reading the ethnographies of gambling machine designers, it becomes clear that such a state has implications beyond that of the immediate gambling industry. Struggling between sticking to the claim of addiction (or 'problem gambling') as something inherent to the individual, most designers nonetheless admit that there are ways to foster addictive behaviours – or perhaps, more accurately, addictive loops[6] – through the point of contact behind users and devices – the user interface. Like in the *Diablo* game, and similar to self-tracking methods of the QS practitioners, the gambling machine simplifies an otherwise messy and random reality into a series of sequential numbers. It is increasingly tied to a permanent user profile that tracks players and rewards them for unbroken play, while continuously adjusting the experience of the machine in order to retain the player for as long as possible.

The experience interwoven into the design of digital maps can also be understood through the machine zone. The map allows for the user to substitute complex thought processes and cognitive unease for a repeated interaction with their physical reality through a pleasant mantle of the familiar. Familiarity, through a sense of cognitive ease, is often interpreted as "truthfulness" by the mind (Lazarsfeld/Berelson/Gaudet 1944; Lazarsfeld/Merton 1948). Familiar actions also have a causal link to affect, meaning that a sense of mastery from performing a familiar task can be felt as pleasant (Zajonc 1968; 1980; Bornstein 1989). This is anchored in the quantifiable nature of the digital media, and relates to another attribute of human perception. The propensity of humans to measure is supplemented by their ability to compare those measures across different, often unrelated, scales and is known as *intensity matching*. Kanhenman (2011) notes that most people from a similar cultural background agree on matching such attributes as the intensity of a colour to the severity of a crime (murder is a deeper shade of red than theft). This also links to the *availability heuristic* (Tversky/Kahneman 1973), which allows one to substitute a question related to frequency or quantity with an easier one.

Why did I do the cumbersome comparison between the supermarkets, described in the opening of the paper? Because I wanted to know which one was closer. To act through a map is often to examine numerical information – whether in units of time or space. But such data has a trace of Ingoldian "cartographic illusions", obscuring the complex spatiotemporal relationship – not only the visible aerial distance on the map, but also the actual turn-by-turn directions that creates the genuinely lived distance of traffic lights and blocked sidewalks. *Thus, if the question that I needed to answer was 'how difficult would it be for me to carry groceries from one place compared to another?', the answer I might end up getting is 'which of the two numbers presented to me by Google Maps is lower?'.*

The Machine Zone through Quantification and Gamification

To summarise the argument so far, the machine zone is a mode of design that uses obfuscation in user interface to entice non-reflexive and prolonged engagement with a digital device. Casual power is the resulting diffused power

---

6   Compare with Stefan Werning (2007) discussion of video games as programmed objects where he draws parallels between the psychological notion of 'behavioural loop' and programming's loop and recursion techniques.

manifesting through multiple small interactions, in simple and repetitive increments. In this last section, I emphasise the role of quantification in such power relations through a comparative analysis of the Google Maps interface with that of the Facebook social media website.

Social media quantifies the basic human relations of the world, allowing one to constantly re-asses his or her position vis-à-vis subjective reality via answering a series of easier questions (How many friends? How many likes?). This happens while experiencing a (misleading) sense of familiarity through the mastery of a user interface designed to foster a disconnect between the ease of an action and its meaning. Artist and critic Benjamin Grosser, inventor of the "Facebook Demetricator" browser add-on that deletes all quantity-related mentions from the popular platform, comments on such constant self-assessment:

"Our need for personal worth is highly dependent on these social interactions, as both relatedness and esteem are necessarily measured in relation to others. If this essential human need can only be fulfilled within the confines of capitalism, then it stands to reason that we are subject to a deeply ingrained desire for *more*: a state of being where more exchange, more value, or more trade equals more personal worth. In other words, our evolutionarily developed desire for worth is an intrinsic need, which translates, through the 'pervasive atmosphere' of capitalist realism, into a desire for more." (Grosser 2014: n.p.)

Grosser's argument is built on the propagation of a neo-liberal managerial culture, and specifically the audit, as an evaluation method rooted in observable metrics, which exceeded its original role in the financial industry and made its way into domains like higher education and public service. Facebook builds upon this culture in two ways: as a driving force, and as a data infrastructure. First, in constantly displaying metrics to the user, it aims at commodifying the social interaction into a manageable structure, while playing on the anxieties of the individual to miss out or lose. The numbers – most often notifications of new events – go up whether the user attends to them or not, thereby maintaining a constant pressure to check what is new in their feed. But the moment she checks (i.e. clicks on the icon which displays the number) the count is gone and the user must attain additional notifications by creating interaction opportunities. This requires engaging others through Facebook to be prompted as they comment or message back, perpetuating the "desire for more". Additionally, based on a list data structure, Facebook's database in itself is geared towards keeping score and assigning a numerical structure, thus "[o]n occasion, this may lead the Facebook interface programmer to include a metric simply because they can" (ibid).

As can be seen from the discussion of the machine zone as a quantitative engagement mode, my argument regarding the casual power of the mapping interface combines several conceptual frameworks. Namely, I recognise the concerns over social media designed towards habituating behavioural automatism (Madrigal 2013) via paths of commodifying quantification (Grosser 2014) in order to create an autotelic mode of being through a playful attitude (Sicart 2014). This allows me to compare how both social media and digital mapping are the offspring of increasingly shortening attention cycles and the unique characteristics of digital objects (Kallinikos/Aaltonen/Marton 2010). Both are often presented as utilities that allow one to extend the existing characteristics of human interaction or spatial perception through improved means. Numbers play a similar function in both as they propagate a sense of the immediate, the calculable, and the objective.

While not as saturated with metrics as the Facebook user interface (Figure 3), Google Maps has similar interface tendencies (Figure 4). Selecting any point on the digital map will give a user several suggestions on the possible ways to interact with it in the physical world, whether by offering quantified (time and distance) ways to reach it or by ranking it compared to other locations in the area. Such suggestions are based on user input, and one's personal preferences are distilled from previous use patterns. Through quantification, the user is presented with clear and discernible information about the world and ways to act in it, making the map into a navigational rather than mimetic reproduction of the world (November/Camacho-Hübner/Latour 2010).

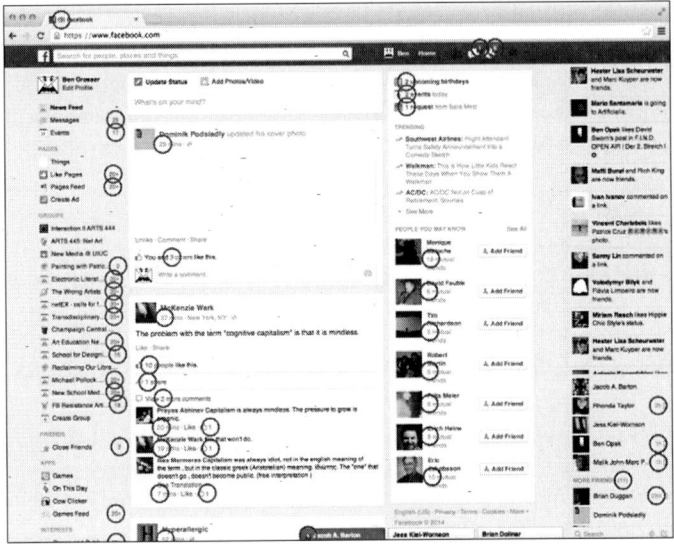

Fig. 3: Metrics location on Facebook User Interface, from Grosser (2015).

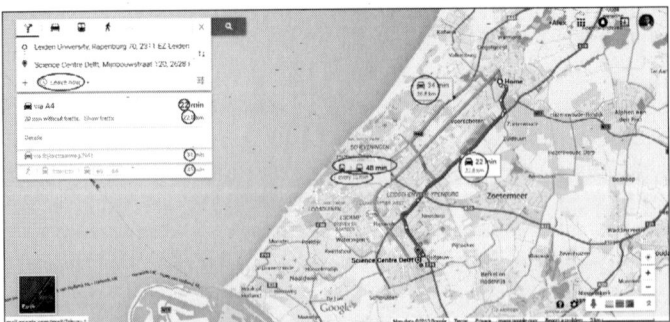

Fig. 4: Metrics location on Facebook User Interface, from Grosser (2015).

Conclusion

While a comparison between an old computer game and a movement centred on self-tracking and self-assessment may seem inane at first, they are both rooted in a cultural shift from analogue to digital platforms. Such a shift prioritises a move to a clear and immediate display of numerical information, giving a sense of purpose to an otherwise messy reality.

My autoethnography of the map was to show how the mundane actions performed on the screen are informed by the necessary reductions that mapped media exert on the physical world. Such reductions are initiated and enabled by user interfaces designed to control and guide user attention. Designers aim to simplify and streamline user interactions with the system and such practices are built on tracking the user and habituating the actions she does through the screen.

Understanding this mapping interaction requires one to consider the nature of play and playfulness, a quality rarely associated with the serious world of task-oriented navigation. Yet, by utilising the ideas of playfulness as an attitude that can be embedded in an object and of the machine zone as an example of non-reflexive engagement with such an object, a theoretical analysis can be performed. The notion of cognitive fluency helps to elucidate the ease and pleasure I received from performing repeated actions on the map. The theory of propensity matching explains how the numerical elements of the user interface allowed me to substitute difficult questions with simpler ones, provided the answer could be expressed in quantifiable and comparable units. Comparing a map's numerical elements with that of a social media website allows us to recognise repeating design patterns in both, that simplify and automate repeating daily actions.

Throughout the paper, I used the term *casual power* to describe this effect: the way digital objects are made to fit into quotidian practices and the ways people *casually* use them while they track him or her in order to continuously improve their user experience and propagate additional time spent using device. This echoes the warning of media philosopher David Berry against

"new forms of invisible interface/ubiquitous computing/enchanted objects which use context to present user with predictive media and information in real time. The aim, we might say, is to replace forethought by reconfiguring/replacing human 'secondary memory' and thinking with computation. That is, the crucial half-second of pre-conscious decision-forming processes whereby we literally 'make up our own minds' is today subject to the unregulated and aggressive targeting of the programming industry." (Berry 2014: 211)

This exercise employed the example of my own Google Maps use for broader critical consideration of quantification in society. In the venue of critical auto-ethnography I strive to provide an analysis that "recursively draws upon our personal experiences and perceptions to inform our broader social under-standings and upon our broader social understandings to enrich our self-understandings" (Anderson 2006: 390). This theoretical framework opens up potential research into the ways media interfaces are produced, how users experience them, and particularly the role and power of quantifiable elements in this communicative practice.

References

Akrich, Madeleine (1992): "The De-scription of Technical Objects." In: Wiebe E. Bijker/John Law (eds.), Shaping Technology/Building Society, Cambridge: MIT Press, pp. 205-24.

Alpers, Svetlana (1984): The Art of Describing: Dutch Art in the Seventeenth Century. Reprint edition, Chicago: University Of Chicago Press.

Anderson, Leon (2006): "Analytic Autoethnography." In: Journal of Contemporary Ethnography 35/4, pp. 373-95.

Badger, Emily (2015): "What Maps Will Look Like When We Need Cars to Read Them." In: The Washington Post March 9 (http://www.washingtonpost.com/blogs/wonkblog/wp/2015/03/09/what-maps-will-look-like-when-we-need-cars-to-read-them/?tid=sm_tw).

Berry, David M. (2014): Critical Theory and the Digital. Critical Theory and Contemporary Society. London, UK: Bloomsbury.

Blizzard Entertainment. (1995): Diablo. PC

Bornstein, Robert F. (1989): "Exposure and Affect: Overview and Meta-Analysis of Research, 1968-1987." In: Psychological Bulletin 106/2, pp. 265-89.

Brown, Barry/Moira McGregor/Donald McMillan (2014): "100 Days of iPhone Use: Understanding the Details of Mobile Device Use." In: Proceedings of the 16th International Conference on Human-Computer Interaction with Mobile Devices & Services, MobileHCI'14. New York, NY, USA: ACM, pp. 223-32.

Dalton, Craig M. (2015): "For Fun and Profit: The Limits and Possibilities of Google-Maps-Based Geoweb Applications." In: Environment and Planning A 47/5, pp. 1029-1046.

Della Dora, Veronica (2012): "A World of 'Slippy Maps': Google Earth, Global Visions, and Topographies of Memory." In: Transatlantica. Revue d'études américaines. American Studies Journal 2 (http://transatlantica.revues.org/6156).

Dodge, Martin/Rob Kitchin/Chris Perkins (2009): "Mapping Modes, Methods and Moments: A Manifesto for Map Studies." In: Martin Dodge/Rob Kitchin/Chris Perkins (eds.), Rethinking Maps: New Frontiers in Cartographic Theory, New York: Routledge, pp. 220-43.

Elden, Stuart (2007): "There Is a Politics of Space Because Space Is Political: Henri Lefebvre and the Production of Space." In: Radical Philosophy Review 10/2, pp. 101-116.

Ellis, Carolyn/Adams, Tony E./Bochner, Arthur P. (2011): "Autoethnography: An Overview." In: Historical Social Research/Historische Sozialforschung 36/4/138, pp. 273-90.

Ellis, Carolyn/Bochner, Arthur P. (2000): "Autoethnography, Personal Narrative, Reflexivity: Researcher as Subject." In: Collecting and Interpreting

Qualitative Materials, Communication Faculty Publications, pp. 733-68 (http://scholarcommons.usf.edu/spe_facpub/91).
Fuchs, Mathias (2012): "Ludic Interfaces. Driver and Product of Gamification." In: G|A|M|E Games as Art, Media, Entertainment 1/1 (http://www.gamejournal.it/ludic-interfaces-driver-and-product-of-gamification/).
Grosser, Benjamin (2014): "What Do Metrics Want? How Quantification Prescribes Social Interaction on Facebook." In: Computational Culture a Journal of Software Studies (http://computationalculture.net/article/what-do-metrics-want).
Hepp, Andreas (2013): Cultures of Mediatization, Cambridge/Malden: Polity.
Hind, Sam/Gekker Alex (2014): "'Outsmarting Traffic, Together': Driving as Social Navigation." In: Exchanges: The Warwick Research Journal 1/2, pp. 165-80.
Ingold, Tim (2000): The Perception of the Environment: Essays on Livelihood, Dwelling and Skill. Reissue edition, London/New York: Routledge.
Juul, Jesper (2010): A Casual Revolution: Reinventing Video Games and Their Players, Cambridge, MA: The MIT Press.
Kahneman, Daniel (2011): Thinking, Fast and Slow. Reprint edition, New York: Farrar, Straus and Giroux.
Kallinikos, Jannis/Aaltonen, Aleksi/Marton, Attila (2010): "A Theory of Digital Objects." First Monday 15/6 (http://journals.uic.edu/ojs/index.php/fm/article/view/3033).
Kitchin, Rob/Dodge, Martin (2007): "Rethinking Maps." In: Progress in Human Geography 31/3, pp. 331-44.
Kitchin, Rob/Gleeson, Justin/Dodge, Martin (2013): "Unfolding Mapping Practices: A New Epistemology for Cartography." In: Transactions of the Institute of British Geographers 38/3, pp. 480-96.
Lammes, Sybille (2009): "Transmitting Location: Digital Cartographical Interfaces as Transformative Material Practices." In: Proceedings of the 6th Media in Transition Conference. MIT: Cambridge, MA.
Latour, Bruno (1987): Science in Action. Cambridge, MA: Harvard University Press.
Latour, Bruno (2005): Reassembling the Social: An Introduction to Actor-Network-Theory. Oxford: Oxford University Press.
Law, John (1992): "Notes on the Theory of the Actor-Network: Ordering, Strategy, and Heterogeneity." In: Systems Practice 5/4, pp. 379-93.
Lazarsfeld, Paul F./Berelson, Bernard/Gaudet, Hazel (1944): The People's Choice. How the Voter Makes up His Mind in a Presidential Campaign. New York: Columbia University Press.
Lazarsfeld, Paul F./Merton, Robert (1948): "Mass Communication, Popular Taste, and Organized Social Action." In: Lyman Bryson (ed.), Communication of Ideas, New York: Institute for Religious and Social Studies, pp. 95-118.
Lefebvre, Henri (1992): The Production of Space. Oxford: Wiley-Blackwell.
Madrigal, Alexis C (2013): "The Machine Zone: This Is Where You Go When You Just Can't Stop Looking at Pictures on Facebook." In: The Atlantic, July 31 (http://www.theatlantic.com/technology/archive/2013/07/the-machine-zone-this-is-where-you-go-when-you-just-cant-stop-looking-at-pictures-on-facebook/278185/).

Miller, Greg (2014): "Autonomous Cars Will Require a Totally New Kind of Map." In: WIRED, December 15 (http://www.wired.com/2014/12/nokia-here-autonomous-car-maps/).

Nafus, Dawn/Sherman, Jamie (2014): "This One Does Not Go Up To 11: The Quantified Self Movement as an Alternative Big Data Practice." In: International Journal of Communication 8, pp. 1784-1794.

November, Valérie/Camacho-Hübner. Eduardo/Latour, Bruno (2010): "Entering a Risky Territory: Space in the Age of Digital Navigation." In: Environment and Planning D: Society and Space 28/4, pp. 581-599.

Perkins, Chris (2008): "Cultures of Map Use." In: The Cartographic Journal 45/2, pp. 150-58.

Perkins, Chris (2009): "Playing with Maps." In: Martin Dodge/Rob Kitchin/ Chris Perkins (eds.), Rethinking Maps: New Frontiers in Cartographic Theory, London/New York: Routledge, pp. 167-188.

Raessens, Joost (2006): "Playful Identities, or the Ludification of Culture." In: Games and Culture 1/1, pp. 52-57.

Raessens, Joost (2012): Homo Ludens 2.0 The Ludic Turn in Media Theory, Utrecht: Utrecht University (http://igitur-archive.library.uu.nl/oratie/2012-0918-200528/UUindex.html).

Rolighetsteorin (2009): Piano Stairs – TheFunTheory.com – Rolighetsteorin.se (https://www.youtube.com/watch?v=2lXh2noaPyw).

Schüll, Natasha Dow (2014): Addiction by Design: Machine Gambling in Las Vegas. Reprint edition. Princeton: University Press.

Sicart, Miguel (2011): "Against Procedurality." In: Game Studies 11/3 (http://gamestudies.org/1103/articles/sicart_ap).

Sicart, Miguel (2014): Play Matters. Cambridge, MA: The MIT Press.

Tversky, Amos/Kahneman, Daniel (1973): "Availability: A Heuristic for Judging Frequency and Probability." In: Cognitive Psychology 5/2, pp. 207-32.

Woolgar, Steve (1990): "Configuring the User: The Case of Usability Trials." In: The Sociological Review 38/S1, pp. 58-99.

Zajonc, Robert B. (1968): "Attitudinal Effects of Mere Exposure." In: Journal of Personality and Social Psychology 9/2, Pt. 2, pp. 1-27.

Zajonc, Robert B. (1980): "Feeling and Thinking: Preferences Need No Inferences." In: American Psychologist 35/2, pp. 151-75.

My Quantified Self, my FitBit and I
The Polymorphic Concept of Health Data
and the Sharer's Dilemma

Argyro P. Karanasiou and Sharanjit Kang

Abstract

The rise of wearable tech, namely devices with sensors measuring the user's daily activities and habits seems to be suggesting a paradox in the post-Snowden era: On one hand, it is generally accepted that unauthorised use, storage and processing of the user's private data by the state directly clashes with our fundamental rights for privacy; on the other, the user seems to be keen on self-recording and storing one's own data by willingly using sensors, enabling him to learn more about one's habits, general health status or even personality. In the era of wearable tech we seem to be accepting that measuring data is not a privacy infringement but a self-surveillance exercise in a quest to get to know ourselves better, most acute to exercising one's right to free expression. Yet, how is this addressed in legal terms? The focal point for this paper is to address the nascent phenomenon of users actively partaking in the QS movement by wilfully sharing health related datasets. Part 1 notes the transition from the "right to be let alone" to the right to own one's data as the underlying rational for QS: is it a form of expression regarding a tradable commodity in a free market or a matter of greater public importance? Part 2 dissects the dilemma in sharing health data for public health and/or research purposes exceeding the strict limits of private sphere. The unfortunate case of Google Health, the unconstitutional purchase of Iceland's national datasets by deCODE and the mishap of the Care.data are studied to shed light to the many faces of our Quantified Selves: Is the current legislative approach fit for facilitating the QS movement, as a type of self-expression? The paper critically examines self-measurement technologies from a legal perspective and calls for urgent reforms in self-measured data protection.

My Quantified Self, my FitBit and I: Performing Self-Surveillance Exercises in the Post-Snowden Era

The rise of wearable tech, namely devices with sensors measuring the user's daily activities and habits seems to be suggesting a paradox in the post-Snowden era: On the one hand, it is generally accepted that unauthorised use, storage and processing of the user's private data by the state directly clashes with our fundamental rights for privacy; on the other, the user seems to be keen on self-recording and storing one's own data by willingly using sensors, enabling oneself to learn more about general habits, health status or one's own personality. In this sense, it has been suggested that privacy has gradually changed its meaning: in the era of wearable tech we seem to be accepting that measuring data is not a privacy infringement but a self-surveillance exercise, most acute to exercising one's right to freely express oneself. As a result, wearable technology seems to be holding great potential for moving us from the concept of "online surveillance" towards the concept of "sousveillance" (Kurzweil et al. 2013), namely inverse community-based surveillance instead of a state organised act for the public good. In 2003, Mann, Nolan and Wellman published a pioneering study (Mann et al. 2003), whereby it was demonstrated that wearable tech can aid user empowerment and suggest alternative ways of surveillance. Almost twelve years later, it seems that the user is mostly treated as a mere consumer, wanting not to express oneself through the use of wearable tech but simply to get to know himself better (Rettberger 2014).

The focal point of this paper is to establish a broader understanding of the legal right to privacy, identify links and overlapping areas with other fundamental human rights, such as free speech, and explore these within the scope of autonomy-based legal theories. Premised on the hypothesis that privacy in the digital era has a wider reach than a mere entitlement to non-disclosure or identification, the main aim of the paper is to highlight the limited understanding of this right and further demonstrate how this can be problematic, once applied in health-related data. It is therefore intended to critically study here an often overlooked issue: the many faces data can have and how this tends to challenge conventional legal thinking regarding data sharing. To this cause, health-related data furnishes us with a great study case: The polymorphic concept of health data is used in this paper to validate the hypothesis that the legal understanding of privacy is limited and ought to be revised in the digital era. To demonstrate this, the Quantified Self (QS) movement shall serve as a point of departure. Not only is self-monitoring a perfect manifestation of privacy as a right encompassing self-determination but exploring in depth how wearable tech is utilised to monitor one's own data shall further help our understanding of a nascent field of research, which presents a major legal challenge, due to its direct link to health-related data: data sharing. The policy maker is asked to perform a balancing act between privacy *stricto sensu*, and free expression; a redefined legislative framework for regulating health-related data is therefore essential for knowing where to draw the line. Before however this intricate balance is further looked into, it is essential that self-tracking is first explained.

The growing tendency to self-track and quantify has taken off since its start in 2008 when two former *Wired* magazine editors, Gary Wolf and Kevin Kelly, co-founded the "Quantified Self" digital tracking group. The term is now used to describe the mainstream phenomenon of people collecting data as means of recording and analysing their lifestyle (Haddadi/Brown 2014). It is estimated that 60% of US adults are currently tracking their weight, diet and exercise routine (Swan 2013), actively collecting and analysing their data in the context of their individual experiences (Nafus/Sherman 2014). The QS movement has further led on to some revolutionary ways of peer interaction regarding commonly faced health problems: self-measured data can gain added value and potentially provide answers, once joined in larger datasets with similar pools of data. Unlike data mining, data sharing has always been considered as an activity that has the potential to give back to the community. The 2016 Pew Research Center study on privacy and information sharing (Rainie/Page 2016) found that there are a variety of circumstances under which many people would share personal information or permit surveillance in return for getting something of perceived value. With regard to health related information, data sharing can further promote a major public health goal: preventive medicine. As Swan notes "the individual, now through quantified self-tracking and other low-cost newly-available tools, has the ability to understand his or her own patterns and baseline measures, and obtain early warnings as to when there is variance and what to do about this" (Swan 2012: 95). This further translated into a new concept of citizenship: "bio-citizenship", namely people using their self-measured data to promote science and aid predictive medicine, often to the detriment of their own privacy.

The fact that users willingly buy and use wearable tech to monitor their daily activities and overall performance, mood and/or health does not implicitly amount to complete consent to their loss of privacy. They do however often engage in data sharing for reasons of treatment personalisation and crowd-sourcing medicine solutions to common health issues. According to a 2015 study by the University of Southern California's Annenberg Center for the Digital Future and Bovitz Inc. (2015) online privacy and data sharing is an issue of trust for users older than 35, whereas it appears to be a purely opportunistic matter of an informed trade-off for younger users, at an age between 17 and 35. For the latter it is a form of expression regarding a tradable commodity in a free market of online services, for the former data sharing concerns the traditional concept of privacy, namely the right to decide whether to reveal or not personal information to the public sphere.

This suggests clearly that the concept of privacy seems to have changed in the era of wearable tech, its focus shifted from the right to be left alone (Warren/Brandeis 1890) to a right to "own" one's data, either for its value determining a fair trade-off or for its fundamental nature as a human right, enshrined in the constitution. Alex Pentland's "New Deal on Data" (Pentland 2013: 83; Pentland 2011) describes data as an asset that can be "possessed, owned and disposed of" (2011) – this description, reflects the current trend of enabling the user to be in control of his data transactions. Is then data sharing a mere transactional act, perhaps ruled by contractual obligations delineating a tradable commodity or is this strictly a matter of privacy law? Most importantly, each time the user willingly performs a self-surveillance exercise the legal boundaries between free expression and privacy appear somewhat blurred. Would this then seem to be paradoxically suggesting that users are willing to entrust private entities with their data as long as they are free to decide themselves how to trade? And how would this explain the public outcry after the Snowden revelations?

In the remainder of the paper it is suggested that the truth is neither here, nor there. It would be a fallacy, an oversimplified claim to argue that the use of wearable tech amounts to the user's admittance that his privacy rights no longer exist. What is argued instead is that we seem to be moving towards a greater autonomy-based concept of privacy. This explains well why self-surveillance also implies an act of self-expression. This further explains the consideration of ownership rights over one's data (Purtova 2011). The next section provides an account of data sharing as both an act of self-expression with a high social value as well as a transaction involving tradable commodities. It will be shown that – although frequently literature and jurisprudence has discussed data from a privacy angle – personal health data sharing is often dealt with as a legal paradox. From there on the paper urges for a legal framework supporting the safe and secure dissemination of health related data. The next section seeks to elaborate further how personal data entails certain levels of autonomy; a rationale, which underpins both privacy and free expression. It should therefore be noted that user-generated and self-measured data is somewhat broader than a mere right to non-disclosure of personal information and ought to be understood as a clear manifestation of self-determination.

Data as a Manifestation of Autonomy beyond the Realms of Privacy

Following conventional methodology, it would appropriate at this stage to provide a definition of privacy; yet, there is no common consensus among legal scholars as to what this human right might entail (Parker 1973: 275). As Post notes: "Privacy is a value so complex, so entangled in competing and contradictory dimensions, so engorged with various and distinct meanings, that I sometimes despair, whether it can be usefully addressed at all." (2001: 2087). Although privacy is indeed an elusive concept to properly define, it is safe to say that the main concern from a legal point of you is to provide regulative principles for managing the status of one's identity within the overlapping spheres of society, market and the state (cf. Kahn 2003: 372). This understanding of privacy as an entitlement to one's personhood can serve as a point of reference but would still not suffice to provide an accurate definition, especially once privacy is considered within the conceptual scope of another ubiquitous and hardly defined area: big data. The latter, not being touched upon by legal scholars until recently, intensifies the problem of adequately defining privacy in the era of big data (cf. Ward/Barker 2013). The most significant part of the debate though is that data can translate to anything from a legal point of view: information, once seen as data can relate to different rights, not necessarily privacy. What is striking though, is the fact that the principle of autonomy seems to be the underpinning rationale in all these cases. This observation is the argumentative basis for this paper. But before this is further expanded upon with regard to health related data sharing and the QS movement, let's take a closer look at this intricate intersection of privacy and free speech as different sides of the same coin: autonomy.

Free speech theorists have long argued that speech should not be merely considered as a means towards societal progress and collective well-being; it constitutes an intrinsic value indispensable to the individual alone (Rosenfeld 2002: 1535), being an integral part of self-fulfilment and self-realisation of the individual's free potential (Schauer 1982: 49). Applied in the context of big data and wearable tech, these theories document well how the major issue at stake is not the traditional concept of privacy but the wider concept of autonomy, further reflecting on the user's ability to develop and exercise one's own rationality as to how and when to share one's data.

The common ground between the right to free speech and privacy with regard to online data is not identified here for the first time. Jane Bambauer (2014) suggests that, inasmuch data privacy laws control communicatory intellectual interactions among users; data in this context could be treated as speech. This however perplexes matters further when it comes to wearable computing and the QS movement. While users have the ability to monitor themselves and build databases of their daily activities, such data is centrally stored beyond the user's control over data. Should this be regarded speech, then this would effectively grant First Amendment protection to data-brokers and various infomediaries[1], data mining and processing would thus be regarded as expressive conduct to the detriment of the user's autonomy. This scenario would most certainly raise a major constitutional issue, reaching beyond the scope of private sphere, currently reflected in the data protection regime in the EU and the US. Further to this, Seth Kreimer accepts that there seems to be a major overlap between privacy and free speech in data in the sense that whilst data processing can be protected under the First Amendment, there is not always a countervailing privacy interest (Kreimer 2011: 335-409) to limit data processing, mining or storage. This last point highlights well the many faces of personal data, especially when it is health-related: a commodity, which can be very profitable to a handful of players trading datasets, as well as an asset of high societal value.

Alan Westin's work has been influential in linking privacy and autonomy by defining the latter as a right of the individual to define herself for others; privacy in his view, is not merely a matter of disclosure of personal data beyond the private sphere but rather one's right to "information self-determination" (Westin 1967). Westin articulates privacy as the "claim of individuals, groups or institutions to determine for themselves when, how, and to what extent information about them is communicated to others" (ibid: 7). This view maintains a broader scope to a mere right to control one's data: it suggests the ability to self-definition. The latter (right to self-definition) fits comfortably with what has already been discussed thus far with regard to the use of wearable tech and big data, the former (right to control) falls short and cannot be properly applied in an online context (Schwartz 1999: 1609-1701; Schwartz/Reidenberg 1996).

---

1 See for example *Sorrell v. IMS Health Inc.*, No. 10-779 131 S.Ct. 2653 (2011), where the Supreme Court ruled that data mining and pharmaceutical companies exercise their right to free speech under the First Amendment in mining data from clinicians' prescriptions.

The autonomy-based rationale for private data constitutes a paradigmatic shift from the right to be "let alone" (Warren and Brandeis 1890) to a "right to be let to decide alone" how you wish to be defined as an individual. In the context of wearable tech, it becomes apparent that regulation of aggregated data does not balance free speech against privacy but rather aims at defining how liberty-based fundamental rights are to be weighed against the free flow of information for the public (cf. Reidenberg 1999: 1341-1342). In this view, autonomy can be exercised when an individual is presented with choices and makes an informed decision; a concept unfortunately not evident in contemporary data protection regime.

For the time being however, the lawmaker – mostly at a European level – seems to ignore the autonomy argument as a principle underpinning data sharing. The closest legal criterion still in use is consent – this however appears to be narrower than autonomy: A consent-oriented privacy regime unavoidably focuses on the user as a merely passive data subject and not as an active listener/speaker, whose autonomy needs to be guaranteed as a precondition for making informed choices over one's data. The absence of a robust legal framework able to fully protect QS and data sharing has led to a general feeling of fear and mistrust towards processing and storing user-generated health data. The next section examines three cases of health data processing, whereby it is clearly shown that the law is still lagging behind and does not fully perceive nor protect data as an expression of autonomy but regards it a mere tradable commodity.

Trust by Choice: Towards Voluntary Data Heavens

It has so far been contended that privacy seems to have gained a new meaning in the context of the QS movement: the rationale is no longer to keep information secret but to keep a daily log of one's biometric data with a view to learn more about oneself. At the same time, the emergence of various QS communities eager to share and exchange health data for research purposes, adds another dimension to the issue at hand: when shared, data gains added societal value. This, however, does not suggest that data cannot be monetised or be a valuable asset at the same time: the larger the dataset, the more valuable data becomes. At the moment there is a booming industry dealing with storage, processing and mining of health data. Being both a profitable business and a valuable asset for research, health data poses an interesting dilemma: if shared, it is no longer under the user's control; if it remains hidden, research misses out an unprecedented opportunity to significantly contribute to science.

What is suggested here is that data protection should view biometric data within a wider scope of autonomy with a view to maintain the user's autonomy in the era of big data. One of the most significant consequences of the NSA revelations are that the user's trust in the way online communications are handled by the state and the private industry was shaken. The issue of re-establishing trust has been dominating policy making fora ever since: In January 2016, the report entitled "Big Data: A European Survey on Opportunities and Risks on Data

Analytics", commissioned by Vodafone's Institute for Society and Communications (2016), revealed a great gap in trust on how data is being handled online. Under a third of the 8.000 respondents that took part in the survey appear to be convinced that their personal data is being handled in a trustworthy manner: 18 per cent confirmed their trust in telecommunications providers handling data, whereas 43 per cent trust healthcare institutions, 36 per cent trust their employers and 33 per cent trust banks. Trust becomes a delicate matter, especially once health data in particular enters the discussion of big data: the inefficiency of a robust mechanism of protection of such sensitive data plays a key part in the user's absence of trust. The 2015 BMC Medicine report by Wicks and Chiauzzi confirmed this further. Their review of the accredited National Health Service Health Apps Library found "poor and inconsistent implementation of privacy and security, with 28 per cent of apps lacking a privacy policy and one even transmitting personally identifying data the policy claimed would be anonymous" (2015: 205).

The current legal concept of privacy appears to be fairly limited in dealing with this challenge: Health data analytics can be a double edged sword, having a great potential promote science while at the same time posing a great risk to one's privacy. Drawing the right balance between privacy and scientific progress could be a valuable tool towards rebuilding the user's trust as to how his personal data is dealt with online. At the same time, it can hardly be argued that reinstating trust in health data analytics is a task exclusively reserved for either the state or the private sector: both seem to have failed regaining the user's trust online due to the limitations imposed on the user's autonomy. The unfortunate cases of GoogleHealth, Care.data and deCODE's Health Sector Database explored below demonstrate well this point.

Google Health's Unfortunate End: Trust-Building Exercises

In 2008, Google attempted to reach a critical mass of users and interested third parties and offered them the opportunity to self-manage their health information through a summary records platform. After four years of perseverance, the platform was eventually deserted exposing the public's ignorance and lack of interest (cf. Greenhalgh et al. 2010). The official reasons of Google Health failures have never been released and discontinuation in 2011 has since been justified by the lack of participation from its consumers and collaborators[2]. That said, the rejection of Google Health platform signifies that the lack of robust governance and legislative provisions in place to monitor the access and sharing of sensitive data that fuel the anxieties and evidently led to the reluctance in embracing Google Health. A username and password would activate an individual account where participants could enter their health conditions, medications, allergies and lab results and build a personal health records profile.

---

[2] "An update on Google Health and Google PowerMeter", June 24, 2011 (https://googleblog.blogspot.co.uk/2011/06/update-on-google-health-and-google.html).

Medical records and prescriptions from any of Google's partner hospitals and pharmacies could be imported- however, this potentially highlighted another flaw as there were not enough collaborators within the network embracing the platform.

Predominantly, it became clear individuals felt, and arguably still feel, uncomfortable with the idea of a multinational commercial entity accessing personal health records (cf. Spil/Klein 2014). Principally, Google's privacy policy, "We believe that your health information belongs to you, and you should decide how much you share and whom you share it with [...]. We store your information securely and privately"[3] did not offer proportionate procedural safeguards to reassure its users in failing to detail what they meant by 'securely' and 'privately.' Users were given the option to share their health records with third parties friends, family and doctors with the safeguard that they could always see who had access of their information and permission can be revoked at any time. However, the crux was that once permission was revoked it was implausible to monitor and control who had access to the records as Google could not account for any copies made by third parties who were not governed by privacy regulations during the time permission was valid and the websites that had been linked to a personal health records. Therefore, Google claimed not to assume liability for the information. Competitors such as *Microsoft HealthVault* made bold gestures in joining the Coalition for Patient Privacy[4], committing to the seventeen principles for privacy; whereas Google failed to offer the same level of reassurance and relied solely on their website announcements. Further scrutiny of the fine print revealed Google may share the data patients store on Google Health for the purposes of enabling additional features for other Google products (Tanne 2008: 1207-1211). The general consensus was that the benefit to Google Health outweighed any personal benefit the individuals would receive from sharing their data and the lack of trust between the commercial entity and the public inevitably contributed to its downfall.

Ironically, the Google Inc. offering, which on the surface had the advantage of delivering the scalability required, in reality served as a double edged sword as Google did not only fail to achieve the visibility for the platform to gather a substantial following needed to make the project a success; but with a profit making agenda it aroused concerns around the rigidity of the contemporary data protection safeguards in place. The strength of the safeguards that sought to protect the privacy of its consumers in the face of challenge were questioned. Ultimately, there was a lack of confidence in the intentions of Google and suspicion surrounding the possible intentions behind gathering vast amount of health data, stored in central databases.

---

3   http://hexus.net/ce/news/general/13383-google-health-launches-plans-manage-well-being/.

4   "Coalition for Patient Privacy", June 13, 2015 (https://patientprivacyrights.org/coalition-patient-privacy/).

It is clear Google has not admitted defeat due to the announcement of 2015, introducing Google X[5], the company's plans for developing a new wearable wristband able to detect, monitor and store data such as pulse, heart rhythm and skin temperature. However, the approach is now different: the company will be seeking regulatory approval for its use in medical contexts, i.e. as a medical device prescribed to patients are used in clinical trials. In other words, the business model seems to be moving from mere collection of data in a central database to a peer-to-peer (patient to doctor) architecture, whereby data is treated as a valuable asset that can be freely exchanged to serve scientific research as well as the patients themselves. This venture is added to a long list of similar initiatives: Apple's *Research Kit*[6], allowing the use of iPhones as medical diagnostic devices by the user without the company's direct involvement is another such example. All these business initiatives, share a very similar pattern: instead of merely performing data mining exercises (often without the user's knowledge or consent), they are mostly interested in enabling user empowerment to share one's data in a decentralized manner. In doing so encouraging users to participate would only improve the quality and quantity of data and if willingly shared, reduce the red tape on the use.

The implications for the trust relationship between these corporations and individuals have somewhat become obscure and almost ignored. It seems corporations such as Google are attempting to bypass the hurdle of establishing trust with their users organically and the rationale now to further their means seems to utilize the patient and doctor relationship. Mostly, whether the more user activity enhances the transparency of its use is yet to be identified.

Care.data: A National Failure to Build a Database

Contrary to Google Health, Care.data was a state run project that had no involvement of private actors. In a highly data driven society, the debacle of Care.data in the UK, examined whether it is possible to strike the right balance between encouragement of the biotechnology industry and protection of the genetic history of citizens (Rodriguez et al. 2013: 276). Once again, public concern regarding medical data privacy halted the plans of the National Health Service in the UK to create a centralized health-care database. The legal framework in place offered little guarantees for the data subject's autonomy: the Health and Social Care Act 2012 enabled the creation of a central database amassing all clinicians' records, while third party usage was justified under the pretext of

---

5 "Google's new wearable tracks vital signs for medicine", June 23, 2015 (http://www.techradar.com/news/wearables/google-s-new-wearable-tracks-vital-signs-for-medicine-1297586).

6 "Apple ResearchKit Turns iPhones Into Medical Diagnostic Devices", March 9, 2015 (http://techcrunch.com/2015/03/09/apple-introduces-researchkit-turning-iphones-into-medical-diagnostic-devices).

pseudonymised HSCIC[7] datasets. This clearly undermined the right of individuals to make their own informed decisions on healthcare matters.

Moreover, the clinician's lack of clarity and understanding on the legal standards of protection (McGraw 2013: 34) could pose significant privacy threats: in the absence of ample restrictions, other commercial organisations outside the pharmaceutical industry could have unethically and unlawfully accessed the database[8]. Despite the fact that the opt-out policy was later reversed by the NHS, the failures of this project were reflected in the mere 29% of adult population recalling the leaflet[9] and only a total 19% supporting it[10]. The fears amongst scholars that the lack of commitment the government has shown on protection of rights in the Care.data project may compromise public trust in research remain very much valid. At the time of the writing, extraction of data is taking place in the UK while the UK's national data guardian Fiona Caldicott has been entrusted with the task to evaluate the fair processing testing communications. In the meanwhile, Care.data is currently being redesigned, along with a number of additional digital services that the NHS is building, following a "crowd coursed" model of online patient care. Note for example, the *Friends and Family Test* (FFT), a dataset of people's comments and ratings of local hospitals[11].

The 2014 Royal Statistical Society "Data Manifesto" puts particular stress on the importance of data sharing encouraging the free and open access of the citizens to national datasets. In dissecting the Care.data debacle the three core issues that were posed began with the extraction of personal confidential data: the processing of the personal confidential data and finally the onward of disclosure of data. When the opt-in selection has been made, the consent hurdle immediately is forgone. In contrast; the doctrine of autonomy is impacted when the individuals are deprived of further regulating any third parties utilizing their personal data in any which way. As previously noted in the Google Health case, the absence of transparency, guidelines and best practises for clinicians and provisions for health related data exchange, are once again a great hindrance to data sharing. It becomes apparent the more confined the control an individual has over the sharing and use of their healthcare data; the greater the hindrance to their autonomy. However, as it will be shown in the next case study, restoring trust is not merely an issue of being able to build a database relying on a robust infrastructure.

---

7   Health and Social Care Information Center.
8   For example, GE Data Visualization uses information based on 7.2 million patient records from GE's proprietary database, 2011 (http://senseable.mit.edu/healthinfoscape/); Cf. http://www3.gehealthcare.co.uk/.
9   "Adults Unaware of NHS Data Plans", February 14, 2014 (http://www.bbc.co.uk/news/health-26187980).
10 "Three in Four GPs Believe Care.data Should be 'Opt In'", February 26, 2014 (http://www.pulsetoday.co.uk/your-practice/practice-topics/it/three-in-four-gps-believe-caredata-should-be-opt-in/20005954.article).
11 For more details see http://www.nhs.uk/NHSEngland/AboutNHSservices/Pages/nhs-friends-and-family-test.aspx.

DeCODE Disaster: Demystifying the De-Identification Myth

Iceland has been described as "the world's greatest genetic laboratory"[12]: the homogeneity of its population means less genetic variation, which offers an ideal environment for geneticists wishing to conduct medical research based on genome sequencing. Decode Genetics Inc., a for-profit American corporation, published in 2015 four papers in Nature Genetics[13], whereby the findings of sequencing genomes of 2,636 Icelanders (almost 1 % of the total population) were presented. In doing so, the company built one of the most impressive and valuable datasets of genomes, able to contribute significantly towards identifying the genetics of common diseases.

DeCODE's efforts however have been met with lot of scepticism and the way to building their database has not been paved with gold: the company, rose from its ashes in 2012, after it had to file for bankruptcy in 2009 due to its questionable business practises and commercial exploitation of the data mined. The initial plan of the company to raise funds from the public by selling shares to their central database containing health information fell apart, when the law allowing for the creation of their database was found unconstitutional. The company was never able to build the database promised for and did not deliver their public offering.

In order to construct its database, deCODE proposed to collect data from medical records via publicly accessible genealogies, hospitals and health centres and finally from research for which a form of consent was required to be compiled into a *Health Sector Database*[14] The Act on a Health Sector Database (No. 139/1998) was passed by the Icelandic Parliament on December 17th, 1998, after extensive debates in the Parliament and the society at large. The Bill was heavily criticized on numerous counts, including that it lacked provisions for obtaining informed consent of individuals whose information was included in the database, undermined scientific freedom, restrained competition, eroded the doctor-patient confidential relationship, and invaded individuals' right to privacy (Adalsteinsson 2003: 203; Andor 2003: 204). Soon afterwards, DeCODE went into an agreement with the Icelandic State to pay an annual fee in return for being granted a 12 year exclusive license for operating the HSD.

In 2003, the Iceland Supreme Court's Gubmundsdottir v. Iceland,[15] held the compilation of personal health records and available genetic information in one electronic database unconstitutional, unless each individual specifically indicated

---

12   "Why Iceland Is the World's Greatest Genetic Laboratory", March 25, 2015 (http://www.wired.com/2015/03/iceland-worlds-greatest-genetic-laboratory/).
13   "deCODE Publishes Largest Human Genome Population Study", March 25, 2015 (http://www.bio-itworld.com/2015/3/25/decode-publishes-largest-human-genome-population-study.html).
14   From this point on referred to as HSD.
15   No. 151/2003, Part IV.

otherwise in a pre-defined six-month window unlawful.[16] The database was to include information on children, deceased persons, and incompetent individuals, all of whom are unable to legally provide informed consent to the use of their personal information. The Icelandic Supreme Court[17] held that the HSD Bill did not grant a proportionately adequate protection to the information it was set to contain as demanded by the sensitivity of the information.

The fact that genetic information may reveal medical information not only pertaining to the subject herself but also to relatives was used to argue that genetic information is different and more intrusive than other forms of traditional medical information. In its analysis of the HSD Act, the Icelandic Supreme Court found additional flaws with the Act's protection mechanisms of personal privacy; concluding that the one-way coding mechanism established by the HSD Act is insufficient for protecting individuals' privacy. The Supreme Court's reasoning was two-fold: first, the Act provided no specific guidance as to what type of information must be encrypted in this manner; and second, the Court interpreted the license to imply that after the deletion of an individuals' name and address only personal identification number needed to be encrypted. In effect, although records were be 'de-identified' by removing the name and address and replacing with encrypting the social security number, the encryption done outside control of Roche, they would be linked to genetic, family data. As a result identification would be very easy, given that Iceland would provide a tight context for the data under review- Iceland easy to identify. The Act presumed the consent of patients to release their records to deCODE. Individuals thus must affirmatively opt out in order to prevent their data from being recorded in the health sector database[18] (cf. Árnason 2007).

Predominately, deCODE aspired to rely on theoretical protection of de-identification to reap the benefits of analytics, meanwhile avoiding denunciation for breaching individual privacy. The "silver bullet," (Tene/Polonetsky 2012: 257) of pseudonymisation, anonymisation, encryption and various forms of key-coding was relied on by deCODE to distance data from personal identities in order to justify the secondary uses of personal data. There seems to be a presumption that de-identification and anonymisation renders identification impossible (Ohm 2010: 270). However, it needs to be reiterated that it takes only 33 bits of information to identify a human[19]. The practical problems of medical data allows for linking episodes into longitudinal records, most patients can be re-identified through the 'Incremental Effect' (Narayanan/Shmatikov 2008: 119), where any

---

16   The HSD Act provided a six-month grace period beginning with the passage of the Act, in which people could choose to opt-out of the project. HSD Act, supra note 11, art. 8. See also infra section IV.A.3.

17   ibid. 5

18   Cf. "Iceland's Research Resources: The Health Sector Database, Genealogy Databases, and Biobanks", NIH Paper, June 1, 2014 (http://grants.nih.gov/grants/icelandic_research.pdf).

19   Cf. "The End of Anonymous Data and What to Do about It", 33 Bits of Entropy, February 5, 2016 (http://33bits.org/about/).

piece of data that has been linked to a person's real identity breaks anonymity and is irreversible. However, New Zealand, demonstrates such a database can effectively exist only when a small number of health service statisticians are permitted to access limited enquiry results of up to six patients at a time in the National Medical Data Set (Neame 1997: 225). The encrypted social security numbers are not considered alone an adequate inference security; (Anderson 1998: 4; Denning 1983; Information/Privacy Commissioner, Ontario, Canada, and Registratiekammer: 1995) special administrative measures are appointed through regulation and data protection legislation with independent government agencies for protection.

It was not until several years later, in 2015, that deCODE (whole owned and operated by Amgen) managed to accumulate genetic data of almost half of the Icelandic population and thus be able to identify people at risk of potential developing a genetic disease. Having failed at receiving legal approval to mine data without consent, deCODE built a research database using clinical data of a large sample of volunteers. If there are any lessons to be learned from deCODE's mishaps is that open data – when addressed as from the perspective of the user and not merely mined and stored into a centralised database – can be of particular significance for advancing scientific research. De-anonymisation and consent have been proven to be the first point of action when lawmakers are faced with health related data mining; yet, how effective are they for protecting the data subject's privacy? Most importantly: at what cost? It is therefore imperative that we further consider the impediment to scientific progress, especially when voluntary schemes of open data exchange can pave the way towards a new system of collecting health related data for national databases.

The next section dissects the issue of monetisation of personal data and seeks to explain how a narrow concept of privacy will not only restore the user's trust but can further pose a significant threat to the QS movement and open data.

Sharing is Caring?
The Monetisation of Health Data and the Sharer's Dilemma

The unfortunate cases of online data repositories discussed, highlight that health related data, once perceived as a tradable commodity, poses a significant challenge for privacy scholars: it is no longer one's privacy that is at stake but the user's ability to determine the flow of his personal data. As noted above, autonomy has been identified by legal scholars as one of the underpinning rationales for privacy as well as free speech. It can further be argued that not allowing the user to maintain a certain level of "informational autonomy", namely the ability to control one's personal data flow, can be detrimental to his privacy and undermine any benefits that health data analytics might have.[20] The

---

20   "Privacy and data protection laws are premised on individual control over information and on principles such as data minimization and purpose limitation. Yet it is not clear that minimizing information collection is always a practical approach

QS movement are a clear manifestation of how the user's autonomy ought to be the basis of a robust data protection legislative framework.

In the early days of wearable tech, user empowerment was the main objective for building an interconnected environment of things and sensors, able to facilitate the needs of the consumer in an automated manner. In 1998 Mann observed: "The most fundamental issue in WearComp [wearable computing] is no doubt that of personal empowerment through its ability to equip the individual with a personalised, customisable operation space owned, operated and controlled by the wearer" (Mann 1998: 2128). Since then, wearable technology has proven to be a profitable business, an industry expected to reach $11.61 billion in revenues by the end of 2020 (Markets and Markets Report 2015). As a result, data is not simply a private or public matter but also a commercial product; a tradable commodity that is part of the daily transactions of several info-mediaries and data-brokers. The recent FTC[21] report from May 2014 "Data Brokers: A Call for Transparency and Accountability" urges the Congress to enhance transparency and user's control over their data (FTC 2014)[22]. That said, instead of user empowerment, the current legislative framework appears to disregard the concept of autonomy. On the other side of the Atlantic, a series of recently leaked proposals (February 2015) for data protection implementation, show that Member States are determined to carve out major guarantees for online privacy offered in the European Commission's proposal for the purposes of an "overriding public interest" (recital 30) or for "scientific purposes". In fact, the leaked documents go as far as re-introducing profiling (originally deleted after the European Parliament's approved text of the proposal in 2014) as an accepted limitation to privacy on grounds of national security, defence, public security and even "other important objectives of general public interest"[23]. This can be an alarming prospect once examined within the context of wearable tech: as noted in the 2015 Nuffield Council on Bioethics report "the bulwarks that have hitherto protected a satisfactory and workable accommodation of interests, principally, the de-identification of data and the 'informed' consent of data 'subjects', have been substantially weakened in a hyper-connected (or potentially hyper-connectable) 'big data' world" (Report of the Nuffield Council on Bioethics 2015).

to privacy in the age of big data. The principles of privacy and data protection must be balanced against additional societal values such as public health, national security and law enforcement, environmental protection, and economic efficiency. A coherent framework would be based on a risk matrix, taking into account the value of different uses of data against the potential risks to individual autonomy and privacy." (Tene/Polonetsky 2012: 67)

21 Federal Trade Commission, hereafter referred to as FTC.
22 FTC (2015): "Data Brokers: A Call for Transparency and Accountability", May 1, 2014 (https://www.ftc.gov/system/files/documents/reports/data-brokers-call-transparency-accountability-report-federal-trade-commission-may-2014/140527databroker report.pdf).
23 For a detailed analysis on the leaked documents see EDRi/Access/Panoptykon/ Foundation/Privacy International (2015).

The importance of this in the case of wearable tech and QS is evident once we consider the merits of open data for epidemiology (cf. Barrett et al. 2013): open data in the public domain seems to be gaining some ground in the US and the UK (Business, Innovation and Skills Committee 3rd special report 2013). At the same time though, centralisation is identified as the main obstacle for protecting the user's privacy, carrying the danger of data abuses. This is clearly evidenced in the 2015 Nuffield Report, which states:

"Whereas standardisation is desirable and technical interoperability essential for linking separately collected and maintained datasets, the drive towards exploitation of public data in the UK has, additionally, involved the consolidation and centralisation of some data resources in so-called 'safe havens' for health and public sector data. [...] Although centralisation is convenient for the extraction of value through the application of data analysis, consolidated databases create large targets for unauthorised technical access, unauthorised access by insiders, or abuse of authorised access at the behest of powerful lobbyists" (Report of the Nuffield Council on Bioethics 2015).

The Road Ahead: Quantified Selves and Data Protection Policies

The QS movement and the numerous cases of users wilfully sharing data amongst various online fora, show that data sharing is clearly an act of self-expression, which is in need of robust legal protection: de-anonymisation and consent do not help the users to regain trust but appear to be limited measures offering little protection to open data initiatives.

Unfortunately, the current data protection regime appears to be fragmented and distanced from the notion of autonomy. On one hand the US approach to privacy has been market dominated, reflecting a policy oriented towards treating privacy under consumer rights (Reidenberg 1999). On the other, EU policy for data protection, although reflecting at large a rights-based approach, seems most preoccupied with the enforcement of its regulation in the cloud for strengthening national commercial interests and less concerned with maintaining the user's autonomy as such. According to the Data Protection Directive, a company may process private information on the basis of consent of the user (data subject). Article 29 Working Party has further described that consent is required to be freely given, implicitly and most importantly informed (Opinion 15/2011 on the Definition of Consent 2011: WP187). An informed consent although by definition presupposes a certain level of autonomy to reach a decision, is not easy to grant or legally assess when discussing the use of ubiquitous technologies. In its 2014 report the Working Party has expressed concerns over the problematic applicability of consent within the remit of wearable tech: The fact that an automated system prioritises the ease of a seamless system over constantly informing the user about how his data is collected and processed can further pose a significant barrier to demonstrating valid consent under EU law, as the data subject must be informed" (Opinion 8/2014 on the Recent Developments on the Internet of Things 2014: WP223). Is this a structural deficiency of the networked environment or an unprecedented legal challenge? It seems that the truth is neither here nor there: the rapid centralisation of datasets, evident in the case studies mentioned above, when combined with a limited range of choices for the user to control processing of his data lies at the heart of the problem.

This paper has sought to explain how boosting the user's autonomy should be the focal point of data protection. The QS movement is a tangible proof of how users are keen to build own datasets and be part of the data processing cycle, joining state and private entities. In this vein, the need for interoperability (Palfrey/Gasser 2012) and data portability is evident. There seems to be a growing interest in data portability in the EU, namely the user's ability to transfer her own data across platforms. This has now been included in article 15 of the Commission's revised proposal[24], which provides that where personal data is processed by electronic means, the user has the right to obtain a copy of their personal data in a "commonly used", "electronic and interoperable" format. Although the concept of interoperability in general is associated at large with copyright law and perhaps appears loosely linked to data protection, its importance for human rights in the digital era can be best demonstrated through the potential it holds for restoring autonomy in online communications.

This last point, arguing for a user-centric internet, seems to be not only supporting an autonomy-based policy model for free speech but for other rights as well, such as privacy. There seems to be a growing tendency to exploit the internet architecture for allowing the user the right to be in sole control of his data shared online, be it speech or personal data. Take for example the concept of privacy by design[25], namely the adoption of privacy enhancing technologies in engineering systems, set out by the Information & Privacy Commissioner of Ontario, Canada, Ann Cavoukian[26] since the early 1990s. Or consider the latest MIT media lab's venture (cf. De Montjoye et al. 2014) open PDS (Personal Data Store): a system that stores data in a repository controlled by the end user, not the application developer or service provider.

The three case studies explored in this paper demonstrate further how data in itself is thus either a valuable tool or a potential threat to the user's fundamental rights. What is suggested here is a positive rights-based approach to maintain a decentralised encrypted networked environment, able to guarantee a certain level of autonomy for the user. Instead of focusing narrowly on protecting one's privacy at the expense of informational flow and free expres-

---

24 European Parliament legislative resolution of 12 March 2014 on the proposal for a regulation of the European Parliament and of the Council on the protection of individuals with regard to the processing of personal data and on the free movement of such data.

25 "Privacy-Enhancing Technologies: The Path to Anonymity", Information/Privacy Commissioner, Ontario, Canada, and Registratiekammer, The Netherlands, August 2, 1995 (https://www.ipc.on.ca/images/Resources/anoni-v2.pdf).

26 "Cavoukian's Seven Foundational Principles of the Concept of Privacy by Design", March 3, 2015 (http://www.privacybydesign.ca/content/uploads/2009/08/7foundationalprinciples.pdf).

sion, it is imperative to look at the matter in a contextualised positive manner towards boosting autonomy through a user-centric networked environment.

Acknowledgements

We wish to thank the editors and the anonymous reviewers for all the comments provided. All errors and omissions remain the sole responsibility of the authors.

References

Adalsteinsson, Ragnar (2003): "Human Genetic Databases and Liberty." In: The Juridical Review 2004/1, pp. 65-74.

Anderson, Ross (1998): "The DeCODE Proposal for an Icelandic Health Database". In: Loeknabladhidh (the Icelandic Medical Journal) 84/11, pp. 874-875.

Árnason, Garðar (2007): "Icelandic Biobank. A Report for GenBenefit" (www.uclan.ac.uk/genbenefit).

Article 29 Working Party, Opinion 15/2011 on the Definition of Consent (WP 187), 13 July 2011.

Article 29 Working Party. Opinion 8/2014 on the Recent Developments on the Internet of Things (WP223), 16 September 2014.

Bambauer, Jane R. (2014): "Is Data Speech?" In: Stanford Law Review 66, pp. 65-120.

Barrett, Meredith A./Humblet, Olivier/Hiatt, Robert A./Adler, Nancy E. (2013): "Big Data and Disease Prevention: From Quantified Self to Quantified Communities." In: Big Data 1/3, pp. 168-175.

Business, Innovation and Skills Committee 3rd special report (2013): "Open Access: Responses to the Committee's Fifth Report", March 3, 2013 (http://www.publications.parliament.uk/pa/cm201314/cmselect/cmbis/833/83302.htm).

De Montjoye, Yves-Alexandre/Shmueli, Erez/Wang, Samuel S./Pentland, Alex (2014): "OpenPDS: Protecting the Privacy of Metadata through SafeAnswers." In: PLoS ONE 9/7, pp. e98790.

Denning, Dorothy (1983):"Cryptography and Data Security", Boston: Addison-Wesley.

FTC (2015): "Data Brokers: A Call for Transparency and Accountability", May 1, 2014 (https://www.ftc.gov/system/files/documents/reports/data-brokers-call-transparency-accountability-report-federal-trade-commission-may-2014/140527databrokerreport.pdf).

Greenhalgh, Trisha/Stramer, Katja/Bratan, Tanja/Byrne, Emma/Russell, Jill/Potts, Henry W. (2010): "Adoption and Non-Adoption of a Shared Electronic Summary Record in England: a Mixed-Method Case Study." In: BMJ, n. p.

Haddadi, Hamed/Brown, Ian (2014): "Quantified Self and the Privacy Challenge", SCL Technology Law Futures Forum, August 2014 (http://www.eecs.qmul.ac.uk/~hamed/papers/qselfprivacy2014.pdf).

Kahn, Jonathan D. (2003): "Privacy as a Legal Principle of Identity Maintenance." In: Seton Hall Law Review 33/2, pp. 371-410.
Kreimer, Seth F. (2011): "Pervasive Image Capture and the First Amendment: Memory, Discourse, and the Right to Record." In: University of Pennsylvania Law Review 159/2, pp. 335-409.
Kurzweil, Ray/Minsky, Marvin/Mann, Steve/Bell, Gordon/Nissenbaum, Helen (2013): "The Society of Intelligent Veillance." In: IEEE International Symposium on Technology and Society: Social Implications of Wearable Computers and Augmented Reality in Everyday Life, June 2013, Ontario, Canada.
Mann, Steve (1998): "Humanistic Computing: 'WearComp' as a New Framework and Application for Intelligent Signal Processing." In: Proceedings of the IEEE 86/11, pp. 2123-2151.
Mann, Steve/Nolan, Jason/Wellman, Berry (2003): "Sousveillance: Inventing and Using Wearable Computing Devices." In: Surveillance & Society 1/3, pp. 331-335.
Markets and Markets Report (2015): "Wearable Electronics and Technology Market by Applications (Consumer, Healthcare, Enterprise), Products (Eyewear, Wristwear, Footwear), Form Factors and Geography – Analysis & Forecast to 2014 – 2020", March 3, 2015 (http://www.marketsandmarkets.com/Market-Reports/wearable-electronics-market-983.html).
McGraw, Deven, (2013): "Building Public Trust in Uses of Health Insurance Portability and Accountability Act de-identified Data." In: Journal of the American Medical Informatics Association 20/1, pp. 29-34.
Nafus, Dawn/Sherman, Jamie (2014): "Big Data, Big Questions. This One Does Not Go Up To 11: The Quantified Self Movement as an Alternative Big Data Practice." In: International Journal of Communication 8, pp. 1784-1794.
Narayanan, Arvind/Shmatikov, Vitaly (2008): "Robust de-anonymization of Large Sparse Datasets." In: IEEE Symposium on Security and Privacy, pp. 111-125.
Neame, Roderick (1997): "Smart Cards-the Key to Trustworthy Health Information Systems" In: BMJ 314/7080, p. 573.
Ohm, Paul (2010): "Broken Promises of Privacy: Responding to the Surprising Failure of Anonymization." In: UCLA Law Review 57, p. 1701-1777.
Palfrey, John/Gasser, Urs (2012): Interop: The promise and perils of highly interconnected systems, New York: Basic Books.
Parker, Richard B. (1973): "A Definition of Privacy." In: Rutgers Law Review 27/2, pp. 275-296.
Pentland, Alex (2011): "Personal Data: The Emergence of a New Asset Class." In: WEF Report (http://www3.weforum.org/docs/WEF_ITTC_PersonalDataNewAsset_Report_2011.pdf).
Pentland, Alex (2013): "The Data Driven Society." In: Scientific American 309/4, pp. 78-83.
Post, Robert (2001): "Three Concepts of Privacy." In: Georgetown Law Journal 89, pp. 2087-2098.
Purtova, Nadezhda (2011): Property Rights in Personal Data: A European Perspective, Alphen aan den Rijn: Wolters Kluwer.

Rainie, Lee/Duggan, Maeve (2015): "Privacy and Information Sharing", Pew Research Center (http://www.pewinternet.org/2016/01/14/2016/Privacy-and-Information-Sharing/).

Reidenberg, Joel (1999): "Resolving Conflicting International Data Privacy Rules in Cyberspace." In: Stanford Law Review 52, pp. 1315-1371.

EDRi/Access/Panoptykon Foundation/Privacy International (2015): "Data Protection: Broken Badly", Report by Access, EDRi, Panoptykon Foundation and Privacy International, March 3, 2015 (https://edri.org/files/DP_BrokenBadly.pdf).

Report of the Nuffield Council on Bioethics (2015): "The Collection, Linking and Use of Data in Biomedical Research and Health Care: Ethical Issues", March 3, 2015 (http://nuffieldbioethics.org/wp-content/uploads/Biological_and_health_data_web.pdf).

Rettberger, Jill W. (2014): Seeing Ourselves Through Technology How We Use Selfies, Blogs and Wearable Devices to See and Shape Ourselves, Hampshire: Palgrave Macmillan.

Rodriguez, Laura L./Brooks, Lisa D./Greenberg, Judith H./Green, Eric D. (2013): "The Complexities of Genomic Identifiability." In: Science 339/6117, pp. 275-276.

Rosenfeld, Michel (2002): "Hate Speech in Constitutional Jurisprudence: A Comparative Analysis." In: Cardozo Law Review 24, pp. 1523-1562.

Royal Statistical Society (2014): "The Data Manifesto", September 10, 2015 (http://www.statslife.org.uk/images/pdf/rss-data-manifesto-2014.pdf).

Sándor, Judit (2003): "Society and Genetic Information: Codes and Laws in the Genetic Era." Budapest: Central European University Press.

Schauer, Frederick (1982): Free Speech: A Philosophical Enquiry, Cambridge: Cambridge University Press.

Schwartz, Paul (1999): "Privacy and Democracy in Cyberspace." In: Vanderbilt Law Review 52, pp. 1609-1701.

Schwartz, Paul/Reidenberg, Joel (1996): Data Privacy Law: A Study of US Data Protection, Charlottsville: Lexis Law.

Spil, Ton/Klein, Rich (2014): "Personal Health Records Success: Why Google Health Failed and What Does that Mean for Microsoft HealthVault?" In: System Sciences (HICSS) 47, pp. 2818-2827.

Swan, Melanie (2012): "Health 2050: The Realization of Personalized Medicine through Crowdsourcing, the Quantified Self, and the Participatory Biocitizen." In: JMP 2/3, pp. 93-118.

Swan, Melanie (2013): "The Quantified Self: Fundamental Disruption in Big Data Science and Biological Discovery." In: Big Data 1/2, pp. 85-99.

Tanne, Janice (2008): "Google launches free electronic health records service for patients." In: BMJ 336/7655, pp. 1207-1211.

Tene, Omer/Polonetsky, Jules (2012): "Privacy in the Age of Big Data: a Time for Big Decisions." In: Stanford Law Review Online 64, pp. 63-69.

University of Southern California's Annenberg Center for Digital Future and Bovitz.Inc Report (2015): "Surveying the Digital Future", December 10, 2014 (http://www.digitalcenter.org/wp-content/uploads/2013/06/2015-Digital-Future-Report.pdf).

Vodafone Institute for Society and Communications (2016): "Big Data: A European Survey on Opportunities and Risks of Data Analytics", January 3, 2016 (http://www.vodafone-institut.de/wp-content/uploads/2016/01/VodafoneInstitute-Survey-BigData-en.pdf).

Ward, Jonathan S./Barker, Adam (2013): "Undefined by Data: a Survey of Big Data Definitions." In: arXiv preprint arXiv: 1309.5821.

Warren, Samuel D./Brandeis, Louis D. (1890): "The Right to Privacy." In: Harvard Law Review 4/5, pp. 193-220.

Westin, Alan F. (1967): Privacy and Freedom, New York: Atheneum.

Wicks, Paul/Chiauzzi, Emil (2015): "Trust but Verify – Five Approaches to Ensure Safe Medical Apps." In: BMC Medicine 13, n. p.

Entering the Field

How Old am I?
Digital Culture and Quantified Ageing

Barbara L. Marshall and Stephen Katz

Abstract

In previous work we argued that ageing bodies and changes across the life-course were becoming measured, standardised, and treated according to a new logic of functionality, supplanting traditional categories of normality (Katz/Marshall 2004). In particular, the binary between the 'functional' and the 'dysfunctional' has become a powerful tool in mapping and distributing bodies around data-points, functional subsystems, and posthuman informatics. In this paper, we extend this line of analysis by exploring how current developments in self-tracking technologies and the proliferation of digital apps are creating new modes and styles of 'quantified ageing'. In particular, we identify four interrelated fields for inquiry that are specifically relevant in setting out a research agenda on ageing quantified selves and statistical bodies: 1) 'Wearables' and mobile technologies, including both technologies designed for self-monitoring/self-improvement (health, fitness, sleep, mood and so on) and those designed for surveillance of and 'management' of ageing individuals by children, caregivers or institutions. 2) Digital apps, including those that collect and connect data uploaded from wearable devices, and those that deploy various algorithms for 'calculating' age and its correlates. 3) The rhetorics of games and scores in age-related apps such as those used in digital 'brain training' games that track a person's imagined cognitive plasticity and enhancement, while promising protection against memory loss and even dementia. 4) The political economy of data sharing, aggregation and surveillance of ageing populations. Conclusions ponder wider sociological questions; for example, how will the insurance industry acquire and use data from digital health technologies to produce new actuarial standards? How will older individuals plan their futures according to the risks assembled through quantifying technologies? We argue that the technical turn to new ways of quantifying and standardising measurements of age raises a range of complex and important questions about ageism, agency and inequality.

Introduction

Researchers in ageing studies have recently moved away from biological and biomedical models of age to re-imagine the complex subjective and culturally mediated ways in which age is embodied, measured, and expressed in multiple and non-chronological ways. At the same time, the proliferation of new consumer and health technologies aimed at enabling self-knowledge and self-tracking has raised important ethical and sociological questions about measurement, standardisation, surveillance, risk-management, selfhood and sociality. These questions are of great relevance to ageing populations and individuals as their healthcare supports shift from governmental to individual realms of responsibility. However, age has been largely neglected in the rapidly-expanding research community exploring these technologies.

In previous work we argued that ageing bodies and changes across the life-course were becoming measured, standardised, and treated according to a new logic of *functionality*, supplanting traditional categories of normality (Katz/Marshall 2004). In this contribution, we extend this line of analysis by suggesting that current developments in self-tracking technologies and the proliferation of digital apps are creating new modes and styles of 'quantified ageing'.

We begin by drawing on recent work in cultural gerontology on the complexities of measuring age in contemporary biosocial regimes, and then sketch out some interrelated fields for inquiry that are specifically relevant in setting out a research agenda on *ageing* quantified selves and statistical bodies

Cultural Gerontology and the Recalibration of Age

Sociologists of post-traditional society contend that the conventional stages of life have become contingent and negotiable. New work, retirement, residence and intergenerational relations have created conditions whereby the experience of ageing is no longer chiefly defined by chronological age. Cultural gerontologists have argued that the current blurring of life-course identities, the longevity stretch in population ageing, the globalisation of ageing spaces, the popularity of anti-ageing industries and the new contingencies around life transitions have rendered the measuring of human ageing increasingly indeterminate in the wake of a postmodern life course (Gilleard/Higgs 2005; Katz 2005; Katz 2014; Marshall 2015). While even the gerontological sciences have struggled with alternative, non-chronological age definitions (Moreira 2015a; 2015b), age is still being measured and quantified via a pervasive logic of functional age grounded in the aggregation of physical capacities. In particular, the binary between the 'functional' and the 'dysfunctional' has become a powerful tool in mapping and distributing bodies around data-points, functional subsystems, and posthuman informatics, making bodies available to a wide variety of techniques of measurement, standardization and intervention (Katz/Marshall 2004). While functional age may appear to diversify ageing and liberate it from the constraints of chronological biomarkers, its mapping of the ageing body is aligned to our ageist culture that reduces the social determinants of ageing to matters of individual choice and responsibility. What have been termed 'biosocial' technologies produce images of life, including ageing, as infinitely modifiable and open to being optimized (Hogle 2005; 2007; Rose 2007). Neoliberal styles of self-care redistribute the capacities of the body across a wider biosocial order of ageing. Further, the biosocial order is one that encourages people to congregate as biocitizens around various diagnoses (Rose/Novas 2005), and more recently, as quantified selves (Barrett et al. 2013; Nafus and Sherman 2014; Ruckenstein forthcoming). Thus, the biosocial order and its incorporation of functional age becomes the contextual background for understanding how self-tracking, digital and 'smart' technologies for older people integrate populational surveillance, individualized care, agential policies (such as 'active ageing'), marketable health-products and new risk-averse social strata.

The Technologies of 'Quantified Ageing'

Three types of technologies related to tracking and measuring age and age-related capacities are of interest here: a) wearable technologies; b) age-related algorithms; and c) incentivisation through the rhetoric of games and scores.

a) Wearable technologies, one of the key trends at the 2015 Consumer Electronics Show (Bowman 2014), include those linked to self-monitoring and tracking (such as FitBits), and those designed to also permit monitoring and tracking by others (such as Tempo or Lively), with only the latter explicitly linked to age. Lupton (2014b) is instructive in positioning a sociological approach to self-tracking as emphasizing its meaning in relation to "... wider discourses on technology, selfhood, the body and social relations that circulate within the cultural context in which the practice is carried out" (Lupton 2014b). It is these discourses that the research proposed here is aimed at unpacking and analysing, especially since age, while figuring prominently in such discourses, has also been neglected in the growing research on self-tracking and 'quantified selves'.

Wearable tracking technologies designed specifically for ageing individuals are designed less as technologies of self-knowledge than as tools to enable others to monitor and assess such individuals' functions, abilities and locations. For example, the external process of collecting on an individual's movements can issue machine-generated alerts if deviations are noted from established patterns of movement. While some research on these ambient monitoring systems suggest that they may be positively received (Hossain/Ahmed 2012; Sixsmith 2000) questions have been raised about both their ethical implications and efficacy (Lie/Lindsay/Brittain 2015; Mortensen/Sixsmith/Woolrych 2015; Neven 2015; Pritchard/Brittain 2015).

b) In a range of digital applications, algorithms are used to analyse, link and compare data and to identify patterns as the basis of decision-making.

As boyd and Crawford argue, they are part of the mythology of 'big data', purporting to offer "a higher form of intelligence and knowledge that can generate insights that were previously impossible, with an aura of truth, objectivity and accuracy" (2012: 663). The algorithmic logic that underpins digital applications reflects a particular confluence of expert discourses, statistical knowledge and standards which can be met or can set markers of failure or risk. With respect to self-tracking, individual measures (such as step count or heart rate) become part of estimates of risk. In devices designed for tracking others, machine-learning technology is employed to determine deviations from 'normal' routines indicated by, for example, the number of times the refrigerator door was opened or the length of time spent out of bed between hours designated as sleep time. Other apps promise to measure and calibrate age and age-related functions and risks in various ways. For example, Microsoft's Age Robot, unveiled at its 2015 developer's conference, uses facial recognition and machine-learning technologies to predict age from photographs. *RealAge* – a site promoted by popular TV doctor Mehmet Oz – promises to tell you how old you really are on the inside based on information you enter about your family history and lifestyle. Canadian tech start-up Vivametrica feeds chronological age, gender, BMI (body mass index) and average daily 'step count' into its algorithm, and then calculates your relative risk for the four most common age-related chronic illnesses. Because 'BMI' and 'step count' are themselves calculated estimates, self-knowledge gleaned from self-tracking and monitoring are already assumed. These are just a few recent examples of what might be called 'ageing by algorithm'.

c) 'Gamification' increases the consumer appeal of self-trackers and digital tools. The rhetoric of games and scores has been widely deployed to incentivise and represent 'progress' (Millington 2009; Rich/Miah 2014), to produce commercially useful data (Till 2014) and to make surveillance 'pleasurable' (Whitson 2013). Of particular interest here are 'brain training' and cognitive enhancement apps which are marketed to ageing individuals as tracking a person's imagined cognitive plasticity and enhancement, while promising protection against memory loss and even dementia. 'Brain-boosting' computer games such as *BrainAge 2* or those provided by HAPPYNeuron fill the pages of retirement and lifestyle magazines. Research has demonstrated that they exaggerate their benefits, which are mostly imagined into existence through scorekeeping, expert testimonials, and excitedly shared maximal/minimal standards (Millington 2011). Indeed, for older individuals, the entire brainwork enterprise creates ambiguous images of ageing – both positive and improvable, but negative and inevitable. These developments are especially salient in a culture terrified of memory loss and dementia, sensationalised in the media by their negative images of population ageing 'tides', 'tsunamis', 'storms', and 'bombs', along with zombie scenarios of demented 'never-ending funerals' and lost souls (Zeilig 2014).

The Political Economy of 'Quantified Ageing'

All of these technologies of tracking and measuring need to be located in the political economy of data sharing, aggregation and surveillance of ageing populations. Some research suggests that data sharing may produce new forms of sociality, as virtual communities form around common interests (Nafus/Sherman 2014). Little research has been undertaken in this respect with older adults, although previous research on older technologies, such as walking clubs using pedometers, suggests that the sociality was more significant than the technology (Copelton 2010; Oxlund/Whyte 2014). Of particular interest to our research are the implications of data aggregation for monitoring older populations. According to data analytics firm Vivametrica, "wearable activity monitors produce more biometric data than the combined public health surveys of every nation on the planet" (www.vivametrica.com). An entire industry has developed around capitalizing on digital tracking technologies (Rocketfuel 2014) making bodies into nodes, or collections of data points, in the "internet of things". In an era of 'big data' and algorithmic surveillance (Cheney-Lippold 2011; Ball/Murakami-Wood 2013; Lyon/Bauman 2013; Bennett et al. 2014; Klauser/Albrechtslund 2014; Lupton 2014a; Mortensen/Sixsmith/Woolrych 2015) the extent to which the devices and technologies of digital culture we have discussed may intensify dividing practices which categorize us functional/dysfunctional, young/old, active/inactive, fit/frail is an important line of analysis.

Tracking and quantifying technologies have already become part of 'speculative futures' of ageing, linking as they do the biopolitics of ageing populations to the anatomo-politics of ageing bodies. How will the insurance industry acquire and use data aggregated from these technologies to produce new actuarial standards of success in ageing? How will normative conceptions of responsible ageing bodies shift? Will they be those that self-track and self-monitor? Do they offer themselves up to remote monitoring and tracking as a means to maintaining 'independence'? Do they demonstrate measurable efforts to forestall discernible ageing – physical and cognitive? Are they those that conform to algorithmic standards of controlled risk for dependency? How, as they engage with these technologies, do older people themselves contribute to the re-calibration of age and age-related characteristics, and to the reshaping of age as a social category? All of these questions may underpin debates about care policy and the distribution of scarce resources in ageing societies.

To summarize, the proliferation of new technologies aimed at enabling self-knowledge, and the tracking of selves and others, has raised important ethical and sociological questions about measurement, standardization, surveillance, risk-management, selfhood and sociality. However, in the growing body of work on quantification and self-tracking cultures, age still figures mostly as simply a dimension of social inequality that may be associated with less access, interest or skill in using digital technologies (see for example Lupton 2013). We argue that there are much larger questions at stake, and we hope to encourage researchers to explore the ways that current developments in self-tracking technologies and the proliferation of digital apps are creating new modes and styles of 'quantified ageing'. At a time when technological developments, demographic shifts and changing regimes of governmentality conjoin to problematize bodies – and here, specifically ageing bodies – a range of difficulties is presented in how to conceptualize, manage and optimize those bodies. We should not be surprised, then, as Nikolas Rose suggests, "that one response is [...] to seek to discipline these difficulties, to find some algorithms to adjudicate about them, to standardize procedures for the potentially conflictful decisions concerning them" (2007: 256). The technical turn to new ways of quantifying and standardising measurements of age exemplifies this response. Our argument is not to gainsay that new technologies may benefit the lives of older people (Schillmeier/Domenech 2010; Sixsmith/Gutman 2013), but to assert that such technologies cannot be assessed outside the social contexts in which they are developed, promoted, used and capitalized. Technologies that track, quantify and compare may indeed assist older people age more 'successfully', and 'age in place' more securely, but they also raise important questions about ageism, agency and inequality.

References

Ball, Kirstie S./Murakami-Wood, David (2013): "Political Economies of Surveillance." In: Surveillance & Society 11/1 & 2, pp. 1-3.
Barrett, Meredith/Humblet, Olivier/Hiatt, Robert/Adler, Nancy (2013): "Big Data and Disease Prevention: From Quantified Self to Quantified Communities." In: Big Data 1/3, pp. 168-175.
Bennett, Colin J./Haggerty, Kevin D./Lyon, David/Steeves Valerie (eds.) (2014): Transparent Lives: Surveillance in Canada, Edmonton: Athabasca University Press.
Bowman, Dan (2014): "Ces: Remote Monitoring, Self-Tracking Tools among Trending Health Tech." In: FierceHealthIT, October 1, 2014 (www.fiercehealth.com/node/22081/print).
boyd, danah/Kate Crawford (2012): "Critical Questions for Big Data." In: Information, Communication and Society 15/5, pp. 662-679.
Cheney-Lippold, John (2011): "A New Algorithmic Identity: Soft Biopolitics and the Modulation of Control." In: Theory, Culture & Society 28/6, pp. 164-181.
Copelton, Denise A. (2010): "Output That Counts: Pedometers, Sociability and the Contested Terrain of Older Adult Fitness Walking." In: Sociology of Health & Illness 32/2, pp. 304-318.
Gilleard, Chris/Higgs, Paul (2005): Contexts of Ageing: Class, Cohort and Community, Cambridge: Polity.
Hogle, Linda F. (2005): "Enhancement Technologies and the Body." In: Annual Review of Anthropology 34, pp. 695-716.
Hogle, Linda F. (2007): "Emerging Medical Technologies." In: Edward J. Hackett/Olga Amsterdamska/Michael E. Lynch/Judy Wajcman (eds.), The Handbook of Science and Technology Studies, 3e, Cambridge: MIT Press, pp. 841-873.

Hossain, M.A./Ahmed D.T. (2012): "Virtual Caregiver: A Ambient-Aware Elderly Monitoring System." In: IEEE Transactions on Information Technology in Biomedicine 16/6, pp. 1024-1031.

Katz, Stephen/Marshall, Barbara L. (2004): "Is the Functional 'Normal'? Ageing, Sexuality and the Biomarking of Successful Living." In: History of the Human Sciences 17/1: pp. 53-75.

Katz, Stephen (2005): Cultural Aging: Life Course, Lifestyle and Senior Worlds, Peterborough: Broadview Press.

Katz, Stephen (2014): "What Is Age Studies?" In: Age Culture Humanities 1/1, n. p.

Klauser, Francisco R./Albrechtslund, Anders (2014): "From Self-Tracking to Smart Urban Infrastructures: Towards an Interdisciplinary Research Agenda on Big Data." In: Surveillance & Society 12/2, pp. 273-286.

Lie, Mabel L. S./Lindsay, Stephen/Brittain, Katie (2015): "Technology and Trust: Older Peoples' Perspectives of a Home Monitoring System." In: Ageing & Society FirstView, pp. 1-25.

Lupton, Deborah (2013): "Quantifying the Body: Monitoring and Measuring Health in the Age of Mhealth Technologies." In: Critical Public Health 23/4, pp. 393-403.

Lupton, Deborah (2014a): Digital Sociology, London: Routledge.

Lupton, Deborah (2014b): "Self-Tracking Cultures: Towards a Sociology of Personal Informatics." Paper presented at the OZCHI 2014: Designing Futures, The Future of Design, December 2-5, 2014, University of Technology, Sydney, Australia.

Lyon, David/Bauman, Zygmunt (2013): Liquid Surveillance, Oxford: Wiley.

Marshall, Barbara L. (2015): "Anti-Ageing and Identities." In: Julia Twigg/Wendy Martin (eds.), Routledge Handbook of Cultural Gerontology, London: Taylor and Francis, pp. 210-217.

Millington, Brad (2009): "Wii Has Never Been Modern: 'Active' Video Games and the 'Conduct of Conduct'." In: New Media & Society 11/4, pp. 621-640.

Millington, Brad (2011): "Use It or Lose It: Ageing and the Politics of Brain Training." In: Leisure Studies 31/4, pp. 429-446.

Moreira, Tiago (2015a): "Unsettling Standards: The Biological Age Controversy." In: The Sociological Quarterly 56/1, pp. 18-39.

Moreira, Tiago (2015b): "De-Standardising Ageing? Shifting Regimes of Age Measurement." In: Ageing & Society FirstView, pp. 1-27.

Mortensen, W. Ben/Sixsmith, Andrew/Woolrych, Ryan (2015): "The Power(s) of Observation: Theoretical Perspectives on Surveillance Technologies and Older People." In: Ageing & Society 35/3, pp. 512-530.

Nafus, Dawn/Sherman, Jamie (2014): "This One Does Not Go up to 11: The Quantified Self Movement as an Alternative Big Data Practice." In: International Journal of Communication 8, pp. 1784-1794.

Neven, Louis (2015): "By Any Means? Questioning the Link between Gerontechnological Innovation and Older People's Wish to Live at Home." In: Technological Forecasting and Social Change 93, pp. 32-43.

Oxlund, Bjarke/Whyte, Susan Reynolds (2014): "Measuring and Managing Bodies in the Later Life Course." In: Population Aging 7, pp. 217-230.

Pritchard, Gary W./Brittain, Katie (2015): "Alarm Pendants and the Technological Shaping of Older People's Care: Between (Intentional) Help and (Irrational) Nuisance." In: Technological Forecasting and Social Change 93, pp. 124-132.

Rich, Emma/Miah, Andy (2014): "Understanding Digital Health as Public Pedagogy: A Critical Framework." In: Societies 4/2, pp. 296-315.

Rocketfuel (2014): "Rocket Fuel: 'Quantified Self' Digital Tools. A Cpg Marketing Opportunity", (http://quantifiedself.com/docs/RocketFuel_Quantified_Self_Research.pdf).

Rose, Nikolas/Novas, Carlos (2005): "Biological Citizenship." In: Aihwa Ong/Stephen J. Collier (eds.), Global Assemblages: Technology, Politics and Ethics as Anthropological Problems, Oxford, UK: Blackwell, pp. 439-463.

Rose, Nikolas (2007): The Politics of Life Itself: Biomedicine, Power and Subjectivity in the Twenty-First Century, Princeton, NJ: Princeton University Press.

Minna, Ruckenstein (forthcoming): "Beyond the Quantified Self: Thematic Exploration of a Dataistic Paradigm." In: New Media & Society.

Schillmeier, Michael/Domenech, Miquel (eds.) (2010): New Technologies and Emerging Spaces of Care: Ashgate.

Sixsmith, Andrew (2000): "An Evaluation of an Intelligent Home Monitoring System." In: Journal of Telemedicine and Telecare 6/2, pp. 63-72.

Sixsmith, Andrew/Gutman, Gloria M. (eds.) (2013): Technologies for Active Aging, New York: Springer.

Till, Chris (2014): "Exercise as Labour: Quantified Self and the Transformation of Exercise into Labour." In: Societies 4/3, pp. 446-462.

Whitson, Jennifer (2013) "Gaming the Quantified Self." In: Surveillance & Society 11/1 & 2, pp. 163-176.

Zeilig, Hannah (2014): "Dementia as a Cultural Metaphor." In: The Gerontologist 54/2, pp. 258-267.

Games to Live With
Speculations Regarding NikeFuel

Paolo Ruffino

Abstract

In this paper I offer an alternative way to look at games that require no form of play. The player of these games is only supposed to keep them always up-to-date and running, but no specific action is required. NikeFuel is a significant example of this kind of game. NikeFuel, a technology for the quantification of body movement developed by the sports company Nike, is applied in a series of gadgets. The most popular, Nike+, is a wristband that quantifies the movements of the user and converts them into a NikeFuel score, which can later be visualised on a laptop or mobile phone. The act of moving throughout the day is transformed into a game-like experience, according to the principles of gamification. Gamification and quantified-self technologies have been noted for their performative potential and their capacity to control and inform our bodies (Whitson 2015). From a Foucauldian perspective, quantified-self technologies are attempts to rationalise the practices and movements of living organisms, as forms of biopolitical control (Foucault 2005, Schrape 2014). However, these are also spaces of transformation of the conditions under which the self becomes possible. Through NikeFuel, and other examples that I explore in this paper (Farmville, Cookie Clicker, CarnageHug), the player has to come to terms with games that act as parasites on their own lives. Thus, I argue that Nike+ can also be seen to complicate our thoughts about the contemporary digital technologies that surround us on an everyday basis. In this paper I will argue, possibly counter-intuitively, that gamification and quantified-self technologies are not necessarily tools that we use for a specific purpose; these are technologies we carry around with us and live with. As such, we are transformed by them as much as we transform them. Thus, the problem raised in this paper is about how we can co-habit and be hospitable with these "parasites" (Serres 1982).

Introduction

NikeFuel is a technology developed by the sports company Nike. First introduced in 2012, NikeFuel is a system for measuring body movement. Its most notorious application is in the Nike+ Fuelband wristband, a gadget that counts the movements of the body of the user through an accelerometer, and connects via USB and Bluetooth to laptops and mobile phones. But there is more to it than that. NikeFuel, as a "life-tracking device", is a tool for what has been called the quantification of the self. Indeed, according to the sports company, in NikeFuel what comes to be quantified is not just movement, but life itself. This is in fact what Nike states in its advertisement:

"Our minds, our bodies and our experience all tell us that movement is life and that the more we move the more we live. It's something athletes have understood from the beginning. The kind of movement it takes to improve your game is the kind of movement it takes to improve your life. But unlike sport, life doesn't come with convenient ways of measuring movement. So we developed one. NikeFuel: a single universal unit uniquely designed to measure the movement of the entire human body for the entire human race, whatever your weight, whatever your gender, whatever your activity. It's that simple and that revolutionary. So get out there find what fuels you and get moving." (Nike, Inc. 2013)

Nike's attempt at quantifying movement could indeed be seen within a discursive framework where the very definition of life is generated. In this definition, life and the movement of the body are the same. The possibility of measuring, controlling, and informing human bodies is a shared characteristic of many other gamification and quantified-self technologies. Jennifer Whitson has argued that "there is a lot of interest in using gamification as a technology of government that shapes users' conduct in the hope of producing certain desired effects (such as using gamification to increase productivity in call centres) and averting certain undesired events (such as using gamification to reduce employee churn and absenteeism)" (Whitson 2015: 341).

From a Foucauldian perspective, quantified-self technologies rationalise the practices and movements of living organisms, as forms of biopolitical control (Schrape 2014). Certainly, the NikeFuel wristband is a 'thorn in flesh': a power that is at the same time repressive and productive, and that limits the individual who wears it through specific practices of self-production (Foucault 2005).

Gamification can be seen, via Foucault, as being based on, and at the same time bringing about, a specific form of truth (Foucault 2005). The techniques of knowledge of the self, analysed by Foucault with respect to Greek and Latin times and later with respect to Christian and contemporary culture, construct the possibility of arriving at and articulating the truth about oneself. The production of a form of truth is replicated in the discourses surrounding gamification. In these discourses, truth is presented as the equivalent of the collection of all possible data about one's body. For instance, in Jane McGonigal's game *SuperBetter*, a browser based game where players set a real-life goal for themselves and are guided towards its completion, self-improvement is defined through the evidence of statistics and medical research, and the standards for a good life are seen as a direct consequence of this data (McGonigal 2011). In the textbooks on gamification, such as *Gamification by Design*, gamification is presented as a technique based on the collection and analysis of previous experiences in user engagement (Zichermann/Cunningham 2011). Resulting from the systematic analysis of previously successful cases, gamification can be sold as a reliable, trustworthy technique for engaging audiences. It also becomes possible to talk about a correct form of gamification, as opposed to a supposedly wrong kind of gamification, which could be imagined as being based on misleading or incomplete information, or relying on unquantifiable aspects.

Through these characteristics and design principles gamification has become what it is today: a series of practical and operational suggestions on how to involve users (be they customers, citizens, or gamers) and maximise their performance with respect to a specific goal. Gamification tends to take the form of a technique, a precise set of design solutions to gamify a certain experience. Gamification has been invented and narrated with the purpose, in the first place, of being a regulated and regulatory practice. It is born as a topic for design consultants, as a pitch for a new category of user-experience gurus and advertisement strategists.

The Gamified Self

It could then be asked, following Foucault's perspective, what kinds of selves are created through and by this specific technique? The gamified-self is constructed through the collection and archiving of data about the user. Data needs to first be collected and processed in order to later become part of a game, and is collected according to a principle of transparency: gamification plays with the facts about the user, and attempts to assist the user in improving these same facts, these truths about him- or herself.

NikeFuel, for example, is a system that is designed to receive and record already predicted signals; it rewards precise events that are already expected by the simulation, according to the principle of cybernetic systems as "governed by time-reversible causal stories" (Norbert Wiener, quoted in Crogan 2011: 5). The runner/player of NikeFuel is encouraged to comply with a regulatory frame of rules, where only specific events are expected, saved, calculated and evaluated. Through this practice of compliance, the runner/player of NikeFuel is normalised, and regulates him- or herself in order to maintain and progress in a process of constant self-normalisation. Failure to comply with the rules of NikeFuel means not following up on the request to produce information.

What appears at first as a game-like experience is soon revealed to frame a very bizarre kind of play, one where not only there is no final goal, but also where the players play with their own bodies as they conform to what is expected by the game itself. Moreover, the process of complying with the game does not happen through a series of deliberate and meaningful choices. NikeFuel is played as life is lived: by taking care of oneself.

Games With No Players

What sorts of play is this, and how can we look at it? Certainly it cannot be looked at through the most common perception of play – as fun, or as a pleasant activity. Already in *Man, Play, and Games*, Roger Caillois said that play is often not pleasurable, but is instead "an occasion of pure waste: waste of time, energy, ingenuity, skill, and often of money" (1961: 5). But it could be further argued that human agency disappears altogether from NikeFuel. These are games that are played in a condition where humans' deliberate intervention has been eliminated as the game plays by itself.

Indeed, NikeFuel is not the first of its kind as there are other games that do not exactly require any form of intervention to be played. These are games where, even if human players are still present, the act of playing is reduced to a series of actions with no significant choice or calculation. These are in effect games with no play.

I am thinking of the popular Farmville by Zynga, a Facebook game that has been attracting millions of players so far. Farmville is played on social networks and its success relies on the activity of players who use their network of friends and contacts to gain an advantage at the game. Farmville, as do many other games based on social networks, asks its players to receive assistance from their personal contacts, thus encouraging every single player to involve as many friends as possible. Also, and most interestingly, a game like Farmville is played through a series of almost meaningless choices. Every time a possible action is presented, the outcome of that action is always already evident and it is absolutely clear to the player which choice is the optimal one: at any given moment it is always made clear where the player should click to receive the best possible outcome in terms of points scored. In Farmville there are, indeed, human players, but it is a game that could just as well be played by an algorithm.

To proceed towards another example, Cookie Clicker (2013) by Julien Thiennot offers a parody of games such as Farmville and, in doing so, explores the absence of human agency that underlies the game by Zynga. In Cookie Clicker points are earned by clicking on a cookie. After receiving about 10 cookie points, the player can spend those points to buy an automatic clicker that will give them 0.1 cookie points per second. The game starts from this initial purchase and then escalates towards an unlimited accumulation of cookies, automatic clickers, and further bizarre upgrades (including the Grandmas, the Cookie Factory, and a Cookie Time Machine that will travel in time to collect cookies from other ages). Eventually, after about 10-20 hours of play, the game is likely to automatically be generating around a billion cookies per second.

Cookie clicker is an example of a new emerging category of idle games; that is, games that keep playing themselves on a computer browser, in the background of other operations that will not affect the automatic process of accumulation. Cookie Clicker is supposed to be a parody of Farmville, but while exploiting the same mechanics as Facebook games it proves to be equally addictive. These are games where human intervention is reduced to a minimum, or sometimes is not needed at all. Human choices, when these are required to keep the game flowing, could be easily replaced by a macro that clicks on the next available upgrade. In Cookie Clicker, as well as in Farmville, the human has to act as would an artificial intelligence. We could repurpose the slogan used by Amazon to define its Mechanical Turk service for crowdsourcing: in crowdsourcing human actors are required to act as if they had artificial intelligence, and, for this reason, Amazon defines crowdsourcing as "artificial artificial intelligence" (Amazon, Inc. 2015). Likewise, in these games the players are supposed to act as if they were controlled by software, as if they were artificial players.

For a game that has gone even further in this approach to gaming, where human agency is replaced by machines or machine-like actors, we could look at CarnageHug (2007) by Corrado Morgana. CarnageHug, based on the popular First-Person Shooter Unreal Tournament, displays game avatars controlled by an artificial intelligence locked in a small squared room. The avatars kill each other continuously, re-spawn and kill each other again. The automated commands force the bots to kill each other on sight, but the incredibly small environment reduces the actions to a chaotic, hectic and senseless mass murder. The artistic intervention can be seen as a further investigation of the possibilities opened by the disappearance of play from games. CarnageHug has been defined by Mathias Fuchs as a "(games-)world that contains actors who have to work ceaselessly without achieving anything for themselves or for others. The actors in Morgana's game work like the users of Farmville or any other gamification apps work when they think they play" (2014: 15).

The avatars of CarnageHug are not too dissimilar from the imagined users of NikeFuel. In the advertisement for Nike's product, quoted at the beginning of this essay, we see human beings running endlessly and ceaselessly while accumulating points on their wristbands. This is a run with no end and no consumption. The bodies of the players of NikeFuel could keep running forever, as much as new crops can always be harvested in Farmville, cookies can always be clicked in Cookie Clicker, and avatars can always shoot each other in CarnageHug.

Games as Parasites

NikeFuel, as well as the aforementioned examples and most of the representatives of gamification, are problematic for a theory of games and play. In fact, these are games where the activity of play almost completely disappears. However, I prefer not to solve the problem by classifying these experiences as non-games. I argue that these are games, just of a different kind. These are games that are not necessarily played for fun, pleasure, or self-improvement, but are games to coexist with, to come to terms with. Players of NikeFuel are embedded in an environment which they co-inhabit with their wristband, they carry it around, and they get obsessed or get along with it. Likewise, players of Farmville and Cookie Clicker have to comply with these games, get back to them regularly and click as much as possible.

As such, NikeFuel also complicates our common understanding of communication processes. The players of Nike+ are not just participating in a feedback loop with their wristband, they are relating to it, dealing with a symbiotic relation where the two ends of the system (player and wristband), although separate, act as parasites on each other.

Ultimately, it is a theory of parasites that I believe could prove useful for understanding this kind of games. In *The Parasite,* Michel Serres (1982) looks at how communication processes are not just linear exchanges, from the sender to the receiver, but defined by the disturbances that are external to the system of information flow. The parasite, rather than being an element of disturbance, is understood by Serres as necessarily entangled within the system that it exploits and opens to further contamination.

Serres argues that the figure of the parasite, as well as the *hôte* (which means, in French, both host and guest), has both a social and a biological function that cannot be reduced to mere passivity. According to Serres, it is the parasite that makes communication possible. Any system, Serres argues, tends to be corrupted or interrupted by external factors. There is no chance that in the long term it can be kept closed and preserved as it is. In a communication exchange, it is interruption or disturbance that becomes, in the long run, the defining characteristic of the transmission. This disturbance then breeds further disturbances, allowing further waves of noise to again modify the transmission of the message. According to Serres, the alleged linearity of the communication process is not only inadequate, it also subverts the other hierarchy, theorised by the French author, where noise and parasites are the defining factors of communication.

The reason I turn to Serres for an analysis of NikeFuel is because, in his theory, the French author deconstructs the dualism of sender and receiver in communication processes. The third element, the parasite, is not merely an addition to the existing duality but is in fact an external factor that also makes the system itself possible. In Serres' theory, the parasite is not just otherness; it is also what enables a relation within the system. It is a thermal exciter, a disturbance, but also what changes existing relations.

NikeFuel and its player are probably better understood as one being the parasite of the other. This parasitical relation is continuously disrupted by uncountable factors that complicate their co-existence and, with it, the possibility of understanding it as part of a system. Systems constitute a problem in Serres' work, as he suggests that a study of communication should become a study of relations that break the supposed boundaries within which flows of information are imagined to be happening. In Serres' view, the system itself is the object of study of ontology. The system is a result of the narrowing down of a series of parasitic relations, and of the momentary freezing of an existing condition. Serres talks explicitly about the black box, as the intellectual gesture that denies transformation, thus hindering knowledge:

"When we do not understand, when we defer our knowledge to a later date, when the thing is too complex for the means at hand, when we put everything in a temporary black box, we prejudge the existence of a system. When we can finally open the box, we see that it works like a space of transformation. The only systems, instances, and substances come from our lack of knowledge. The system is nonknowledge [sic]. The other side of nonknowledge. One side of nonknowledge is chaos; the other, system. Knowledge forms a bridge between the two banks. Knowledge as such is a space for transformation." (Serres 1982: 73)

If, by opening the black box that is NikeFuel, we can look at it as a space of transformation, then what kind of knowledge can we get? At play in these processes of transformation, which result from the on-going relations between the game and the user, is the very condition of possibility of the self.

Conclusions

NikeFuel does not make much sense as a box, or as a tool to be used to improve one's health. It makes much more sense, instead, as a space of transformation where the truth about oneself is continuously negotiated. As such, NikeFuel is a strange game, one that is not supposed to be played but to live with, as parasites rather than players, as it becomes a parasite in its own turn of our own movement and physical transformation. NikeFuel is representative of a trend in gaming that is much more transversal than the gamification and quantified-self movement. It is in fact a category of games where no significant action is required, but that need to be kept always running and up-to-date. These are not games to play, but to live with.

References

Amazon, Inc. (2015) "Amazon Mechanical Turk homepage", February 2, 2016 (https://www.mturk.com/mturk/welcome).
Caillois, Roger (1961): Man, Play and Games, Champaign: University of Illinois Press.
Crogan, Patrick (2011): Gameplay Mode: War, Simulation and Technoculture. Minneapolis: University of Minnesota Press.
Foucault, Michel (2005): The Hermeneutics of the Subject: Lectures at the College de France 1981-1982. New York: Palgrave McMillan.
Fuchs, Mathias (2014): "Gamification as 21st Century Ideology." In: Journal of Gaming and Virtual Worlds 6/2, pp. 143-157.
Nike, Inc. (2013): "This is NikeFuel. Video. Directed by NikeFuel", October 15, 2013 (https://www.youtube.com/watch?v=bvM0h0DFZ30).
McGonigal, Jane (2011): Reality is Broken: Why Games Make Us Better and How They Can Change the World, New York: Penguin Press.
Schrape, Niklas (2014): "Gamification and Governmentality." In: Mathias Fuchs/Sonia Fizek/Paolo Ruffino/Niklas Schrape (eds.), Rethinking Gamification, Lüneburg: meson press, pp. 21-46.
Serres, Michel (1982): The Parasite, Baltimore: The Johns Hopkins University Press.
Whitson, Jennifer (2014): "Foucault's FitBit: Governance and Gamification." In: Steffen P. Walz/Sebastian Deterding (eds.), The Gameful World: Approaches, Issues, Applications, Boston, MA: The MIT Press, pp. 338-358.
Zichermann, Gabe/Cunningham, Chris (2011): Gamification by Design: Implementing Game Mechanics in Web and Mobile Apps, New York: O'Reilly Media.

Quantified Bodies
A Design Practice

James Dyer

Abstract

Self-trackers are a diffuse and diverse group that quantify their lives. From the ordinary to the extraordinary, intimate and vital happenings that occur on (infra)-empirical planes are cast as legible events. The tracked data consists of blood pressure, heartbeat rate, testosterone levels, posture, diet, muscle tension, social activity or geographical position. These are now happenings to be intervened upon and rendered as units of measurement and comparable variables. These measurements may give insight to help rebuild a recognition of oneself (Catani 2015), or allow a brooding recall of lost moments (Kalina 2012) – this is the manifest quantified body, a body read and a body written. Yet the quantified body is a veneer, it is the outward appearance of control, awareness and care-for-self: we were cynical subjects (Sloterdijk 1987) long before we were quantified bodies. However, self-tracking intrinsically disassociates from the ubiquitous cynical condition. The cynical self-tracker gropes for independence whilst submitting to a life of mediated self-discovery, it is a renunciation of independent vitality so as to act "as if", to appear to be whilst never being – to fall short of realising difference. It is argued here that the quantified body allocates us all to be designers – reading and writing in culture. And as such, our actions must be critiqued as a symptom of a design practice, where the condition of subjectivity is at the forefront of value-making in taste, style and fashion. How does the cynic self-track? What is the value of design in the field of new media and digital culture?

Self-Tracking

Self-tracking constructs intimate and vital events into units of measurement – writing the body into legibility. The intimate is formulated here as the encounter with another person or place, as a quantified relation. This could be relations to and between people, monuments, location, weather, time, and so on. The vital is all essential and belonging to life: heartbeat rate, body temperature, or blood pressure for example. Presenting intimate and vital events as variable units fundamentally alters perspectives of personhood, social relations and the body (Rabinow 1999; Novas/Rose 2000). The expanded (infra)-empirical access to intimate and vital relations has created a new logic of accountability, one that has not been experienced before (Pantzar/Ruckenstein 2015: 14). The emergent popularity of self-tracking demonstrates a strong cultural currency in the reading and writing of the body. As such, self-tracking is not an inconsequential fad, rather it is a phenomenon requiring sensitive attention.

Sensitivity is paramount in a critical study of self-tracking. To concern intimacy and vitality without sensitivity, particularly sympathy, is to shun self-tracking towards the well-established routine of divorced judgement: it deserves more than the "gullible critiques" (Latour 2004: 230) of ideology (Žižek 1989), social control (Foucault 1978) and fetishisation (Pietz 1987). To claim self-tracking is harboured in illusory perception (ideology), manipulation (social control) or false values (fetishisation) is to renounce the fundamental core of the practice, the agent – that is, the "tracker". Whilst predictable concerns of nefarious panopticism are perpetuated – and heightened post-Snowden – there are also encouraging accounts that break away from this dominant discourse – such as a proposed "soft resistances" to biopolitical regimes (Nafus/Sherman 2014: 1790), events such as Lifehack Marathons (Setup 2015) and schools for poetic computations (SFPC 2015). Here, an extend reach of alternative cultural debates is proposed – presenting a different view on quantification. The new perspective is from the position of design, a perspective that is not landlocked in the quotidian shuffle of impartiality and cold sobriety, rather it is deeply connected to the reading and writing of cultures – self-quantification is fundamentally a designerly practice.

Design

Design is defined here as the consideration of significances. The manifested significances – the designed object – is the composition of those considerations. To be clear, the designed object is not necessarily a luxury designer object, but it may be a service, system, machine, body, and much more. Therefore, design is not merely faithful to form or function, but more towards fiction – design is world-making. This definition crucially incorporates two facets of design – action and value. Action is consideration, and the (in)-significances of a designed object are its value. As such, the intensities of a designed object's value-significance make up a potency of argumentation (Cross 1982: 229). That is to say, designed objects contest and concur with their environment and each other by their very existence; minimalism is an argument opposed to ornamentation, just as luxury cars are an argument against sustainability.

The assembly of argumentation in design becomes a design style. In this instance, style is a manner of pursuit, preference in taste, and choice of value, and it is from a particular posture of style that a designer reads and writes in culture. That is to say, disagreements are read and opposing positions are written – in new styles. It is to compose what does not exist via a contestation of what already exists – "one way of doing things, chosen from a number of alternative ways" (Simon 1975: 287). Design is a practice of suggesting and manifesting possible solutions and futures (Cross 1982: 225; Fry 2009). Accordingly, argumentative positions of design are concerned with what has come before, what happens now, and what may happen. Self-tracking and design meet within this spectrum of read-write culture, argumentation, and style.

The quantified "readable" body becomes a body of contestation as it is written into culture. It is a body of interaction, between (inter) operations (action), a body deeply embedded in relations of and to itself via the practice of self-tracking. As considerator (designer) and composition of significances (designed), the body is not solely the valued object of design, but also the acting agent enforcing such design. Via self-tracking, vital variables and intimate relations are read and new ones written, the body is written in acknowledgement of its past, present and future form – this is the quantified body. The culmination of this independent "designerly" agent of self-tracking is clearly seen developing through a brief leapfrog genealogy of electrocardiogram (ECG) devices.

The Quantified Body: A Brief Genealogy

Genealogically, the quantified body may be traced back to the early 1900s with the introduction of telemedicine. Dutch scientist Willem Einthoven developed an early form of telemedicine when he successfully transmitted a patient's ECG signal from a hospital to his laboratory, some 1.5 km away. Einthoven called this a "telecardiogram" (Einthoven 1957), it is an early indication of bodily quantification; it is the interception of a vital event, the heartbeat, for the purpose of transmission, communication and manipulation (medical care).

Notably, the career of physicist Norman J. Holter presents a clear trajectory from Einthoven's work. In 1947 Holter introduced an eighty-five pound backpack – the Holter Monitor – consisting of two batteries and an ECG radio transmitter (Gawlowska/Wranicz 2009: 386). It was later refined to a more compact and portable system in 1962, which the inventor called a "step toward freedom" (Holter 1961: 1214), a freedom from the limits of poor "electronic and mechanical performance" (ibid: 1219). Holter's later inventions allowed up to ten hours of monitored heart activity to be stored on magnetic tape using a portable "electrocardiocaster" and "electrocardiocorder" (ibid), the device was now discreet and the patient was mobile.

Both Einthoven and Holter produced unique equipment to grant specialists an unprecedented access to the body, however this changed with the emergence of e-health in the early 1990s. The dominant motif of e-health was the repurposing of existing devices and their surrounding rhetoric. E-health adopted orbiting ideologies of technological developments and socio-economic aspirations, such as e-commerce and the Internet. In this sense, e-health is not an active development of telemedical services, but is instead an adoption of relevant and proximal trends, particularly ones that charge the user as champion over the specialist. The specialist has been disregarded in lieu of an "informed user".

E-health emphasises the "device-process" as opposed to the telemedical service of "specialist-procedure". The focus is less oriented towards disaster response and urgent needs (Garshneck 1997: 42), and rather aimed towards a vague state of health attention. This can be seen in the addled and prophetic celebrations for e-health's adoption of the "explosion" in email communication in medical care in the 1990s (Pallen 1995). E-health created a growth of "proto-professional" user-consumers (Novas and Rose 2000), they are the "informed patients" (Detmer et al. 2003) and the "worried well" (Frith 2014). The divorce from specialists, and the introjection of mediated independence, still resonates today, it is the "user-model" of the independent agent – designing and designed – called here, the quantified body. However, the cast of an independent self-tracking read-write agent is, on the whole, a myth – that is to say unlived. There is a stagnant slump in necessary action – we are all, still, cynics.

Cynicism

The philosopher Peter Sloterdijk, heralded by social scientist Bruno Latour as being the designers' philosopher (2008: 8), proposed in his seminal book *Kritik der Zynischen Vernunft* (1983) that the dominant human condition is a cynical one. It is a diffuse condition of enlightened false consciousness (Sloterdijk 1987: 5). The cynic acts as if ignorant of their own knowingness, or in cultural critic Slavoj Žižek's maxim "they know very well what they are doing, but still, they are doing it" (1989: 29). As such, self-tracking clearly jars with the condition of cynicism, if the model self-tracker is to know (read) and act upon that knowledge (write) – to change and manipulate – then the cynical self-tracker appears only to know (read) and to reinstate that knowledge (re-write) – to maintain a conservation of behaviour. In illustration: cynical self-trackers know very well that they smoke 200 cigarettes per week, but they are still doing it. This has detrimental effects for the traditions of the critique of ideology, in which the goal has been enlightened consciousness, to liberate the mislead, to unveil the veiled and dismantle illusion. Yet, the dominant cynical subject is not mislead by illusion and requiring enlightenment, rather the subjects are acting "as if" whilst knowing otherwise – this results in a post-ideological Fukuyama-esque tension.

Political scientist Francis Fukuyama notes the development of history is dependant on the conflicts of ideologies (Fukuyama 1989: 4), an ideology being an assemblage of beliefs and values that sanction particular behaviours. The cynical self-tracker does not employ the necessary condition of active conflict – the writing of difference – to create authentic change over their body. As such, if the general goal of self-tracking is to alter, manipulate or better oneself – under the rubric of care, optimisation, or health – then there must be an action of opposition. That is to say, there must be an envisioned alternative of "x" or a potential better version of "y", the self-tracker must contest something so as to mark progress. The cynical self-tracker does not need more intimate and vital data, they need to act, to create friction and genuine change, the quantified body needs to be animated so as to agonise and develop, this is what Sloterdijk calls "kynical" action (1987: 218), a way of acting in knowledge.

For Sloterdijk kynicism is "self-embodiment in resistance", opposing cynicism as "self-splitting in repression" (1987: 218). Through his postmodernist cubist-like style, Sloterdijk delivers existential emphasis on the diffuse being; the Socratic imperative to know thyself is no longer enough, the unexamined life may not be worth living but the examined life is yet to be lived. As such, the cynical strapline of the Quantified Self organisation, "self knowledge through numbers" (2007), presents a transparent inadequacy. An amended kynical strapline would be; "self doing through knowing numbers", that would be a materialised kynical read-write project of "flesh and blood" rather than a cynical read-re-write "dialogue of heads" (Sloterdijk 1987: 104).

Conclusion

In many cases traditional academic rebuttal of self-tracking, and more broadly new media and digital culture, has remained rooted in a well-trodden path of critique, one which champions a dispassionate sobriety and "matter-of-factness". Such critiques have untimely cast self-tracking as a known phenomenon that presents certain predictable variables, almost as if prematurely archived in Bruce Sterling's Dead Media Project (1995) – home to the known and redundant. Employing a design perspective will recast self-tracking as unknown, as an intriguing and unique field requiring sympathetic critique; allowing discovery, error, and debate, rather than inculcating tradition and dominant narratives. Rational conflicts of (enlightenment) reason and logic do not command design, instead it is the sensations of intensities and styles of argumentations with non-absolutist ends that steer and guide it. As such, through the position of design, it is possible to appropriate and reinvigorate lyrical writings (such as Camus, Cioran, Sabato) within contemporary theorisations of design practices (such as Latour, Willis and DiSalvo) to inform an emotive and sympathetically reflective perspective of critique. Further research is needed into the materialist/vital potentials for creating theories of "flesh and blood" (Sloterdijk 1987: 104). This must regard the emergence of self-quantification beyond the false values in fetishism, the misdirection in ideology and the manipulations of social constructions. These theories still have an important place, but room must be made for the free cynical agent, as manipulator and manipulated, and design creates this room.

References

Camus, Albert (2013): "The Sea close By", London: Penguin Classics.
Cioran, Emil M. (1996): "On The Heights of Despair", trans. Ilinca Zarifopol, Chicago: University of Chicago Press.
Cross, Nigel (1982): "Designerly Ways of Knowing." In: Design Studies 3/4, pp. 221-227.

Catani, Damien (2015): "Tracking 7,459 Dreams", September 2, 2015 (http://quantifiedself.com/2015/07/damien-catani-dream).

Detmer, Don E./Singleton, Peter D./MacLeod, Alison/Wait, Susan/Taylor, Mary/Ridgwell, Jolyon (2003): "The Informed Patient: Study Report." Cambridge: Judge Institute of Management.

DiSalvo, Carl (2012): "Adversarial Design", Cambridge: The MIT Press.

Einthoven, Willem (1957): "The Telecardiogram." In: American Heart Journal 53/4, pp. 602-615.

Sabato, Ernesto (2011): "The Tunnel", New York: Penguin Classics.

Flusser, Vilém (1995): "On the Word Design: An Etymological Essay." In: Design Issues, pp. 50-53.

Foucault, Michel (1978): "The History of Sexuality, Volume 1: An Introduction", R. Hurley, Trans. New York: Vintage.

Frith, Maxine (2015): "Are you one of the rising numbers of the 'worried well'?" September 2, 2015 (http://www.telegraph.co.uk/lifestyle/wellbeing/diet/10977877/Are-you-one-of-the-rising-numbers-of-the-worried-well.html).

Fry, Tony (2009): "Design Futuring: Sustainability." In: Ethics and New Practices, Berg, Oxford.

Fukuyama, Francis (1989): "The End of History?" In: The National Interest 16/1, pp. 3-18.

Garshnek, V., J. S. Logan/Hassell, L. H. (1997): "The Telemedicine Frontier: Going the Extra Mile", In: Space Policy 13/1, pp. 37-46.

Gawłowska, Joanna/Wranicz, Jerzy Krzysztof (2009): "Norman J. 'Jeff' Holter (1914-1983)." In: Cardiology Journal 16/4, pp. 386-387.

Holter, Norman J. (1961): "New Method for Heart Studies Continuous Electrocardiography of Active Subjects over Long Periods is now Practical." In: Science 134/3486, pp. 1214-1220.

Latour, Bruno (2004): "Why has Critique Run Out of Steam? From Matters of Fact to Matters of Concern." In: Critical Inquiry 30/2, pp. 225-248.

Latour, Bruno (2008): "A Cautious Prometheus? A Few Steps toward a Philosophy of Design (with special attention to Peter Sloterdijk)." In: Proceedings of the 2008 Annual International Conference of the Design History Society, pp. 2-10.

Kalina, Noah (2012): "Noah takes a photo of himself every day for 12.5 years", YouTube video, 7:47, posted by "Noah Kalina", September 4, 2012 (https://www.youtube.com/watch?v=iPPzXlMdi7o).

Nafus, Dawn/Sherman, Jamie (2014): "This One Does Not Go Up To 11: The Quantified Self Movement as an Alternative Big Data Practice." In: International Journal of Communication 8, pp. 1784-1794.

Novas, Carlos/Rose, Nikolas (2000): "Genetic Risk and the Birth of the Somatic Individual." In: Economy and Society 29/4, pp. 485-513.

Pallen, Mark (1995): "Guide to the Internet: Electronic Mail." In: Bmj 311/7018, pp. 1487-1490.

Pantzar, Mika/Ruckenstein, Minna (2015): "The Heart of Everyday Analytics: Emotional, Material and Practical Extensions in Self-Tracking Market." In: Consumption Markets & Culture 18/1, pp. 92-109.

Pietz, William (1987): "The Problem of the Fetish, II: The Origin of the Fetish." In: RES: Anthropology and Aesthetics, pp. 23-45.
Quantified Self (2007): "Quantified Self | Self Knowledge Through Numbers", September 2, 2015 (http://quantifiedself.com/).
Rabinow, Paul (1999): "From Sociobiology to Biosociality." In: The Science Studies Reader, pp. 407-416.
Setup (2015): "LIFEHACK MARATHON #1", September 2, 2015 (http://setup.nl/content/lifehack-marathon-1).
SFPC (2015): "SFPC | School for Poetic Computation", School for Poetic Computation. September 2, 2015 (http://sfpc.io/).
Simon, Herbert A. (1975): "Style in Design." In: Spatial Synthesis in Computer-Aided Building Design 9, pp. 287-309.
Sloterdijk, Peter (1987): "Critique of Cynical Reason" Michael Eldred, Trans. Minneapolis: University of Minnesota Press.
Sterling, Bruce (1995): "The Dead Media Manifesto", September 2, 2015 (http://www.deadmedia.org/modest-proposal.html).
Willis, Anne-Marie (2006): "Ontological Designing." In: Design philosophy papers 4/2, pp. 69-92.
Žižek, Slavoj (1989): "The Sublime Object of Ideology", London: Verso.

Quantified Faces
On Surveillance Technologies, Identification and Statistics in Three Contemporary Art Projects

Mette-Marie Zacher Sørensen

Abstract

The article presents three contemporary art projects that, in various ways, thematise questions regarding numerical representation of the human face in relation to the identification of faces, for example through the use of biometric video analysis software, or DNA technology. The Dutch artist Marnix de Nijs' Physiognomic Scrutinizer is an interactive installation whereby the viewer's face is scanned and identified with historical figures. The American artist Zach Blas' project Fag Face Mask consists of three-dimensional portraits that blend biometric facial data from 30 gay men's faces and critically examine bias in surveillance technologies, as well as scientific investigations, regarding the stereotyping mode of the human gaze. The American artist Heather Dewey-Hagborg creates three-dimensional portraits of persons she has "identified" from their garbage. Her project from 2013 entitled Stranger Visions involves extracting DNA from discarded items she finds in public spaces in New York City, such as cigarette butts and chewing gum. She has the DNA that is extracted from these items analysed for specific genomic sequences associated with physical traits such as hair and eye colour. The three works are analysed with perspectives to historical physiognomy and Francis Galton's composite portraits from the 1800s. It is argued that, rather than being a statistical compression like the historical composites, contemporary statistical visual portraits (composites) are irreversible and complicated amalgams. The article furthermore examines questions regarding the agency of the technologies used by the artists.

In her book *Face Politics*, Jenny Edkins describes how much of the scientific work on "face processing" is based on the initial assumption that the face identifies someone, either as an individual or, for instance, as a member of a group, population or race, and at the same time expresses an emotional state (2015: 55). In this article I will examine the former, namely the identification of faces. Jenny Edkins further describes how face processing concentrates on how people who see a face process it (ibid). What concerns me here, however, is what I would call machinic face processing, and I will present three examples of how contemporary media art examines issues concerning new technologies and the identification of faces, for example through the use of biometric video analysis software or DNA technology. Via a description and brief analysis of three art projects, I will investigate possible consequences that arise when the human face is transformed into numeric representations. In my critical analysis of the three works I particularly focus on questions concerning the statistical face, the bias and stereotyping associated with the identification of faces, and in continuation thereof, issues related to the agency of technologies in the monitoring of faces.

The installation *Physiognomic Scrutinizer* was designed by the artist Marnix de Nijs in 2008 and further developed under the name *Mirror_Piece* in 2010. It is an interactive installation that uses biometric video analysis software to identify who the viewer most closely resembles, out of a database of 250 notorious personalities. When I experienced the work at the transmediale festival for new media art in Berlin in 2011, I was told by the interface that I looked like the famous early developer of computer science, Alan Turing (1912-1954), who was persecuted because of his homosexuality. The work plays satirically on the historical science of physiognomy, where the face is seen as a sign system (i.e. with a connection between a special type of nose and personal character). The comparison with infamous personalities establishes references to Cecare Lombroso's physiognomical criminal anthropology of the 1800s and Otto Weiniger's misogynist and anti-Semitic theory of human morphology in the book *Sex and Character* from 1903. In this light, it is no wonder that physiognomy has been largely eradicated. In 1999, the art historian James Elkins described how physiognomy as a science had entirely vanished (Elkins 1999: 73). But *Physiognomic Scrutinizer* raises the question of whether physiognomy, or at least the practice of reading the face as a structure, is somehow returning with face recognition technologies.

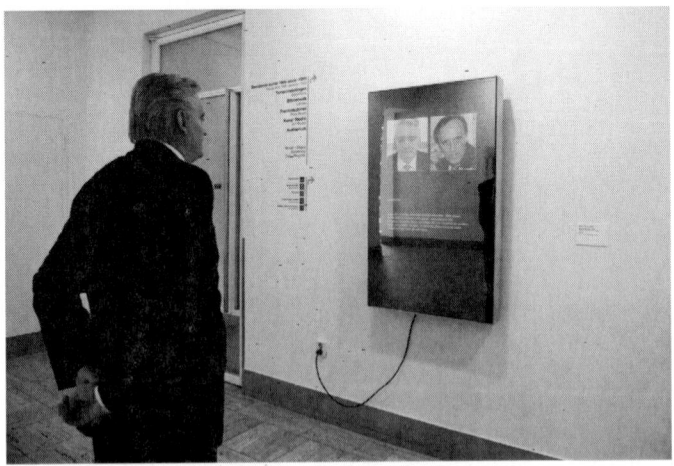

Image 1: Marnix de Nijs *Physiognomic Scrutinizer/Mirror_Piece* (2010). Photo by Lotte Stekelenburg.

Another artist who thematises this type of question regarding statistical faces is Zach Blas, who has produced three-dimensional portraits in his *Facial Weaponization Suite* project, including *Fag Face Mask* from 2012. The portraits here are blurred pink plastic masks containing data for 3D scans from 30 gay men's faces. The masks and a related video produced by Zach Blas are an explicit response to contemporary scientific experiments with the phenomenon of "gaydar", the intuitive registration of homosexuality, as carried out in the study of "Accuracy and Awareness in the Perception and Categorization of Male Sexual Orientation" by Nicholas O. Rule et al. (2008). The art project is, at the same time, a critique of the bias of biometric surveillance and the myth of objectivity in machinic face processing. It is not only machinic face processing that is programmable and works with pre-coded stereotypes. According to media scholar Bernadette Wegenstein (2013) and her theory of a human cosmetic gaze, we look at ourselves and others as incomplete and with an abstract yet ideal face outside the concrete face. The cosmetic gaze is subject to historical and media contexts, meaning that the technological possibilities at hand are likely to affect the human perception of the face. Blas himself also sees a resemblance between biometric surveillance and the historical physiognomy: "Capture technologies and their global standards of identification insidiously return us to the ableist, classist, homophobic, racist, sexist, and transphobic scientific endeavours of the 19th century, like anthropometry, physiognomy, and eugenics, albeit with the speed and ubiquity of 21th century digital technologies." (Blas 2014)

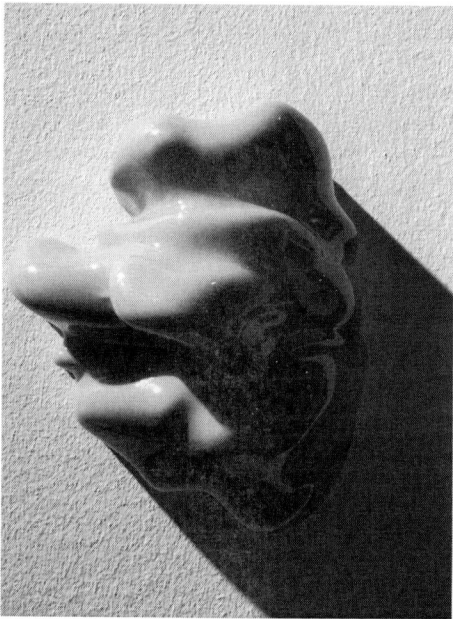

Image 2: Zach Blas *Fag Face Mask*
(Courtesy Ursula Drees)

In the *Fag Face Mask*, opacity and anonymity gained from the composite portraits of several individuals are used as a protest and a weapon. The masks are not portraits at all, according to the art theorist and philosopher Cynthia Freeland's definition of portraits as a "representation or depiction of a living being as a unique individual" (2010: 5). There is a quite explicit avoidance of the depiction of singular faces, due to the irreversibility of the relation between portrait and origin in the *Fag Face Mask*. It is not a portrait in the traditional sense, but could be characterised as a composite portrait comparable to the historical photographic composites deployed in 1865 by the eugenicist Francis Galton; his composite images were made by a series of photographs of faces superimposed so that they constitute a "single-face" which aims to reveal the common features of the faces. With the composite portrait Galton attempted to demonstrate that certain types of offenders, for example, shared the same physical characteristics (Kemp 2004: 116). His technique of sandwiching multiple faces gained new possibilities with computer-generated portraits. In 2000, Time had a front cover to illustrate the "New Face of America" by combining the features of Anglo-Saxons, Middle Easteners, Africans, Asians, etc. (ibid: 118). Bernadette Wegenstein points to the fact that while the historical examples of composite portraits display a before and after, the integrated technologies of the 21st century have "blurred the line of the assemblage" (2013: 371).

My third example of current artworks in new media art which thematise monitoring and surveillance issues by configuring statistical faces is the artist Heather Dewey-Hagborg, who creates three-dimensional portraits of persons she has "identified" from their garbage. Her project from 2013 entitled *Stranger Visions* involves extracting DNA from discarded items she finds in public spaces in New York City, such as cigarette butts and chewing gum. She has the DNA extracted from these items analysed for specific genomic sequences associated with physical traits such as hair and eye colour. Heather Dewey-Hagborg describes:

"I can tell if you have African ancestry or European, but I can't tell precise shades of darkness. From other parts of the genome, I can get some information about the dimensions of a person's face – small things about whether your eyes are close together or farther apart; other things, like eye color, or if you might have freckles. Gender, of course, and whether you might be overweight." (Wilkinson 2013)

One of the three-dimensional portraits from *Stranger Visions* (entitled Sample 2) depicts a Caucasian-looking man with dark hair and a dark eye area. He has bushy eyebrows that almost go down over his eyes. He has a fairly symmetrical face, an oval head shape, a well-formed nose and a little narrow, pinched mouth, where the lower lip is slightly fuller than the upper lip. He looks very kind, although at the same time his features give him a seemingly rather brusque appearance, perhaps due primarily to the dominant eyebrows. He makes me think of a shy athlete: healthy, strong and introverted. He is about thirty years of age and clean-shaven, but I think that he would have a thick beard, if he let it grow. Back in 2004, in the book entitled *Future Face*, Alf Linney wrote

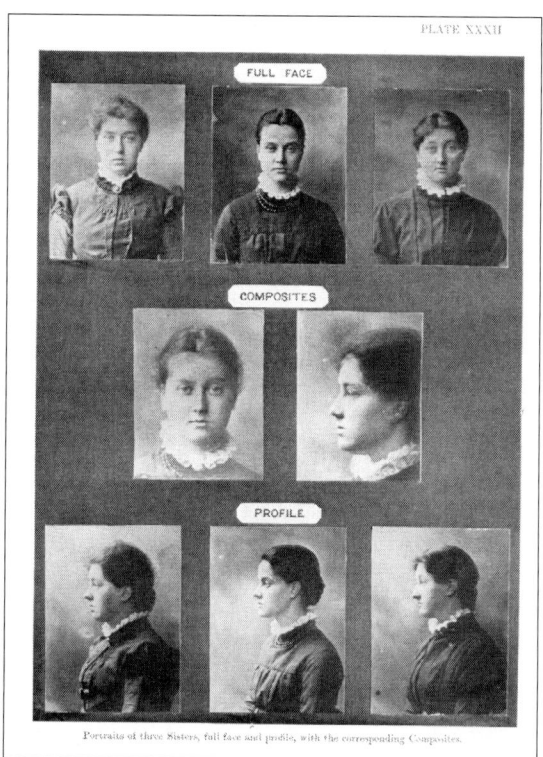

Image 3: Francis Galton, Composite photographs of three sisters, from the second half of the 19th century. Source: galton.org

Image 4: Heather Dewey-Hagborg *Stranger Visions*, 3D face prints and sample boxes at Art Miami, 2014 (Courtesy the artist)

the chapter "medicine face" in which the following quote appears: "If we are able to learn enough about how genes control the shapes of our faces, it might even be possible one day to construct someone's face from a sample of DNA. Just think of the impact this would have on crime scene investigations." (2004: 176) Hagborg's *Stranger Visions* project has been given a lot of attention, also more widely than in the art world (cf. Wilkinson 2013; Dawsey 2013), because the project has proven to resemble some potentials that may soon become reality in the scientific world. Hagborg's own framing of the project is very much focused on the dystopian prospect of being able to use this technique for monitoring and surveillance.

Dewey-Hagborg's faces are at best a guess about the source of the DNA. They are crude portraits with a probabilistic nature – so far nobody has recognised himself or herself. The portraits do have an origin, even though it is irreversible. The portrait-sculptures with an aura of forensics could be compared to identikits, but with new technologies in the role as the human witness. When one wishes to understand and analyse this work, it is relevant to relate to the phenomenological experience of the portraits, but also to seek to understand the technologies used to produce them, and to explain their logics by the best possible means. What are the logics of the DNA technology used by Heather Dewey-Hagborg? Can the relation between structure and singularity be discussed in a nuanced way? In my preliminary attempt to describe Sample 2, I am confronted with a number of issues that are linked to the genre of portraiture in general, and to this type of statistical DNA portraits in particular. Questions regarding the production of the face such as "does he have a beard?", "Does he smile?" "How old is he?" (It is possible, however, to extract knowledge of age based on DNA (cf. Callaway 2010)). The portrait is based on statistical potentialities, rather than singular actualities, and the relation between structure (genes, DNA) and actual presence is complicated. Does Sample 2 smoke, does he eat many vegetables? Does he use an expensive day cream? Does he have any acquired micro-gestures? The following quote is from the biologist Kun Tang. About reconstructing faces based on DNA, he says: "One thing we're certain of: there's no single gene that suddenly makes your nose big or small [...] The task is complicated further [...] by environmental factors, such as exposure to specific climates, which is hypothesized to influence the structure of faces." (Reardon 2014). The media scholar N. Katherine Hayles also describes how "recent work in evolutionary biology has acknowledged the importance of epigenetic changes – initiated and transmitted through the environment rather than through the genetic code" (2012: 10).

The relationship between the phenomenological experience of the work and an awareness of the DNA technology that has been used to carry out the portraits also pertains to a relationship between the artist and the technology used. How is agency distributed between the two agents that have control? This is an issue that we see in all the three works considered here. In Dewey Hagborg's work we find a probabilistic nature, and thus a statistical range of possibilities and openness in the identification. The same type of openness is also seen in de Nijs' *Physiognomic Scrutinizer* project, where the limited number of faces in the database provides a very gaping statistical space and thereby an imprecision.

The system identified me as a man, even though I am a woman. With de Nijs' performance with the biometric surveillance software, there is also a gesture aimed at showing abilities, but also to a very high degree the weakness of the technology. One can also say that the artists outsource some responsibility and this helps to identify the technologies and their logics as active participants.

Physiognomic Scrutinizer and *Stranger Visions* are types of projects in which the artists have not, as such, developed finite artworks: they have also been developing techniques for production (the use of DNA equipment in the development of the three-dimensional portraits in the work by Dewey-Hagborg, and the algorithms structuring the search of similar faces in the work by de Nijs). According to Vilém Flusser, they meet his definition of being tool-makers, as well as artists (Hayles 2014: 165). The process has moved from object to tool, as it becomes more sophisticated. With the right technologies, they trigger preconditions for the processes which their works constitute. The three art projects make use of and reflect on new technologies and their practice explores the potentials, but also the dystopian problems that arise when the human face is translated into numerical data. The projects have in common that they use the irreversible portraits as something subversive – either to demonstrate the uncertainty of the technologies or, as with Blas, to gather so much data that the collective and composite become a defence against surveillance. So the space of statistics can, paradoxically, be a place where biased and stereotypical face processing is avoided.

I have mentioned examples of composite historical, statistical portraits which, according to Wegenstein (2013), clearly display one before and one after, i. e., they display the number of parts (the singular faces), and then their compressed whole, in a single portrait. One can say that the historical composites are a visual statistic or generalisation with some sort of transparency in the representation. The three contemporary works of art, on the other hand, have a complex, irreversible or impossible relation to an "original" singular face and demonstrate how the amount of data allows for visual statistics to be complicated amalgams, rather than, as in the historical examples, being a transparent compression. It would be relevant to examine further how the implications of this potential for statistics and quantitatively complicated data volumes affect the issues briefly mentioned here with regard to the bias, stereotypes and agency of the technology vis-à-vis the human producer in face processing.

References

Blas, Zach (2014): "Informatic Opacity." In: The Journal of Aesthetics and Protest 9 (http://www.joaap.org/issue9/zachblas.htm).

Callaway, Even (2010): "The birthday candles in your veins." In: Nature, November 22, 2010 (http://www.nature.com/news/2010/101122/full/news.2010.625.html).

Dawsey, Josh (2013): "Art Emerges From DNA Left Behind." In: The Wall Street Journal March 10.

Edkins, Jenny (2015): Face Politics, Abingdon/New York City: Routledge.

Elkins, James (1999): Pictures of the Body: Pain and Metamorphosis, Stanford: Stanford University Press.

Freeland, Cynthia (2010): Portraits and Persons, Oxford: Oxford University Press.

Hayles, N. Katherine (2012): How We Think – Digital Media and Contemporary Technogenesis, Chicago: The University of Chicago Press.

Hayles, N. Katherine (2014) "Speculative Aesthetics and Object Oriented Inquiry (OOI)." In: Ridvan Askin et al. (eds.), Speculations V: Aesthetics in the 21st Century, Brooklyn: punctum books, pp. 158- 179.

Kemp, Sandra (2004): Future Face: Image, Identity, Innovation, London: Profile Books.

Linney, Alf (2004): "Medicine Face." In: Sandra Kemp (ed.), Future Face: Image, Identity, Innovation, London: Profile Books, pp. 170-181.

Reardon, Sara (2014): "Mugshots built from DNA data: Computer program crudely predicts a facial structure from genetic variations." In: Nature, March 20, 2014 (http://www.nature.com/news/mugshots-built-from-dna-data-1.14899).

Rule, Nicholas O. et al. (2008): "Accuracy and Awareness in the Perception and Categorization of Male Sexual Orientation." In: Journal of Personality and Social Psychology 95/5, pp. 1019-1028.

Wegenstein, Bernadette (2013): "Machinic Sutures: From Eighteenth-Century Physiognomy to Twenty-First-Century Makeover." In: Ulrik Ekman (ed.), Throughout: Art and Culture Emerging with Ubiquitous Computing, Cambridge: MIT Press Books, pp. 365-379.

Weininger, Otto (2005 [1903]): Sex and Character: An Investigation of Fundamental Principles, Bloomington: Indiana University Press.

Wilkinson, Alec (2013): "Mask Crusader." In: The New Yorker July 1, 2013.

Coupling Quantified Bodies
Affective Possibilities of Self-Quantification beyond the Self

Robert Cercós, William Goddard, Adam Nash and Jeremy Yuille

Abstract

The main promise behind the idea of self-quantification is to transform our lives through the continuous collection of numerical evidence about the body and its activity. Although this process may help boost self-knowledge, everyday life also involves a complex network of relations with other bodies that exert a significant, sometimes determining, influence on our behaviour. To address this concern, we suggest that self-quantification data can be modulated as perturbations to other human and non-human bodies that, in turn, may directly affect the everyday practices of the self. By coupling quantified bodies, we transform existing practices by disrupting the elements that realise, perform and reproduce existing practices. In order to explore and further understand the affective potential of this idea, we designed a system that creates unfamiliar, digitally enabled couplings between two quantified bodies: a human and a plant. In particular, in this design experiment we modulate walking activity data into perturbations to a quantified plant. How does this coupling transform the way we look at self-quantification? Are we bringing forth a new space of responsibility and ethical concern? What if the plant dies because someone did not walk enough? In this article we discuss the implications of creating such a coupling keeping a critical distance to current forms of self-quantification, which are often focused on change through prescriptive solutions rather than through the fostering of self-determined growth. With this work we aim to expand the current understanding of the affective possibilities of self-quantification in the context of social change.

Introduction

One of the promises behind the idea of self-quantification is to transform the ways in which we live our lives through the continuous collection of numerical evidence about the body and its activity. By quantifying ourselves, we are able to observe, compare, analyse, and reflect about data that represents our current patterns of living, transforming the body into a "different kind of knowable, calculable and administrative object" (Shove et al. 2014: 100), which may contribute to bettering ourselves.

But has this promise of improvement come true in a "datafied life" (Ruckestein/Pantzar 2015)? With less than half of *Fitbit* buyers actually wearing the device after 6 months (Fitbit Inc. 2015), it seems that these devices are not playing their part in the long-term embrace of healthier ways of living. Moreover, self-quantification may result in fear and anxiety (e.g. Huniche et al. 2013) which are detrimental to people's health. Sjöklint et al. (2015) suggest that self-quantification devices are currently being used for self-exploration rather than as an actual commitment to change. Furthermore, looking at collected self-quantification data usually ends with users postponing change and finding excuses that rationally explain or neglect the data as a coping tactic to deal with broken expectations (ibid). Perhaps an explanation of these findings is provided by Pantzar and Ruckenstein (2015), who suggest that, in order to become integrated in our lives, self-quantification needs to not only *measure*, but also *matter*. For example, by measuring our heartbeats using a heart-rate monitor, we might change our relationship with our heart, becoming more emotionally attached to it, therefore "hearts and their beating start to matter more" (ibid). Although relevant, it seems that those current affective encounters enacted by self-quantification are not significant enough (i.e. its affective power is limited) to the "selves" yet, at least not enough for enabling lasting change in their lives.

We also believe that it is problematic to consider individual behaviour as the first and foremost thing that needs to be changed, which is arguably a common assumption behind self-quantification systems. When individual behaviour becomes the focus of enquiry, self-quantification tends to be used to rationally convince individuals to change beliefs and attitudes that inform behaviour choices. This approach disregards the complex network of relations – social context, materials, meanings, and so forth – of which the individual behaviour is but a small part. In other words, this approach tends to disregard the significance of self-quantification in relation to its broader context. In response, social practice theory suggests that behaviours and the contexts in which they occur have no separate existence, being both "sustained and changed through the ongoing reproduction of social practice" (Shove 2010). Therefore, more than influencing individual attitudes and beliefs, we should think in ways to affect the complex dynamics that emerge from the relations between the elements that define a social practice: materials, socially shared meanings and practical knowledge (Shove et al. 2012: 22-25).

In this paper, we explore ways in which self-quantification can become more meaningful and therefore – we will argue – more affective. In particular, we draw on the relatedness between humans and non-humans that participate in the broader context in which practices are enacted; in other words, self-quantification that has significance beyond the self.

The Affective Power of Coupling

It may sound paradoxical to try to push self-quantification beyond the self, however, if we distinguish the produced data from its subsequent modulation into different display modes (e.g. numbers, graphs, game inputs, audio, video and so on) (Nash 2012), the paradox fades. The affective power of self-quantification is not associated with the data itself ("data-as-data") – which has no ontological difference from the data that comes from other sources (ibid), such as, say, weather data. Its affective power relies ultimately in the way the data is transformed into a display state that can be perceived ("data-as-display"). This distinction is also useful to understand the association between self-quantification and the *self*. For example, in the heart-rate monitor example discussed above, the emotional attachment comes from the fact that a modulation is explicitly showing that the data has a direct relation to the *self*. Therefore, self-quantification's association with the *self* that is being quantified comes from the display modes that highlight self-oriented meanings. In sum, extending self-quantification beyond the self only requires of adequate display modes.

Self-quantification is limited not only in terms of self-centred display modes, but also in a somewhat restricted understanding of what a *self* is, which only considers *human selves*. What if we attach an activity tracker to a dog? Or if we monitor the photosynthesis process of a plant? Is it still a form of self-quantification? We believe that there is a great opportunity in including other ways of being into the *selves* that might be quantified. As we will show, extending our understanding of what a *self* is enable us to observe self-quantification from different, unfamiliar perspectives.

But what are the possibilities that this approach brings forth? If we embrace exploring different modulations that go beyond the self (including other ways of being) we are able to create *structural couplings* between quantified-selves. A *coupling* is enabled when self-quantification data is modulated as perturbations to other human and non-human bodies that, in turn, may directly affect the everyday practices in which the self participates. If the other body is also being quantified, these perturbations can operate in both ways. Humberto Maturana and Francisco Varela denoted this dynamic as *structural coupling*, which occurs "whenever there is a history of recurrent interactions leading to the structural congruence between two (or more) systems" (Maturana/Varela 1987: 75), involving reciprocal perturbations that change the structure of the involved organisms without destroying their organisation and autonomy as autopoietic (i.e. living) systems (Maturana 1975; Maturana/Varela 1980). By coupling quantified bodies, a coevolving dynamic between the coupled bodies is enabled.

Coupling Quantified Bodies: Human-Vegetal Play

In order to explore and further understand the affective potential of coupling bodies using self-quantification, we designed a system that creates unfamiliar, digitally-enabled couplings between two quantified bodies: a human and a plant.

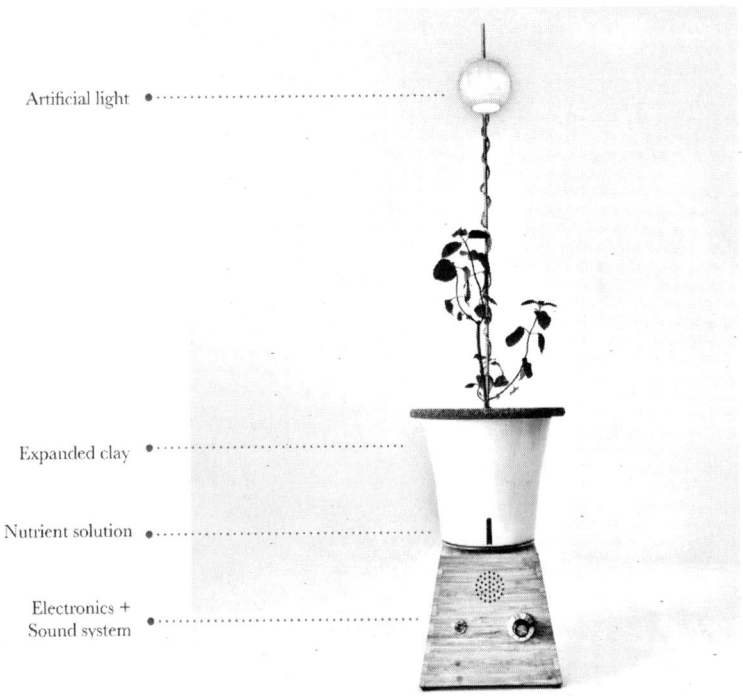

Fig. 1: The components of Dataponics: Human-Vegetal Play

In "Dataponics: Human-Vegetal Play" (Fig. 1), we map human physical activity measured by a *Fitbit* to the amount of light and water fed to a potted plant. Also, the system measures the moisture in the growing hydroponic medium (in this case, expanded clay) that surrounds the plant's roots, and plays different internet radio stations accordingly.

We consider the emerging dynamic of interactions between the human and the plant to be *play*, using the notion of "free movement within a more rigid structure" (Salen/Zimmerman 2004: 304). This notion provided us with a frame that guided our design decisions; our design aims to respect and preserve players' autonomy ("free movement") although the digital coupling (part of the "more rigid structure") may be sometimes disruptive for both the human and the plant.

In order to illustrate how framing the interactions as play influenced our design decisions, we can think of two relevant scenarios. For instance, what if a player does not want to be coupled? Based on the idea of play that preserves the players' autonomy, we chose to design a coupling that is *voluntary* from the human perspective; the human player needs to check-in by pressing a button every day in order to get coupled. Furthermore, we can extend our first scenario to the non-human player: what if the human player does not walk enough? Should the plant just die? Using the same principle, the coupling is *conditional* from the plant's perspective; the plant decouples if it is not getting enough light or water. In this design, none of the players are enforced to participate in the coupling; the plant always gets what it needs to survive, and the human player can choose whether to be coupled or not. In other words, the interactions are not a matter of life or death, but rather an opportunity of affecting, and being affected by, the other player.

Besides preserving autonomy, the system's design also aims to resignify the "reward and punishment" approach based on positive or negative reinforcements. Providing water and light to a plant may be considered as a form of reward, yet the effects are slowly embodied into the plant in a non-linear, uncertain way (i. e. it is difficult, if not impossible, to directly link the state of the plant to each particular action). This shifts the focus from this complex, indirect form of reward and puts it into the other body's wellbeing. The slowness of the process and the uniqueness of the effects reframe the reward as such. Furthermore, the "benefits" of this complex reward go to the non-human player, which also avoids the "intensely individualistic focus of quantifying the self" (Lupton 2013), moving away from conceiving the human as a self-interested agent that only pursues maximising his/her individual benefit.

Finally, another interesting dimension of enabling a coupling with other living species is to enrich our perspective about our everyday practices. What does the plant know about us after playing for a while? Under this light, the non-human players become "epistemic objects" which "embody what one does not yet know" (Miettinen/Virkkunen 2005: 438). In our example, the plant – as a sentient organism (Chamovitz 2012: 6) – becomes "aware" of the routines and rhythms of the human player's life. Just as someone that lives in the same house, the plant suddenly "knows about us" and slowly changes accordingly.

Conclusion

The design of "Dataponics: Human-Vegetal Play" allowed us to observe self-quantification from a different perspective and raises questions about its limits. By applying Maturana's notion of structural coupling, we were able to explore the implications of coupling bodies using self-quantification, triggering structural transformations in the involved quantified bodies.

We discussed how our design embraces play-based design values, such as preserving players' autonomy ("voluntary coupling") and limiting potential life-or-death effects of the digital coupling ("conditional coupling"). This approach helped us dealing with some critical issues that our system highlights; when other living species take part into self-quantification systems, the extremely narcissistic focus of current forms of self-quantification becomes problematic. The idea of coupling quantified bodies allowed us both facing and going beyond the utilitarian approach toward social change, in which other humans and non-humans are just means to a desired end. In summary, this research enriches the notion of self-quantification, extending it beyond the self through embracing play-based design values.

In this work, we explored unfamiliar forms of relatedness to a broader context that can be enacted using data about the self, which we hope contribute to critically evolve the ways in which we design and experience self-quantification in our everyday lives to enact social change.

References

Chamovitz, Daniel (2012): What a Plant Knows: A Field Guide to the Senses of Your Garden-and Beyond, Oxford: Oneworld Publications.

Fitbit Inc. (2015): "Form S-1 Registration statement, Fitbit Inc.", May 7, 2015 (http://www.sec.gov/Archives/edgar/data/1447599/000119312515176980/d875679ds1.htm).

Huniche, Lotte Birthe/Dinesen, Carl Nielsen/Ove, Grann/Toft, Egon (2013): "Patients' use of Self-Monitored Readings for Managing Everyday Life with COPD: a Qualitative Study." In: Telemedicine and e-Health 19/5, pp. 396-402.

Lupton, Deborah (2013): "Understanding the Human Machine". In: Technology and Society Magazine, IEEE 32/4, pp. 25-30.

Maturana, Humberto (1975): "The Organization of the Living: A Theory of the Living Organization." In: International Journal of Man-Machine Studies 7/3, pp. 313-332.

Maturana, Humberto/Varela, Francisco (1980): Autopoiesis and Cognition: The Realization of the Living, Dordrecht: Springer Science & Business Media.

Maturana, Humberto/Varela Francisco (1987): The Tree of Knowledge: The Biological Roots of Human Understanding, Boston: Shambhala Publications.

Miettinen, Reijo/Virkkunen, Jaakko (2005): "Epistemic Objects, Artefacts and Organizational Change." In: Organization 12/3, pp. 437-456.

Nash, Adam (2013): "Affect and the Medium of Digital Data." In: The Fibreculture Journal 21, pp. 10-30.

Pantzar, Mika/Ruckenstein, Minna (2015): "The Heart of Everyday Analytics: Emotional, Material and Practical Extensions in Self-Tracking Market." In: Consumption Markets & Culture 18/1, pp. 92-109.

Ruckenstein, Minna/Pantzar Mika (2015): "Datafied Life." In: Techné: Research in Philosophy and Technology 19/2, pp. 191-210.

Salen, Katie/Zimmerman, Eric (2004): Rules of play: Game Design Fundamentals, Cambridge: MIT Press.

Shove, Elizabeth (2010): "Beyond the ABC: Climate Change Policy and Theories of Social Change." In: Environment and Planning A 42/6, pp. 1273-1285.

Shove, Elizabeth/Pantzar Mika/Watson, Matt (2012): The Dynamics of Social Practice: Everyday Life and How it Changes, London: Sage Publications.

Sjöklint, Mimmi/Constantiou, Ioanna/Trier, Matthias (2015): "The Complexities of Self-Tracking – an Inquiry into User Reactions and Goal Attainment." In: ECIS 2015 Complete Research Papers, paper 170.

In Conversation with

I Think it Worked Because Mercury was in the House of Jupiter!

Tega Brain and Surya Mattu in Conversation with Pablo Abend and Mathias Fuchs

Tega Brain is an artist and environmental engineer from Sydney, Australia working at the intersection of art, ecology and engineering. She is an Assistant Professor of New Media at SUNY Purchase and also teaches and organizes at the School for Poetic Computation. She has been an artist in residence at Eyebeam, New York and a member of New Inc, New Museum. She has recently exhibited work at the Science Gallery, Dublin and at the Australian Centre for Design.

Surya Mattu is an artist and engineer based in Brooklyn. He is currently a fellow at Data & Society where he is investigating infrastructure with a focus on wireless as a way to better understand bias in technology. He is also a contributing researcher at ProPublica. Previously he has worked as an engineer at Bell Labs and is a graduate from the New York University's Interactive Telecommunications Program. He has a degree in Electronics and Telecommunication from the University of Nottingham in the United Kingdom.

Mathias Fuchs (MF): It seems to us that you both are knowledgeable and substantiated in the arts and in critical media. You seem to be hovering in between the arts and technology and innovation. What is your position in these fields?

Tega Brain (TB): I describe myself as an artist, but Surya and I both come from engineering and technology backgrounds and that very much informs our work in the arts. To me being an artist gives you the freedom to address the cultural context of technology. This is not an easy thing to do from within the field of engineering. It is often under considered within the industry and there is hardly a language to address questions of the ethical and political dimensions of emerging technologies. Predominantly now I work as an artist and also as an educator to do this.

Surya Mattu (SM): I am interested in exploring the implications of new technologies and I basically have three ways of engaging with them: Teaching, journalism, and also through art. Each of these provides different ways of tackling the subject matter. With teaching you go into details of these technologies and

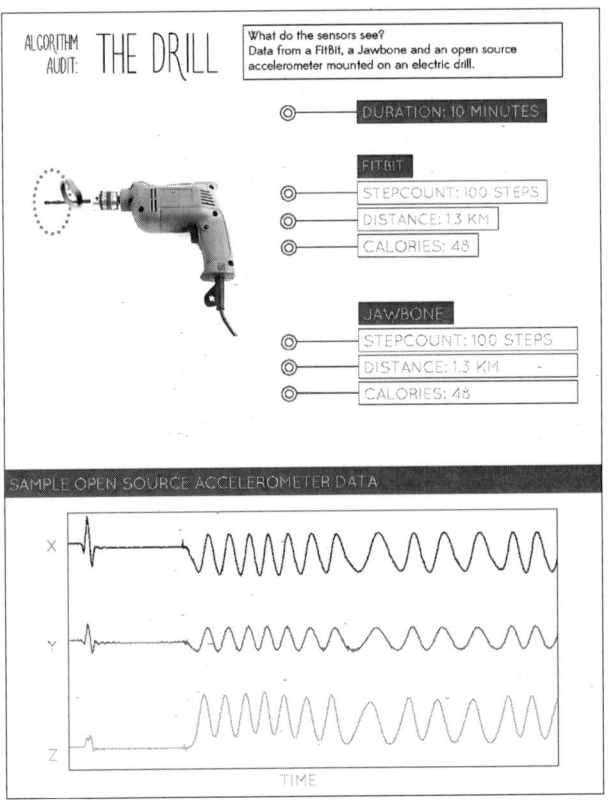

with investigative journalism you're addressing the public. I am a contributing researcher at *ProPublica* and I am also member of *Data and Society*, a think tank that started one and a half years ago. I am trying to bring these different approaches together and I think art can accomplish this. Art doesn't require the level of detail that journalism requires, and it need not be as didactic as teaching.

TB: I think we are both interested in unconventional ways of discussing these ideas and that is why we made *Unfit Bits*.[1] It's a project that addresses questions concerning a technology like fitness trackers in a form that is open. In it we very deliberately present ideas and questions within the framework of the tech start-up, which is of course a very techno-utopian environment.

SM: We do presentations where we pitch data spoofing products as a start-up, with all the phrases and assumptions that characterize this community.

Pablo Abend (PA): ... And people can also buy your product?

---

1   Cf. http://www.unfitbits.com/.

SM: You can buy it, like all things on the art market. (laughing)

TB: I am very interested in thinking about these technologies outside the very narrow utilitarian and commercial borders that define how they are usually developed. Back during the time when I was still working as an engineer dealing with clients, I found it always very hard to ask the questions about whom certain technologies serve and what agendas they are furthering. The way Surya and I work now, broadens this scope and allows us opportunity to ask questions about how they enact power and how this could be different, we're doing a kind of eccentric engineering. Media art provides a unique context to explore, stretch and subvert how emerging technologies are deployed and this is important as unlike most traditional art practices it occurs and on a system's level, on a functional level, as well as on a symbolic level. To me it is not enough to only address these phenomena on a representational level.

MF: Do you consider yourselves critics from outside, or would you say you are users as well. Do you have loads of *Quantified Self* equipment? Do you do your daily tracked running miles in Central Park?

SM: Well I am a smoker, so that is out of the question. (laughing)

TB: Not at all! To be honest I am not excited about the *Quantified Self* promise at all. Even if I had all of the information to tell me what I should be doing, it does not compel me to go out and do it. The problem with the idea that data will automatically lead to behaviour change, is that it leaves out so many other constraints that influence my behaviour.

SM: I also don't think that more data necessarily means better decisions. If I knew everything about myself, would I be the best version of myself? No, not at all. Attempts to quantify the self through tracking are always somewhat wrong – if I can track where I have been, what does that actually say? What can be seen of me from tracking data is never going to be a complete representation of my life, because I am much more complex and individual than that. It's also important to remember that the sensors we use to measure our environment and ourselves are always biased towards picking up certain signals better than others.

For example, one thing we came across when looking into how the *FitBit* tracker does peak detection and how it determines how long your steps are, was that initially the data used to train their algorithms had all been collected from tall Western men, because this was the type of researchers who developed the system. All their algorithms were therefore biased to this data. You can't take the culture out of the technology!

TB: Also, as we are talking about fitness and health data, it is often also assumed that there is medical expertise involved, because these apps are labelled as *health* apps. This can be dangerous and misleading as these apps have not really come

out of medical and health research and yet they are often assumed to have this authority.

SM: There have been cases where people accused *FitBit* of not having used the right heartbeat monitoring algorithms and a lawsuit is currently underway about this. It's particularly interesting as if you want to use *FitBit* software you usually accept to agree for arbitration, which means you cannot sue them for anything. The loophole that the lawyers have found in this case is that it is perfectly legal to sue *FitBit* if you bought the equipment in a store rather than on the Internet and therefore have not yet signed the agreement. So people are doing this and are suing *FitBit* for providing shitty heartbeat detection.[2]

TB: The relationship these technologies have to medicine is really interesting. I went to the doctor yesterday and of course I couldn't help asking him what he thinks about the *Quantified Self* movement. He said that he has patients who come to him with their *FitBit* statistics, and also others who come with a full diagnosis that they got from the Internet. Yet no matter how much information you have, you still need to be a very experienced, trained specialist to get the full picture of a patient's condition and make meaning out of the data. The data-only narrative is skewed and there is so much more nuanced interpretation involved in diagnosis.

PA: It seems people are trying to circumvent interpretation by correlation. In the *Quantified Self* movement it is all about correlation. But do you see a playful side to the *Quantified Self*? The community is tinkering with the technology and is correlating all kinds of senseless data. Is there a playful side?

SM: It is like astrology, it is a good way to engage people, and there is a really good playful community aspect with it that I like. But when it is assumed to be the truth, or when it is used as the truth, that's when it becomes problematic. You can use the tool if you put the investment into it and if you are honest with yourself about it, but the tool is agnostic without you.

MF: Coming back to your example of astrology: Do you mean that most people use the *Quantified Self* half-believing that it is not true?

2 Cf. http://www.fastcompany.com/3055198/fast-feed/a-class-action-suit-claims-fitbit-devices-inaccurately-measure-heart-rate and http://www.technologyreview.com/news/543716/your-doctor-doesnt-want-to-hear-about-your-fitness-tracker-data/.

SM: I come from India and my father is an astrologer. I see people coming to him asking important questions: When should I buy a house? Is X the right person for me to marry? And he gives them advice based on their horoscopes. Then they come back after a year and say: "Thank you, it helped me." Who is to say that the stars did or didn't help, if believing in them helped the individual make a difficult decision in life? And it is the same with *FitBits*. If wearing a fitness tracker helps you take better care of yourself I can see the value in that. However, that is not the same as saying the data they collect is *always* telling the empirical truth. We shouldn't be able to use them in a court of law because that could set a dangerous precedence. Believing in *FitBits* as the undisputed truth is similar to saying, I think I didn't get the apartment I was looking for because Mercury was in the house of Jupiter. (laughter)

TB: I mean obviously it also becomes very problematic when this data becomes conflated with finance such as when you get discounts if you share your data. It reinforces inequality and who gets to live with privacy and who doesn't. It seems like every few months an insurance company, or an airline, or a department store is launching new initiatives to try and get people to share their data. That is a big issue for us as well.

SM: We want to prompt people to consider the agenda that is driving all these companies encouraging us to use all these devices

PA: With regards to your other works, do you first look at emerging technologies and the impact on society, and then you start criticising it? Does this critical stance characterise your work?

SM: For me new technology always raises questions. I did a project digging into WiFi and I wanted to understand how the protocol works on a technical level and then understand the implication on a cultural level. For me, I do think about a lot of this stuff from a critical perspective and a lot of it starts off as a playful exploration. I'm always asking why do things work the way they do?

TB: Often the way emerging technologies are rolled out is with a sort of solutionism in mind, through the story that technology improves our lives and makes us better people. They are not typically rolled out with precaution or critique particularly here in the US at the moment. (laughter) I feel like the critique that we are interested in is really important as it points to the fact that there is another conversation here that is not being accounted for by marketing and promotional narratives for obvious reasons. I don't see

a lot of other spaces where you can start conversations about emerging technologies outside of academia. And this whole idea that technologies are political is still something that is not widely discussed in fields outside of the arts or humanities. I have come out of a civil engineering practice which is probably the most conservative flavour of engineering and in my experience, this discipline typically describes what it does as solving problems to make the world better. The idea that technologies are inherently social and political is not readily discussed because engineers frame their activities as predominately technical. All the theory within Science and Technology Studies is unfortunately not part of a regular undergraduate engineering degree this is a problem. I think it is very important to think about ways to bring theoretical ideas from STS into commercial and industrial contexts, especially in ways that are not white papers in journals which only academics read.

I've also been very interested in the public reaction to our project and at times I am a little troubled by it. Like many artists making critical work, we claim for this project to start certain conversations and it really does. But at times I worry about the way we present it as if it is a real thing and a real company acting in that industry. On one hand this is important as it causes people to question reality and question their assumptions and ask, "Is this real? How do I feel about this? Do I want my society to be heading in this direction?" We get mentioned in *Twitter* all the time when insurance companies, banks airlines and most recently universities launch new deals involving tracking technologies. People write things like "Don't worry! *Unfit Bits* is taking care of it." I worry that articulating the appearance of resistance, encourages a certain complacency as we are giving the people the idea that someone is on it and taking care of it – someone is keeping corporate entities in check. So of course the question then becomes, how to have this type of work bolster real change and real resistance. I think we need practices like ours *as well as* traditional activism and structures that protect employees, and vulnerable communities such as unions and regulations.

SM: Another consistent thread in making creative works like *Unfit Bits* is that we spend a lot of time diving deep into technical protocols but then also into how these technologies impact different communities. And when we're doing this we're spending a lot of time thinking about how people can better understand these complex and often black boxed systems. It's always a process of thinking about an audience in the creation of the work. One trope we always avoid is the hacker. We don't want the people to look at our work and think "oh these guys can do it, but we couldn't do that" – and I think this is an important thing to keep in mind. An important aspect of our research is making these complex systems understandable. This is especially important since the Snowden leaks and the public realization that we are actually living in a surveillance dystopia. We no longer need to spectacularize the sinister possibilities of networked technologies as we now know that this is the world we live in. And so recently it has become important for us to try and present work that is empowering, inviting and didactic rather than impressively technical which inevitably alienates a non-technical audience.

PA: Yeah, your work *Unfit Bits* is very hands on and has a very accessible DIY look to it. But when I look at your other works – for example *From The Dark*[3] or *What the Frog's Nose Tells the Frog's Brain*[4] – the question of tangibility and access becomes a lot more difficult. When you look at the visualisation or the objects, these works are not quite self-explanatory. How do you deal with this?

SM: That is a good question (laughs) …

TB: There is a tension. As an artist you try to create spectacular things and draw attention and one way to do that is by creating technologies that have some magic in them because they are not fully explained. Yet you also want to talk about critique, empowering your audience and inviting people into conversations in different ways. And so there is a tension between these two agendas. You try to occupy the role of the expert albeit an unconventional one, but at the same time you are also what Claire Pentecost calls the "public amateur" (Pentecost 2008: 2) – someone who is learning in public and trying to educate by being a stand in for the every person. It gets complicated with technology-based practices like ours because inevitably a lot of expertise and technical knowledge is required to build much of this type of work.

SM: We're not trying to translate these practices into things that are existent in and of themselves and that is why the audience plays such a big part in the process. Recently I have been working on a curriculum for middle schools about the question of what the Internet is and it is really helpful to talk to people who do not live in this art and technology world because you realize that it can be quite a bubble. I am always terrified about getting so wrapped up in it and forgetting that people outside are likely to have a different interest level in this stuff.

TB: But it is important for us and people in this community to be doing this work outside of companies and to not be designing the next big thing for *Intel* or whoever. It is an interesting position to occupy because we have no power and thus can explore things in different ways. Artists are trusted in a way someone at *Google* might not be because we are doing our projects for different reasons.

SM: … you can scream and shout and do crazy things!

---

3 Cf. http://suryamattu.com/FROM-THE-DARK
4 Cf. http://tegabrain.com/The-Frogs-Nose

MF: But let's do a thought experiment. If the MOMA invited you to show it in a gallery room or *Google* invited you to show it in a gallery, or if *Nike* said well that is a nice thing, we want to present it in a nice white cube gallery. Would that be a possibility? Do you think you can undermine the system by working with its tools? Is it a subversive act or a statement or is it an appropriation piece?

SM: I think it is definitely subversion. For me this is a motivation. I am not sure how I would feel about Nike wanting it. That would be a weird conversion to navigate. The idea of it is making me uncomfortable. What I like about *Unfit Bits* is that you see it and you get it right away and it is a sign of protest. It is quite clear what the statement is and this is a good thing to engage people.

TB: We definitely like to show it in art contexts, mostly in galleries that are research oriented such as those within universities. The project is a little ambiguous in its relationship to the *Quantified Self* and tracking industry because it uses their aesthetics and it uses their language and this makes it less obviously activist. In many ways it is a continuation of their weird logic to a point where it becomes ridiculous – we're proposing to disrupt fitness tracking that in itself proposes to disrupt fitness! But in seriousness, this is an interesting position because I think you cannot create change by being completely at odds with someone. It is more interesting to try to get into their space and then provide a different perspective or draw attention to some of the ridiculous stories that are being told about these things. If *Nike* wanted to talk to us about it I would be excited to have that conversation because I am also fascinated how they see these contradictions and the problems afforded by the technologies they are making. Really, we should be making art for policy makers and for people who are running these companies rather than for the ambiguous general public, but it is very complicated. If *Google* came to me and said we want to commission you to do a project for $20,000 it would be tempting but I probably wouldn't do it because it is extremely difficult to be funded by the people you are trying to critique. But then I have done work for galleries such as the *Science Gallery* in Dublin who got a million dollar grant from Google three years ago. I think you have to be transparent and honest about these issues. An important part of what we are doing is exploring our own hypocrisy because there are no black and white positions here.

PA: Would it be interesting for you to confront the *Quantified Self* movement directly with your critique?

SM: I am not really that critical of the *Quantified Self* movement because I think the movement has a bigger role. This notion that we can control our habits and our lifestyle through these sensors is really interesting as an experiment and I hope the people keep doing that. It is an interesting study of how people interact with technology. For me the bigger problem is the claim – and I have to come back to this – that the technology is telling the truth and that there are no other consequences of *Quantified Self* for society as a whole than positive ones. The scary trend coming from tech companies right now is *AirBnB* saying they are only a platform and they are not a rental service, *Uber* claiming it is not a taxi service but a platform. The conversation that is happening a lot in the field of new technologies is one of disruption and what this actually means is a lack of accountability. Industry is using networked technologies to try to sidestep existing checks and balances and this is the criticality I would like to focus on.

TB: Part of the problem is that all the risk; the risk of this data being used in the wrong way; the risk that it will be used in different and yet unknown ways in the future or the risk for people's privacy. All this risk falls to the individual and there are no consequences for the entity involved. This is part of the problem with these tracking programs. These devices and their data further already starkly asymmetrical power relationships. For example, say my health data is available to my employer and that it plays into decisions regarding my future employment, this is a problem particularly as I may not even get to know that this is happening.

SM: We are getting to the point where everyone agrees that we need more transparency concerning the use of the data and that this cannot be just a business secret. Before we can actually explore how bad it is we need access to what is actually happening because this is getting harder to know. It's like crystal ball gazing with the lights off. Until we have more transparency on how the datasets companies collect are being used, trying to find the effects of the bias in technology remains a bit of a vision quest.

PA and MF: Thank you for the conversation.

References

Pentecost, Claire (2008): "Beyond Face." In: Elizabeth Chodos (ed.), Talking With Your Mouth Full: New Language for Socially Engaged Art, Chicago, IL: The Green Lantern Press and Three Walls, pp. 31-45.

Biographical Notes

Pablo Abend is a postdoc at the project *Modding and Editor-Games* (DFG Priority Program 1505) at the *Institute for Media Studies and Theater*, University of Cologne.

Marie-Luise Angerer is chairholder for *Media Theory/Media Science* at the *Institute for Arts and Media*, University of Potsdam.

Jill Belli, Ph.D., is an assistant professor of *English* at New York City College of Technology, CUNY.

Andréa Belliger is director at the Institute for *Communication & Leadership IKF* in Lucerne, Switzerland and pro-rector of the *Teachers Training University* of Central Switzerland.

Bernd Bösel is an assistant professor at the *Institute for Art and Media Studies*, University of Potsdam.

Tega Brain is an artist and environmental engineer. She is Assistant Professor of *New Media* at SUNY Purchase and teaches at the *School for Poetic Computation*.

Robert Cercós is an industrial engineer and interaction designer. He is a doctoral researcher in *Media and Communication*, RMIT University.

Stefan Danter is a doctoral student at the *American Studies Department*, University of Mannheim.

James Dyer is a PhD candidate contributing to the *Research Group G, for Graphic*, University of Huddersfield.

Mathias Fuchs is an artist, musician and media scholar. He is Senior Fellow at the *Institute of Advanced Study on Media Cultures of Computer Simulation* (MECS) at Leuphana University, Lüneburg.

Alex Gekker is a PhD candidate and researcher in the European Research Council (ERC) project *Charting the Digital*, University of Utrecht.

William Goddard is a game designer. He is currently a doctoral researcher in *Media and Communication*, RMIT University.

Sharanjit Kang is a research student in Open *Data at Centre for Intellectual Property Policy & Management (CIPPM) – Media & Communications School (Law)*, Bournemouth University.

Argyro P. Karanasiou is a senior lecturer at the *Centre for Intellectual Property Policy & Management (CIPPM) – Media & Communications School (Law)*, Bournemouth University.

Stephen Katz is a professor of *Sociology and Distinguished Research Award Recipients*, Trent University, Peterborough, Canada.

David J. Krieger is director at the *Institute for Communication & Leadership* in Lucerne, Switzerland.

Alex Lambert is a lecturer in *Communications and Media Studies* at Monash University, Melbourne and an honorary research fellow at the *Research Unit in Public Cultures*, at the University of Melbourne.

Barbara L. Marshall is a professor of *Sociology and Distinguished Research Award Recipients*, Trent University in Peterborough, Canada.

Surya Mattu is an artist and engineer. He is fellow at the *research institute Data & Society*, New York, and contributing researcher at *ProPublica*.

Adam Nash is an artist, composer, programmer, performer and writer. He is a lecturer at the *Bachelor of Design (Games)* and Program Manager of the *Bachelor of Design (Digital Media)*, RMIT University.

Ulfried Reichardt is chair for *American Literature and Culture*, University of Mannheim.

Paolo Ruffino is a lecturer at *Goldsmiths and London South Bank University* and a member of the art collective *IOCOSE*.

Regina Schober is assistant professor at the *American Studies Department*, University of Mannheim.

Jeremy Yuille is an interaction designer, digital media artist and academic. He is a co-founder of the *Design Futures Lab* and Program Manager of the *Master of Design Futures*, RMIT University.

Mette-Marie Zacher Sørensen is a postdoctoral fellow at the *Department of Art and Cultural Studies*, University of Copenhagen.